The Illustrated History of Europe

The   Illustrated

With photographs, paintings, prints, drawings and maps.

general supervision
ROBERT LAFFONT

supervision of text and illustrations
JACQUES BOUDET

editor-in-chief
EDMOND POGNON

text by
**JEAN AMSLER
JACQUES BOUDET
LOYS MASSON
JACQUES NOBECOURT
EDMOND POGNON**

captions
GASTON BONHEUR

technical supervision
PAUL RUDLOFF

dummy and layout
PHILIPPE GENTIL

History of Europe

editorial secretary
JEAN-PAUL DEUDON

illustrations, documentary research
**JOSETTE BONDUELLE
NICOLE LEVY
DOMINIQUE RAOUL-DUVAL**

planning committee
**PHILIPPE BRUNET
ROBERT BOURILLET
JACQUELINE BERARD
HUGUETTE REMONT**

translated by
RICHARD GRAVES

original maps
MICHEL FONTAINE

photographs : listed individually at the end of the book

DOUBLEDAY & COMPANY, INC. GARDEN CITY, NEW YORK

Other Editions of this Book

In Dutch by
J. M. MEULENHOFF - UITGEVER, AMSTERDAM

In English by
THE BODLEY HEAD LTD, LONDON
(for England)

In Finnish by
WERNER SÖDERSTRÖM OSAKEYHTIÖ, HELSINKI

In French by
EDITIONS DU PONT ROYAL, PARIS

In German by
ALFRED SCHERZ VERLAG, BERNE - STUTTGART

In Italian by
VALENTINO BOMPIANI & C., MILANO

In Spanish by
COMPAÑIA GENERAL FABRIL EDITORA, BUENOS AIRES

In Swedish by
BOKFORLAGET NATUR OCH KULTUR, STOCKHOLM

Norwegian Edition in Preparation

First published in the United States of America 1960
Planned and printed by les Editions du Pont Royal,
Paris, France
Copyright ⓒ by Editions du Pont Royal 1959
English translation ⓒ The Bodley Head Ltd 1959
First published in England 1959
Library of Congress Catalog Card Number 60-6125

PREFACE
BY H.R.H.
THE PRINCE OF THE NETHERLANDS

DOES THERE EXIST A SATISFACTORY INTERPRETATION OF THE WORD ' CULTURE '? AND CAN ANYONE CLEARLY DEFINE WHAT EUROPE IS? TO WRITE A WORK ON EUROPEAN CULTURE AND THE GENIUS OF EUROPE IS CLEARLY AN ADVENTURE. IT IS, NEVERTHELESS, ESSENTIAL THAT WE SHOULD STUDY THE ELUSIVE PAST OF OUR CONTINENT, FOR THE CONSCIOUSNESS OF OUR HISTORY IS ONE OF THE INDISPENSABLE ELEMENTS OF EUROPEAN CULTURE AND THE FUTURE EVOLUTION OF EUROPE WILL INEVITABLY BEAR ITS IMPRESS.

WHAT GREATER DIVERSITY CAN BE FOUND THAN IN THE PERIOD OF PRE-HISTORY RESOLVING ITSELF INTO THE ' MIRACLE OF GREECE ', THE RISE OF CHRISTIANITY PROCEEDING TO THE EMPIRE OF CHARLEMAGNE, THE GRADUAL TRANSITION FROM BYZANTIUM TO THE RENAISSANCE AND FINALLY THE DEVELOPMENT OF CAPITALISM IN WESTERN EUROPE? OUR HISTORY PROVIDES A CULTURAL IMPULSE SO RICH AND VARIED THAT ONE CANNOT BUT ASK WHAT ARE THE ESSENTIAL ELEMENTS WHICH DISTINGUISH THE GENIUS OF EUROPE FROM THE GREAT CULTURES OF ASIA.

DOES THE PROGRESS OF EUROPEAN CIVILISATION TO THE PEAK OF ITS PRESENT DAY SUPREMACY DATE BACK TO THE RENAISSANCE? OR WERE THE GERMS OF THIS ASTONISHING VITALITY ALREADY DORMANT IN A PREVIOUS EPOCH?

IT WOULD BE A GRAVE ERROR TO CONCENTRATE SOLELY ON THE FIVE CENTURIES SEPARATING THE RENAISSANCE FROM THE CHAOS OF THE TWO WORLD WARS. THE TRUE FOUNDATIONS OF OUR HISTORY GO BACK FAR BEYOND THE MODERN TIMES WITH WHICH WE ARE FAMILIAR. THE GENIUS OF EUROPE EMBODIES A LIVING PAST IN WHICH PRE-HISTORY PLAYS A ROLE SIMILAR TO THAT OF CLASSICAL CULTURE IN THE MEDIAEVAL THEOCRACY. IT IS PALPABLY IMPOSSIBLE TO PRESENT ALL THE RICHES OF OUR PAST HISTORY. THAT IS WHY IT HAS BEEN NECESSARY, IN THIS WORK, TO MAKE A VISUAL PRESENTATION, NOT FOR THE MERE PLEASURE OF THE EYE BUT IN ORDER TO CLARIFY AND COMPLETE THE PICTURE OF EUROPEAN GENIUS.

THE TEXT AND ILLUSTRATIONS OF THIS BOOK, WHICH DO HONOUR TO THE ENTERPRISE OF THE FRENCH PUBLISHING PROFESSION, CALL TO MIND A GOBELIN TAPESTRY, WHERE THE BRIGHTLY COLOURED THEMES CORRESPOND FAITHFULLY WITH THE ARTISTS' THOUGHTS. BUT THIS TAPESTRY IS NOT DESTINED TO ADORN THE WALLS OF A ROYAL RESIDENCE. IT HAS BEEN PLACED IN THE HANDS OF THOUSANDS OF READERS THROUGH THE MEDIUM OF MODERN PHOTOGRAPHIC REPRODUCTION. THIS FACT IN ITSELF MAKES THE BOOK A SYMBOL OF ONE OF THE ESSENTIAL FEATURES OF EUROPEAN CULTURE, FOR IT DISPLAYS CONFIDENCE IN THE SPIRIT OF MAN WHICH ALONE CAN SPREAD ABROAD THE DOCTRINE OF FREEDOM AND WHICH LEADS US BACK TO THE SPRINGS OF HISTORY WITHOUT CRAMPING OUR GENIUS FOR CREATION.

PRINCE OF THE NETHERLANDS.

Once upon a time there was Beauty, and the Beast, - a nymph and a bull -

a legend at the dawn of our history.

Even today Europe is not yet a nation, but from the first she has been a focus of civilisation. She is the heir to the culture of Greece, the organising genius of Rome and the Judeo-Christian conception of life. She has also benefited from the fruitful energies of the Germanic and Scandinavian races. For the past fifteen centuries she has been engaged in an adventure unique in history. Her annals, read at too close quarters, resemble those of a jousting-ground or a jungle. But seen from above and placed in its proper relation to the whole world, her evolution appears as an astonishing revelation of man's transfiguration and the conversion of the land to the service of man. By the efforts of Europe during the last fifteen hundred years the world has progressed incomparably faster than during the previous millennia.

Today, as a result of the lessons she has given to other peoples, Europe is no longer the only crucible in which the future is prepared. But, in spite of the all-too-numerous differences that divide them, Europeans should realise that since their origins they have been called to fulfil an incomparable human mission, which has always made of them a single people. They should turn back to review their past, not to bask in the memory of vanished glories but to conjure fresh light from their embers.

A legend brightens the dawn of this history. Europa was a very beautiful girl with a pure white skin. She lived in Phoenicia where her father, Agenor, was king. As she was playing with her companions on the shore, Zeus perceived her and became inflamed with love. Taking the form of a white bull he approached her. Unafraid she climbed on to his back. Immediately he galloped away and bore her over the sea to the island of Crete. Of their union four sons were born: Sarpedon, one of the heroes of Asia, and three law-givers so famous for their judgments that they became the Judges of the Underworld. They were Minos, Aeacus and Rhadamanthus... At this point legend turns into history.

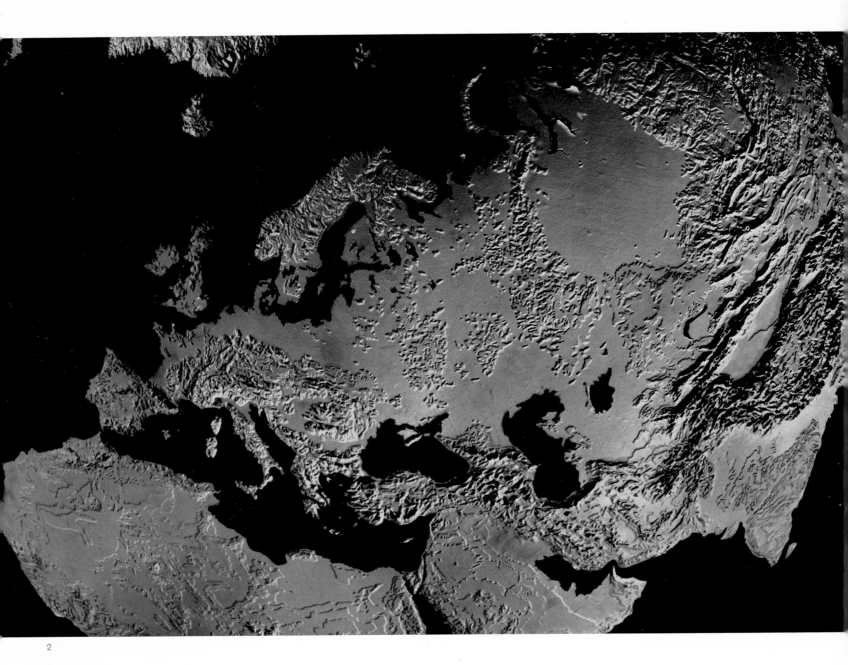

A promontory of the Asiatic continent—that is how Europe appears to anyone examining a globe-map of the world in relief. But this promontory is a world in itself. With its bony ridges, its nervous systems, its vast water-supply, it is a living body. Only the eastern steppe is flat and monotonous. Elsewhere mountain ranges have provided the face of the continent with perfect features. Their steep ridges divide and protect, and their snowy crests give rise to rivers both fertilising and navigable. By a bounteous dispensation the Alps coordinate all the essential parts of the West—the Germanic world to the north, the Latins to the south, to the west Gaul, and the Greeks and Slavs to the east. The Alps link them together and bring them nearer to one another without forcing them to mingle. Their passes and their valleys are the channels of intercourse and influence. Thus even if Western Europe is a land of diversity, of particular-

ism and of strife, it is also one in which the good of each nation is seen to be the good of all.

And from the Arctic Ocean to the Black Sea, what a multitude of capes, of gulfs, peninsulas and islands, great and small! No shores in the world possess outlines so denticulated. No place in Europe, even in the heart of the Continent, is really far from the sea. Europe has more than 4 kilometers of coastline for every 1000 square kilometers of area. Asia has less than two. So this continent, so well able to live on its own resources, in its own particular ways, is, at the same time, the most prone to cast its eyes out to sea. Its intimacy with the Atlantic has long since opened to it the sea-ways of the world, and its familiarity with the Mediterranean links it with the most ancient civilisations. As she reaches out towards the future, Europe is conscious of the unexampled richness of her inheritance from the past.

This History starts with Geography : Cape Europe with its countless bays.

Asia, where all is inscribed and all erased, already had its ruins and tombs.

3

4

In fact Asia is the homeland of the world's oldest historic civilisations. In the fifth millennium the first organised states appeared in the valleys of the great rivers—Indus, Tigris, Euphrates, Nile and on the shores of the Eastern Mediterranean.

The end of the fourth millennium saw the invention of writing, arithmetic, geometry and astronomy in these regions.

About the year 3000 B.C. Mohendjodar, one of the oldest known cities, was founded on the banks of the Indus. In its early days art was already
3 flourishing. This sculptured head reveals a type of man altogether different from the Aryan invaders who, about 1300, were to assimilate this ancient civilisation.

In Mesopotamia, in the third millennium, the Sumerians extended their empire and created a highly developed art, as can be seen from this

bas-relief, in which the king of the city-state of 4 Lagash (about 2000 B.C.) is carrying on his head the first bricks of the temple whose foundation he is celebrating. At the end of the second millennium the Semitic Assyrians subjugated the Mesopotamian peoples, but Assyrian art owes much to the tradition of the vanquished from whom the conquerors also borrowed the art of cuneiform writing.

As early as the middle of the 4th millennium Egypt, which in the eyes of the ancients was a part of Asia, had erected, between the Nile and the desert, the Pyramids—a monument for all eternity. 5

At the other end of Asia the Chinese came into history. They boast that by 3300 B.C. they had invented music. Towards 2500 B.C. they had perfected the system of writing which is practised today.

5

Deep in the clay and the moss, our life before history began.

6

7

Europe, at a time when important civilisations flourished in Asia, was still in the period of prehistory. Nevertheless certain gleams come to us from the darkness. Those figures of Venus, all breasts and belly, date from the Aurignacian epoch, tens of thousands of years before our era. Examples of these have been found at Irkutsk and at Willendorf in Lower Austria, as well as at Lespagne and Brassempouy in the Landes in France. These are fertility emblems, perhaps even the effigies of the Mother-Goddess worshipped everywhere at the beginning of the historical epoch.

The wall-paintings in the caves of Lascaux, in the valley of the Vézère or in Cantabrian Spain are the work of artists dating from the Magdalenian times, more than 12,000 years before Christ. In them wandering hunters have represented with life-like realism the great beasts of their epoch—mammoth, aurochs, bison, reindeer and stag. Doubtless they hoped to bring good luck to their hunting expeditions by painting in advance pictures of their success, for in those subterranean regions they must have felt themselves in contact with supernatural forces. Art and magic came into being at the same time.

An immense chronological abyss separates these pictures from the megalithic monuments —dolmens and menhirs—which were erected ten thousand years later in a great many parts of Europe. These form the relics of a religion about whose propagation we know nothing. In the cromlech of Stonehenge, on Salisbury Plain, a circle of menhirs has been set up to represent the image of the sun.

8

But a wind from the East was already filling the sails of the Cretan ship.

Europe with its megaliths had reached the Bronze Age. This new metal spread from south to north. It was already known in Gaul at the opening of the second millennium, but did not reach Scandinavia until the beginning of the Christian era. This little archer shows what good use the Sardinian artists 9 could make of bronze. The fact is that during this period Sardinia, like all the lands of the Mediterranean basin, was influenced by the enlightenment of a civilisation born between Asia and Europe — the civilisation of Crete.

Here history confirms legend. The true ancestor of Europe is this Crete, where the white-skinned Europa was set down by the divine bull. Towards 2400 B.C. the Cretans, a seafaring people, imported copper from Cyprus and tin from Spain, perhaps even from Britain. Their skilful hands produced a multitude of bronze pieces which they exported far and wide. Possessed of a powerful navy they soon became rulers of the Aegean. These little dark men not only had a great talent for industry and commerce; they were also extremely gifted as artists. They constructed in Cnossos, their capital, great palaces adorned with frescoes. This black-eyed 'Parisienne', with rouged lips and an elegant 10 hair-do, bears witness to a state of society in which women lived in public and made much of their charms. This 'Prince with lilies' was no doubt 11 named Minos, like all the Kings of Cnossos, after Europa's first-born son.

9

11

10

Here we see agile acrobats baiting a giant bull. 12 That is the traditional theme of Cretan circus performances and religious dances. One finds scenes of this nature painted on vases and the walls of the palaces. The bull, a divine animal, is the incarnation of the virile principle. But the Cretan Pantheon is dominated by the figure of the Great Mother, Goddess of fertility, whose primitive aspect is curiously reminiscent of the Aurignac Venuses. Her profile becomes more refined, as time goes on, but all the paintings represent her with bare, full breasts. It was in her honour that the Cretan women and the priestesses bared their breasts during the great festivals.

The enterprise and military successes of the Cretans led them to explore all the shores of the Mediterranean. Towards 1700 B.C. they landed on the Hellenic peninsula, where they met and subdued for a while the Achaean invaders. The latter, originally northerners, appear in history as the vanguard of the Indo-European hordes, who had come down from the cold regions of the Baltic or the Caspian. While preserving certain features of their Nordic civilisation, these barbaric warriors became conditioned, as time went on, to the Mediterranean. The example of the Cretans taught them to become navigators and traders. The profits of their flourishing trade justified Homer in calling their capital, Mycenae, 'the city rich in gold'. Their art, at this time, was mainly concerned with warlike pursuits. They built strategic roads in 13 shaped stone, fortified castles, great cemeteries in which they laid their dead with their faces covered with golden masks according to the northern 14 custom.

The Asian Minotaur crosses the islands and enters Europe through Mycenae.

14

Strong by virtue of their newly acquired maritime science and animated by a sense of military vocation, the Achaeans were always ready for fresh conquests. One day in the 15th century B.C. a host of warriors resembling those in the illustra-
15 tion landed in sight of Cnossos. The city was set on fire and Crete lost for ever its Aegean kingdom.

Mycenae now became the central point of a mixed civilisation at once Mediterranean and continental, which was destined to extend from Sicily to Cyprus and from Anatolia to Thessaly. This is the starting-point of the history of Greece and the history of Europe.

Victorious in war, the barbarians civilised by Crete became conscious of their standing as Aegeans and displayed a confused antagonism to the older peoples of the Orient. This antagonism appears as the initial and still very rudimentary symptom of a European consciousness.

At this point we enter the domain of written tradition by the royal door of the Homeric poems —the Iliad and the Odyssey. The date of the Trojan War, one of the episodes of which is the theme of the Iliad, is assumed to be about 1180 B.C. This is the first great historic event in the records of Europe, and it was, in fact, an offensive against the Orient.

If the Iliad illustrates the warlike aptitude of the Achaeans, the Odyssey, a truly Mediterranean poem, celebrates the cleverness and cunning of the men of the isles. During his journey home Ulysses
16 prudently has himself tied to the mast of his ship, so as not to be lured by the song of the Sirens.

Thus the first great European literary monument represents exactly the Greek society born from the fusion of the two races, Achaean and Cretan.

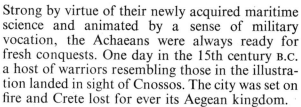

15

16

Homer wrote of arms and men - the first epics.

17

Six centuries later the Greek miracle materialised. Athens, as the foremost of the Hellenic cities, had flung back the Asiatic invader and now became supreme. From its Acropolis radiated a beauty which was to remain for the whole of Europe the standard of true beauty. Its harmoniously proportioned temples and porticoes compose the 17 most perfect urban landscape in the world. This paradise became the home of the Gods, whom the Greeks chose to see in the image of man. They mingled in the lives of mortals, and heroes were born from their union with women. The most celebrated of the Greek heroes, Achilles, shared with the humblest citizen of Athens a passion for gambling. His partner, portrayed on this vase, is 18 Ajax.

Over the Acropolis the sun stopped for this moment of perfection.

If Zeus reigned on Olympus, Athene reigned in the Acropolis. Athens was her town and its hill was consecrated to her.

19   She led the Athenians to victory at odds of one to a hundred when they flung the Persians back into the sea. She is the personification of victory and the temple of Athene the Victorious is dedicated to the spirit which conquers blind force, the spirit of wisdom.

Not far away the Erectheum housed a statue of the Goddess in olive wood, which was said to have fallen from heaven. And it was for Athene that Pericles had the Parthenon built. Balanced and austere, the Doric style of this building accords with the Genius of the Goddess who, proceeding from the brain of Zeus, incarnates reason.

20   Every four years the Athenians marched up to the temple of their Goddess in a long procession, as they celebrated the great Panathenian festival of which Phidias has left a living and harmonious picture in marble. Youths on horseback escort the long train of citizens, magistrates, priests, musicians and girls bearing offerings to present to the Goddess — a new tunic and a golden crown.

21   The town and the port with its traders and merchants were under the protection of Hermes, the cunning and ingenious God of commerce. He it was who watched over the prosperity of Athens.

Above him, as befitted the god of all the Greeks, came Apollo, embodiment of the sun. His oracles were transmitted by the Delphic priestess. The 'Amphictyonic League' at Delphi was one of the first attempts at federation in Europe. The member-states sent delegates to it twice yearly to discuss questions of common policy. A non-aggression pact subsisted among them, and they undertook to unite against any attack from outside.

Victory over Asia was the victory of Greece and Reason.

Man, 'the measure of all things', was the central figure of Greek art. Painters and sculptors possessed a perfect knowledge of the human body. They studied with minute care the play of the muscles and the sequence of attitudes in order to be able to suggest natural movement. They glorified the grace of maidens in their rippling robes and the beauty of athletes naked in the sunlit stadium. One example out of many is the famous discobolos.

The physical exercise, the games, the athletic contests, showed the pleasure the Greeks took in enhancing the beauty and the suppleness of the body—instrument of the mind. In pursuing physical culture methodically, in the gymnasium and at

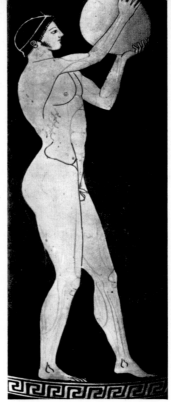

22

24

the stadium, they were exercising their reason and their free will.

In describing the passions and sufferings of their heroes, the tragedians display the same exactness and vigour of expression. Aeschylus, Sophocles and Euripides have set a standard of psychological observation and elegant style for all succeeding European dramatists. Aristophanes created a comic tradition to which the western world is still

loyal. Every year new tragedies and satiric pieces were played in the great theatre of Dionysus, to celebrate the festival of the God.

The full scope of Athenian democracy was revealed at this festival. There was nothing like the theatre, where the crowds were swelled by even the poorest, to unite a whole people: together they were moved by the terrors of a tragic scene, the gaiety of a comedy; all were equally gripped by the problems and conflicts presented to their imagination.

While Sparta was offering the first example of a totalitarian state, Pericles, at Athens, was consolidating the institutions of democracy. This regime favours the development of eloquence, for which the Greeks have a natural bent.

Demosthenes, who succeeded in checking the rivalries of his compatriots and inducing them to unite against Philip of Macedon, was the most famous of the Attic orators. 'He would have saved Greece if the Greeks had been willing to be saved', but it was too late. Torn by internal strife Greece could no longer resist the foreign enemy and, reduced to servitude, she gradually disintegrated.

The Greeks invent democracy : in the arena, in the theatre, at the polls.

27

26

Fortunately classical Greece had endured long enough to provide, in the creations of her genius, the sources of what the West today calls civilisation. In addition to enriching the patrimony of mankind by her treasures of plastic and literary beauty and establishing the principle of democracy, the shield

26 of human liberty, with the voter's pebble for its curious symbol, she gave to the world the admirable philosophy, which in the words of Cicero

27 'Socrates first caused to descend from heaven'. This great man, having studied all the known sciences, concluded that they were all of relative and incurably provisional significance. He did not despise them; far from it, he loved them, but the study of man was his great interest. It led him to the discovery of introspection and self-knowledge through the dialectical method. He distrusted systems and the great fabrics of the metaphysicians and confined himself, with his simple method, to the double goal of determining truth and discovering virtue. The only true values are those of the mind; beauty, wealth, reputation count for nothing. The outward man is nothing—his true identity is to be discovered in his soul.

Socrates wrote nothing, but he inspired, in the person of Plato his pupil, an apostle who was one of the greatest philosophers and poets of all time. With Plato came into being the philosophy of the spirit, which so greatly influenced early Christian thought. His disciple, Aristotle, evolved a more rigid and logical system, in which the sublime functions of man are contemplation and rational reflection, anticipating the Catholic theology of St Thomas Aquinas. The influence of Plato and Aristotle on European thought inspired Raphael in the 16th century to portray them as the central

28 figures in his fresco 'The School of Athens'.

28

At the fountainhead of philosophy stand Socrates and Plato.

The columned cradle of our civilisation awaits the birth.

30

31

Seafarers and traders created all over the coasts of the Mediterranean little Greek settlements which expanded in course of time. Pushing northward they founded Byzantium and established trading-posts among the Scythians in Southern Russia. In Provence they founded Nice and Marseilles, and Malaga in Spain. Round the coasts of the Ionian Sea and in Southern Italy and Sicily, a new Greece came into being—Greater Greece.

These lands, rich in wheat, wine and oil, with their powerful cities—Tarentum, Sybaris, Crotona, Syracuse, Agrigentum, Naples, Cumae, Paestum —gave the mainland Greeks a new world, not unlike what America was to become later in the eyes of Europeans. Exiles, malcontents and adventurers rushed to these new territories. Temples were built, as towns sprang up. That of Segesta, 29 constructed in the purest Doric style, is dedicated to Demeter, the Goddess of agriculture.

Commerce flourished in oversea Greece and each city had its own coinage. The coins, often of a striking beauty, reflect the bustling life of cities like Tarentum, Rhegium and Syracuse. Passing from 30 31 hand to hand from the Pillars of Hercules to the Euxine they carried far and wide images showing the beliefs and achievements of a civilisation.

29

God-like Alexander died at 33, but the Asia he conquered remembers him.

32

At the end of the 4th century the Hellenic world set out to conquer the Orient. Philip, King of Macedon, had united the cities of Hellas under his guardianship. He conceived the notion of concentrating the whole force of the Greek world against Persia and of cementing by a common victory the union of Macedonia and Greece. But he died in 336 B.C. leaving his son Alexander to carry out his great project. At the head of a small army of 35,000 men, Alexander crossed into Asia.

32 There his irresistible *élan*, pictured centuries later in a mosaic at Pompeii, routed the innumerable armies of the Great King. Encouraged by his victory at Issus, he conquered Egypt, founded Alexandria and then launched his forces at the heart of the Persian empire. Babylon, Susa, Perse-

polis fell in turn. After the death of Darius, Alexander continued his victorious advance. He reached Bactria (Turkestan), where he founded cities, and then, turning south, crossed the Indus. He would have pushed eastwards to the Ganges, had his troops not refused to go on. At his death, age thirty-two, he had already transformed Western Asia.

Everywhere he sowed the seed of Hellenism. In India the Greco-Buddhist style with its curious Apollos flourished for a few seasons. 33

In the kingdoms established throughout the dismembered Empire, Pergamos, Antioch and Alexandria took, each in turn, the place of Athens. At the entrance to the harbour of Alexandria gleamed 34 the Pharos, one of the seven wonders of the world.

34

33

He founded twenty cities, - Alexandria, the empire's brand and dying ash.

35

36

Alexandria, henceforward the seat of the Ptolemies, became the centre of the new Hellenistic culture. Artists and poets ceased to show themselves in the life of the market-place. They began to appeal to a mundane society. People no longer went to see tragedies. They read them at home. The great library of Alexandria, continually enriched by gifts from the Ptolemies, contained as many as 700,000 volumes.

In the precincts of the museum, one might have encountered Eratosthenes, Euclid, Aristarchus or Theocritus. The most famous Ptolemy was an Alexandrian of the 2nd century A.D. His system of astronomy remained in vogue for centuries. A portrait of him survives from the middle ages. He 35 is wearing a crown with his spouse, Astronomy,

at his side. The artist, misled by a contemporary error, thought him a member of the Royal House.

Alexandria bred not only scientists but also engineers. It was there that man invented the lever and the water-wheel and discovered the properties of compressed air and of steam.

Contact with the Orient had its effect on artistic expression. The pure and sober Attic ideal was succeeded by excess and over-emphasis. Examples are this group from Pergamos showing a Gaul killing his wife, or the mannered languor of 36 this hermaphrodite from Alexandria. Hellenistic 37 civilisation, the child of Aristotle, grew to maturity on the soil of Asia and was finally to reach Europe by way of Rome, Byzantium and the Arabs.

37

38

39

The European continent which stood outside the Greek world was a self-centred unit. Civilisations which grew up with the rapidly expanding metal industry had created a vast system of communications which crossed the continent, linking the Baltic with the Mediterranean. But the Scythians who descended on Europe from Southern Siberia around A.D. 500 and penetrated as far as Alsace, promptly broke up this trading network. They were forced back into Romania by the Celts. The so-called Celts were neither a nation nor a race. These migrant peoples who, towards 350 B.C., were occupying Gaul, Western Germany up to the Elbe, Bavaria, Bohemia, Hungary, Serbia, Northern Italy, Spain and the British Isles, acquired in the course of their wanderings through Europe common traditions, a common language and a common religion—the elements of a civilisation. The Greeks gave the name of Celts or Gauls to these wanderers.

Early in the 3rd century B.C., after plundering Greece, one of their armies crossed the Bosporus and created in Asia Minor the kingdom of Galatia. More than once they menaced Rome. Their manner of building survived for long in regions as different from one another as Provence and Ireland. 38 39

They were known for their bravery, pride and readiness to take offence. Inconstant in thought and action, bold but easily disheartened, they filled the ancient world with movement and trouble. They were the *enfants terribles* of antiquity. Possessing no genius for organisation, they could never unite, and so became subject to the Romans in Italy, the Germans west of the Elbe and the Dacians along the Danube. But though subjugated they did not lose their vitality and they preserved the spirit of their traditions. Their temperament remains an important component of the European character.

Formerly nomads, they invested their wealth in what they could lead or carry with them—flocks and herds and gold. They knew how to preserve wine in casks and meat in salt. They were remarkable wheelwrights and glass-workers. They created an art which was original but susceptible to many outside influences. What is there in common between these two heads found one at Mseche Zehrovic in Czechoslovakia and the other near Nîmes in France? 40 41

40 41

Europe has a Grecian nose, but the changing eyes of her Celtic mother. Wine

24

This little dancing girl recalls the Sardinian bronzes, 42 while this horseman hunting a boar shows traces 43 of Iberian influence. But the most remarkable relic of Celtic art is the great silver bowl discovered at Gundestrup in Jutland. It is carved with a double frieze, inside and out, adorned with figures in relief showing battle scenes, sacrifices and busts 44

representing the Gods of the Celtic Year. The Celts worshipped springs, trees, the stars, and certain animals. This coin shows Epona, the Mare- 45 Goddess, poised above a boat bearing the solar wheel.

The druids, who were both soothsayers and doctors and who wielded great political and religious power, used to preside at the human sacrifices and feasts in honour of the Earth Mother, the source of all life.

in the cask, timid souls and boastful hearts attest our peasant origin.

The great gateway is Etruscan, open for Rome to pass through.

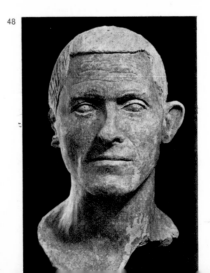

During the second millennium, while the Achaeans were establishing themselves in Greece, other peoples, also of Indo-European stock, invaded Italy. These were the Italiots. Next, in the 9th century, came the Etruscans, who had probably journeyed by sea from Asia Minor. This was a race of warriors, who extended their rule from Etruria to Latium, the Campagna, the valley of the Po and even to Corsica. Their towns, which they built on the tops of hills, were fortresses. Surrounded by stone ramparts with great vaulted gateways, they remind us of Mycenae and Tiryns. The citadels of Volterra and Perugia are still upstanding under the Tuscan sky. At Tarquinia and other places they built indestructible cities of the dead, often decorated with frescoes.

From their lofty strongholds they ruled over the submissive plainsmen, to whom they taught the principles of irrigation. The marshes were drained and the soil became rich and fertile. The Etruscans were skilled goldsmiths and bronze-workers. They exploited copper and silver mines and extracted iron-ore in Elba. Their vessels ploughed the Mediterranean and their merchants crossed the Alps, traversed Germany till they reached the Baltic and penetrated to the heart of the Danubian plains.

A new form of art spread from the Arno to the Tiber. In this bronze dancer of the 5th century one can recognise the influence of Greece and the Orient, while this terra-cotta head of the 1st century is obviously Roman. The difference in style is obvious, but is not this dancer with his pathetic movements and his unclassic shape somehow closer to modern art? Today many think that Etruscan, like Celtic, art kept alive the archaic and expressionist tendencies which preceded the austerities of classical art and emerged once more triumphantly when the Middle Ages succeeded to antiquity. Thus Etruscan civilisation may be considered as a bridge between two opposing but equally European styles of art. In more obvious and direct fashion it fertilised Rome. Early in the 3rd century Rome broke the power of Etruria, but the Etruscans, in defeat, became the mentors of their conquerors. Their architects made a town of Rome and their magistrates and priests a city.

49

50

In the great days of Etruscan civilisation Rome still cut an insignificant figure. We have, indeed, every reason for thinking that in the second half of the 6th century Rome was actually ruled by her powerful neighbour. The house of Tarquin was Etruscan.

There is no better known legend then that of the founding of Rome. Aeneas, fleeing from Troy in flames, lands on the coast of Latium. His son, Ascanius, founds Alba Longa. Later Romulus and Remus, the twins born of the union of Mars with the king's daughter, are abandoned on the banks 49 of the Tiber and suckled by the she-wolf. Next we see Romulus in 753 B.C. tracing the first plan of Rome on the soil of the Palatine. The outlaws of the region flock to inhabit the new town and need-

ing to supply themselves with wives, seize the Sabine women. Mythical, no doubt, but it is worth while remembering that the Albans possibly came in Homeric times from Asia Minor and that Rome sprang from an alliance between the Albans of the Palatine and the Sabines of the Capitoline. This legend contains traces of ancient myths from all round the coasts of the Mediterranean. The story of the she-wolf was current in Crete and Arcadia. In this version the wolf was doubtless the totem of an ancient tribe of Latium.

A tremendous adventure was beginning. As time went on the town on the seven hills was destined to be covered by a forest of monuments growing ever richer and more splendid. It was to become 50 the first capital of Europe.

Rome at last, nourished on wolf's milk, Rome, the first capital of Europe.

53

The Albans of the days of Romulus were Indo-Europeans. They had brought with them into Italy the same toughness, energy and taste for war which enabled the Achaeans to conquer the Cretans. The Sabines, from the oldest Mediterranean peoples, were remarkable for their finesse, their vivacity and imagination. The Romans issued from a blend of these two elements.

Rome grew to greatness slowly. It took her four centuries to conquer the peninsula. By her tenacity she overcame the resistance of the Latins, the Etruscans and the Greek cities of the south, as well as the Gallic invaders. Her victory over Carthage established her dominion over the whole of the Western Mediterranean. In the 2nd century B.C. Macedonia, Greece, Asia Minor and the south-east of Gaul and Spain became Roman provinces. The legions, commanded by great captains, who 51 had made signal advances in the arts of war, imposed Roman law and order everywhere. In Rome itself the Senate worked out the broad political and administrative principles which, already at this stage, were moulding Europe. Gaul, conquered by Caesar, did not struggle for long in her chains, like the captive Gauls one can see on the triumphal arch at Carpentras. Romanised, the 52 Gauls became the most stable and, at the same time, dynamic element of the Empire. Caesar profited by his conquest of Gaul to become a dictator. The Republic crumbled. The huge Roman Empire needed a single head. When Julius Caesar 53 was murdered, who was to succeed him?

51

52

Rome's power and brightness are personified in Caesar.

Mark Antony, Caesar's second, a blunt soldier, or Octavianus, Caesar's great-nephew and heir, a quick-witted intelligent young man? At first they divided the provinces between them. Mark Antony took Greece and the Orient and Octavian Italy, Gaul and Spain. In Egypt Mark Antony conquered Cleopatra, while in Rome Octavian secured the favour of the Romans. He was clever enough to give the inevitable clash with Mark Antony the aspect of a war between Rome and Egypt, the West against the East. In 31 B.C. his victory at Actium established the supremacy of the West. Julius Caesar had already assumed the title of

54 *Imperator* and Octavian accepted from the Senate the appellation of Augustus, a style hitherto reserved for the Gods. All the military, civil and religious powers of the State were concentrated in his hands. At thirty-two the heir of Julius was the absolute master of the civilised world. Everywhere his statue was set up beside the images of the Gods.

In countless regions, formerly blood-drenched by the internecine struggles of citizens and tribesmen, the Pax Romana was established. A new society, subject to Roman law, came into being, but man's inhumanity to man was not abolished.

55 Slaves were numerous and often ill-treated. Peace brought a remarkable expansion to the economy of the state. Commerce and banking flourished as far as the remote Germanic confines of the Empire. Here we see boatmen rowing their cargoes of

56 barrels on the Moselle and here money-changers
57 counting their coins at Trèves.

54

56

57

55

Rome of Augustus, the Imperial city, imposes her gods and her laws.

Rome, the modeller, leaves her mark on Europe from Spain to Roumania.

60

In order the better to assure the peace of the Empire, Augustus aimed to extend his frontiers to the Elbe and the Danube. Long and bitter campaigns were fought in which Tiberius and Germanicus, the conqueror of Arminius, distinguished themselves. The greater part of Europe was now 58 Roman. The Great Cameo of France, displaying Germanicus surrounded by his illustrious ancestors as well as by the Emperor Tiberius and the Imperial Family, celebrates this victory.

In the 2nd century under the Antonines the Empire ceased to expand. It already stretched from Scotland to the Tigris and embraced the whole of North Africa and Dacia. But beyond the Danube the Germanic world was already in turmoil.

During these fruitful years Europe was romanised and transformed. The territories of the Empire were intersected by high-roads and aqueducts as far as Segovia in the heart of Spain, while thermal 59 stations, triumphal arches and arenas, copied from the Coliseum, still display their monumental walls at Verona, Nîmes and Arles. Numerous, richly 60 decorated villas adorned the provincial countryside. This mosaic, which represents the sadness of 61 winter, was found in a villa in Sussex.

By means of her language, coinage, institutions, couriers, armies, outposts and administrators, her wealth, banks, public works and works of art, by her laws and her practical genius Rome was able to mould the still malleable clay of Europe. The waves of barbarian invaders were still threatening to submerge her, but her civilisation was destined to survive the Empire and become the common property of the new world.

61

59

These roads enabled Rome to keep the countries conquered by the legions and to practise administrative and economic centralisation. The Appian Way, built in 311 B.C., linked Rome with Capua. The Gallic network was completed by Augustus. Tiberius and Vespasian made roads in Spain, Claudius in Dalmatia and Nero in Thrace. At the end of the Empire the total length of the Roman roads was over 56,000 miles, of which about half was in Europe.

These highways were practically indestructible walls of cemented flagstones resting on a bed of concrete which went down as far as the basic rock. As far as possible they followed a straight line and avoided the steeper slopes. Hence the necessity for numerous bridges, viaducts and tunnels. The distances were marked every 1000 double steps (about 1620 yards) by cylindrical milestones, on which was inscribed the name of the reigning emperor.

THE ROMAN ROADS WERE THE ARTERIES OF EUROPE WHICH MADE THE CONTINENT A LIVING BODY.

(1) *Alcantara Bridge on the Tagus.* (2) *Thermal station, Bath.* (3) *Aqueduct of Gard.* (4) *The Black Gate at Trèves.* (5) *Gate of Augustus at Rimini* (27 B.C.). (6) *Arch of Janus Quadrifrons at Rome.*

These roads, triumphant and vain, awaited the messengers of the Word.

63

But Rome had no spiritual message for her peoples. Her best thinkers had assimilated the philosophy of the Greeks without contributing anything new. In this field, as in the arts and technical sciences, the Romans invented nothing. Moral decadence gradually overtook all the romanised peoples. In the big towns an unproductive proletariat spread like a cancer. Economic conditions became chaotic and the Empire barricaded itself behind its frontiers.

The time had come when the historian Florus could ask if Rome would not have done better to content herself with Sicily and Africa, or even to do without them in order to govern Italy more effectively.

Grinding poverty or unsatisfying luxury led people to hope for a religion that would meet their highest aspirations. They abandoned their old Roman Gods and sought comfort in the religions of the East. The soil was ready for Christianity, a sudden breakaway from the synagogues of Palestine. (The illustration shows the Jewish

62 pentagram, which figured on the shield of David.)

Christianity brought to the world the word which was to provide unfailing inspiration to artists and writers through the centuries.

63 This bas-relief from the cathedral at Hildesheim shows man in the bondage of sin, since God expelled him and Eve from Eden, but this mosaic

64 from Daphni adds that the sacrifice of Jesus, the Messiah or Christ, frees men, if they so will, from the ancient curse. It only depends upon them to attain eternal life.

The peoples of the Empire, and foremost among them the Greek-speaking citizens, received the glad tidings with gratitude and joy. History had started to inscribe a new chapter to succeed the Epics of Greece and Rome.

62

64

33

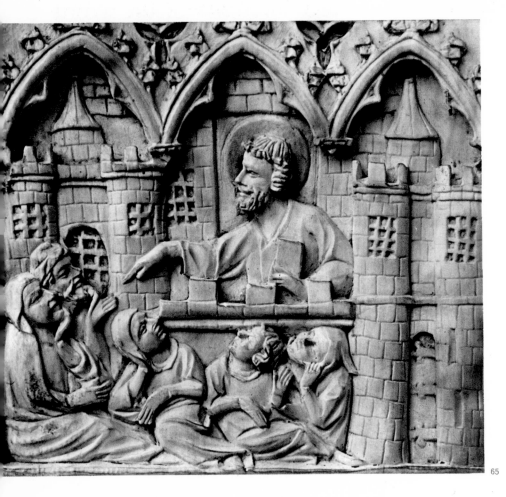

65

66

At Rome the message of Christ at once clashed with the policy of the State. In the capital, where all strange religions were received with favour, only the Christians were persecuted, for the reason that their doctrine appeared to threaten revolution and endanger society. Its adepts refused to adore the Emperor as a God. They endured every form of punishment rather than sacrifice their faith in a single universal God. Meanwhile the voices of the first apostles spread the good tidings abroad.

Peter, a disciple of Jesus, preached the Gospel in Judaea, Galilee and Asia Minor, before coming to Rome, where he evangelised the Jewish colony and laid the foundations of the primitive Church. Paul, a fanatical defender of Judaism, first became known for his zeal in persecuting the Christians.

As the result of a vision he had on the road to Damascus, he became the Apostle of the Gentiles. His journeys through Asia Minor, Greece and Macedonia, where there was no lack of brigands and scoffers, his heroic sea-voyages, his apostolate in Rome, where he met Peter, combined to make Paul the first and greatest missionary. His sermons and epistles to the different communities teach the first Christian dogmas.

He is first of all a teacher and that is how he is most often depicted. Meanwhile Peter, considered as the first of the Popes, holds the keys of Paradise. Both of these saints died as martyrs to their faith, and in spite of the activity of the disciples of Christ during the three ensuing centuries, the new religion remained a secret cult. The Christians, who rejected cremation, buried their dead in the catacombs which they decorated with symbolic signs such as the fish, $i\chi\theta\nu\varsigma$, a word formed from the initial letters of the Greek words for Jesus Christ, Son of God, Saviour.

65
66

67

67

Peter and Paul offer mankind martyrdom and the Keys of heaven.

Constantine's Cross became a banner matching Byzantium with Rome.

68

At the opening of the 4th century there were in Rome only 30,000 Christians, most of them Jewish or slaves or Greek-speaking freedmen, but the aristocracy also provided recruits. The cause of Christianity was won when in 313 the Emperor Constantine, who had long been tormented by 68 unsatisfied religious longings, and even superstitions, opted for Christ. The Edict of Milan gave Christians the right of citizenship. Disputes over dogma arose immediately. Constantine embraced the Arian heresy. Just before his death he had himself baptised by an Arian bishop. But the essential thing, as the Middle Ages decided, was that he was the first Christian Emperor. At Rome, in the Church of the Four Crowned Martyrs, is a fresco showing his baptism in the prime of life. 69

Helen, Constantine's mother, made the first historical pilgrimage to the Holy Land. At Jerusalem she unearthed the wood of the True Cross. Thus the taste for relics, so widespread in the Middle Ages, was already apparent. The finding of the Holy Cross became the theme of 70 numerous miniatures.

But the unity of the world under the Sign of the Cross was disintegrating. Constantine turned Byzantium, a Greek city on the Bosphorus, into a new capital—the rival of Rome. And so the Eastern Empire was born and grew up beside the Western.

69

70

Not even after its conversion to Christianity could the Empire alone establish Europe as an entity. The remote regions of the continent remained inaccessible by reason of the resistance of the different barbarous tribes, such as the Sarmatians, often beaten but never conquered, who are 71 depicted on Trajan's column.

The year 395 marks the end of Roman unity. Theodosius, before his death, had divided the Empire between his two sons. The Eastern Empire was to survive for a thousand years, but the Western disappeared within a century, shattered by the blows of the barbarians. In order to combat depopulation and impoverishment, Rome had long since admitted Goths and Vandals to citizenship and made colonists and soldiers of them, and the barbarians were imperceptibly colonising the Empire. Soon Europe began to feel the repercussion of the great revolutions in Asia. The Huns fled before the Chinese; the Alains and Goths before the Huns, driving before them the Germans and Vandals. In Gaul, Italy, Spain and even 72 in North Africa, the tribal chiefs partitioned the territory of Rome. They did not regard themselves as the enemies of the Empire, whose civilisation they admired and respected, but their migrations were not effected without destruction. Rome was pillaged in 410 by Alaric's Vizigoths and again in 455 by Genseric's Vandals. The fusion between invaders and Romans took place in an atmosphere of uncertainty and danger.

This influx of strangers changed the face of the Roman world. New models were provided by the Steppes to replace Greek art. The barbarians introduced new treasures into the West, such as this Scythian panther in hammered gold dating 73 from the 6th or 7th century B.C., or this horseman 74 with tracery ornamentation, of uncertain date.

The age of the great chieftains, prompt to push aside proud Rome, yet ready

75 The invaders marched across the whole of the Western Empire, sooner or later settling down permanently. Wherever they went they found, firmly established upon the ruins of Roman institutions, the religious, social and administrative structure maintained by the Christian clergy. The bishops perceived that, if they wished to save the Church, they would have to make Christians of their new masters. So the barbarians were converted, and this conquest of the victors by the faith of the vanquished assured the foundations of
76 Europe. Only Attila's Huns held out against this contagion of the spirit. And now the world of antiquity was dead and the Middle Ages came into being.

76

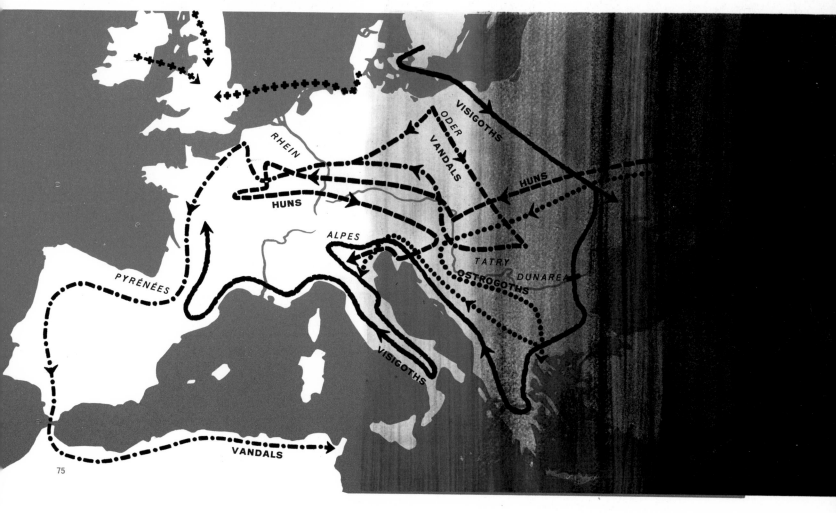

75

to be baptized. Beauty and the Beast allied : This is the real Europe.

73

37

Pope Gregory will change imperial Rome into the Christian capital.

77

78

Rome and the chief cities of the West were filled 77
with ruins, which no one attempted to rebuild. The
fiction of the Roman Empire remained, but the
barbarian kings were the real masters of the West.
Ostrogoths ruled in Italy, Vizigoths in Spain,
Burgundians and Franks in Gaul, Angles and
Saxons in Britain.

In Italy Theodoric, who had been educated in
Constantinople, strove to continue the Roman
tradition. He resided at Ravenna, but revived the
old relations with the Senate and people of Rome.
For a short time Italy revived. This eagle, a Roman 78
symbol, treated in his own national style by an
Ostrogoth goldsmith, shows that a new civilisation
—a synthesis of the Germanic with the Mediterranean genius—was taking shape.

Spain enjoyed a similar respite from war in the
reign of Euric the Vizigoth. After his death Spain
became an Ostrogoth protectorate until the day
when King Recared repudiated Arianism and
founded the Iberian Catholic monarchy. Meantime Clovis created an united Frankish kingdom
stretching from the Loire to the Weser. By his
conversion to Catholicism, he secured the support
of the Church. A new adventure was brewing in
these Gallo-Germanic lands.

The reconquest of Italy by the Emperor
Justinian had ruined the country. Rome, which
formerly possessed a million inhabitants, was
reduced to a population of 50,000. After this the
Lombards arrived, but never succeeded in having
their kings crowned at Rome with their famous
diadem, for now, with Gregory the Great as Pope, 79
the Papacy became in its turn a Temporal Power.

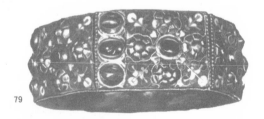

79

At Constantinople the Imperial idea flourished in full vigour. In the 6th century it was personified by Justinian, splendidly seconded by his wife Theodora.

This indefatigable ruler aimed to restore the Empire to what it was in the time of Augustus and Trajan. His campaigns against the Arian Ostrogoths and Vandals can also be considered as Catholic crusades against heresy. He recovered Italy, North Africa and South-East Spain for the Empire, but only his legislative achievements were destined to survive him. Thanks to his Code, his Digests, his Pandects and his *Institutiones*, Roman law has outlived the centuries of barbarism. The texts of his works were rediscovered in the 12th century and were to serve as the foundation of the laws of the European nations of the Mediterranean.

During his campaigns on many fronts undertaken to maintain the heritage of Greece and Rome, Justinian set himself to enrich the Empire. In his reign innumerable castles, aqueducts, hospitals, churches and palaces sprang up. Saint Sophia was the most splendid of these. At Constantinople there was an immense accumulation of treasures from the ancient world, such as the famous horses, cast in the 3rd century B.C., formerly in Rome and Alexandria, which now stand in front of St. Mark's at Venice.

A form of Christian art, which has been strongly influenced by the Orient, began to spread throughout the Empire. Examples of this can be found in the splendid mosaics at Ravenna, and later in those of Rome and Sicily, and in the domed churches of Greece and the Middle East. Poised above the barbarian world and astride on the hinge between two continents, Constantinople shone with incomparable brilliance.

The Empire spread overseas, to survive on the Bosphorus.

85

The country districts of the West were converted to Christianity much more slowly than the towns. In those European languages which are derived from Latin—the Romance languages—we get (in French) *paysan=paganus=païen*. The peasant was attached to the soil which he cultivated. His mind, little inclined to speculation, easily confused natural with supernatural forces. Prehistoric fertility cults had left their traces on him. He worshipped trees and springs. Moreover, the monuments inherited from the great neolithic religion and utilised by that of the Druids—the dolmens and menhirs—remained the objects of veneration and superstitious attachment, as did the host of Greek and Celtic gods.

It took many centuries to christianise the countryside and conversion took the most varied forms. In Gaul and Britain, dolmens and menhirs bearing the sign of the Cross bear witness to the ⁸⁵ intention of the missionary to imprint the new faith on the monuments before which the common people had long been accustomed to worship a divine power Springs also became recruits to Christianity.

Most of the pioneers of the Cross in the country districts remain obscure, forgotten and unknown. In the 4th century there is mention of Nicetas, who converted the Dacians, a savage tribe dwelling in the lower reaches of the Danube; in Northern Italy we hear of the missionaries sent out by Vigilius, Bishop of Trent; while in Flanders Victricius of Rouen left his mark. But Gaul could boast of the most illustrious of them all, St Martin.

The Cross is planted in pagan earth to become both guide and conscience.

A mystical Europe arises with the monasteries to shed its light.

86

87

86 As a young officer in the Roman army, he started his career as a Christian by sharing his cloak with a beggar—an act of brotherly love commemorated by painters throughout the ages. Before he died in 397 he had evangelised almost all the provinces of Gaul. In 360 he founded at Ligugé, near Poitiers, the first of the Gallic monasteries.

Nothing during the early Middle Ages was more effective in planting Christianity in the soil of Europe than the network of monasteries which grew up everywhere. The monks of the West were not merely, like their brothers in the Eastern Empire, men who had withdrawn from the world. They craved for an active rather than a contemplative spiritual life. Heirs of the Roman tradition, they dreamt of a united world; in the twilight that brooded over Europe they kept the flame alive.

Consciousness of such a mission is visible in the strongly stylised features of this likeness of St Matthew depicted in a copy of the Gospel of the 7th century. This type of art, which is also illustrated by this chalice of the 8th century, comes from Ireland. That country, evangelised by St Patrick in the 5th century, soon became a great centre of missionary effort. Monks, with St Columba at their head, set out in crowds from its monasteries to conquer the Continent. 87 88

St Benedict, in the first half of the 6th century, provided a Rule for European monasticism. It was owing to the influence of his disciple St Maurus, whom we see here presenting a book in homage to his master, that the Benedictines spread so rapidly in the West. Pope Gregory the Great was a member of the Order. 89

89

88

43

At the end of the 6th century Europe was torn by political and military conflicts. The Emperor of the East had no longer any authority in the West, although the clergy and the Pope himself continued to appeal to him. Gregory the Great, elected Pope in 590, declared himself 'Subject to the Emperor's orders' though he well knew that he faced the barbarians alone.

What he did was to approach the latter resolutely giving them the status of Europeans. Whether they were Arians or pagans, they had to be brought into the Catholic fold. He made plans for the conversion of the heretic Lombards. He despatched to the pagan Anglo-Saxons missionaries under the leadership of Augustine, who achieved a total success. Aided by Queen Bertha from Paris, this monk baptised, on Whitsunday 597, King Ethelbert and a great number of his officers. He had himself consecrated Archbishop of the English Church and at Christmas baptised 10,000 English converts on one day. The King, eager to be of service, gave him his own palace at Canterbury. In the 7th and 8th centuries the Anglo-Saxon Church became the centre of science and learning in the West. Augustine contemplated a mission to Germany, but a century had to pass before St Willibrord founded in Luxemburg the Abbey of **90** Echternach, in 698, the starting-point of a fresh campaign of expansion. Finally, in order to gratify the faithful and retain their allegiance, he increased the attractiveness of the services. Plainsong or Gregorian chant characterises the youthful power of the Roman Church.

Gregory the Great, one day while he was celebrating mass, had a vision of Jesus, which Christian art has commemorated, but his political **91** vision was not less inspired. In the ruins of the old Western world, still prostrate on the Rome-Byzantium axis, he visualised young Europe on its feet, advancing to greet the virgin forces of the North.

91

A great Pope dreams of young Europe leaning for support on the barbarian

But the hour had not yet come for the realisation of Gregory's Grand Design. He died in 604 and his successors quickly slipped back into the Byzantine rut. The first apostles to Germany, left to themselves, became gradually exhausted by unco-ordinated efforts. A tombstone of the 7th century found near Bonn attests the force of German paganism. Graven on it is an image of the serpent resisting the Cross.

Meantime a new power was threatening Europe —that of Islam. In less than a century, between 634 and 713, the Arabs established by conquest an immense Empire stretching from India to Spain, where they were to remain for nearly eight centuries. In 718 they were defeated before Constantinople and in 732 Charles Martel drove them back to the Pyrenees, but the religious unity of the Mediterranean was effectually broken and Christianity lost its hold on the Near East and Africa.

As a set-off against these losses St Boniface, an Englishman, evangelised Germany. He stabilised his spiritual conquests by founding great monasteries and nunneries and at Geismar he cut down the sacred tree of Wotan. When he suffered martyrdom, the German Church was already closely attached to the Holy See. From 740 onwards Boniface reorganised the Frankish Church and, in 752, in the name of Pope Zachary, he anointed Pippin the Short, the son of Charles Martel, on his accession to the throne.

Of great importance was the fact that Pippin I was king by the will of God, which gave him standing as the official protector of the Church, therefore it was to him, and not to the Emperor at Constantinople, that Pope Zachary appealed against the Lombards. Pippin wrested from them the Exarchate of Ravenna and gave it to the Pope, thereby creating the first of the Papal States. He also drove the Arabs out of Languedoc and subdued the Aquitanians. He traced the path his son was to follow, giving reality to Gregory's dream.

North. Wotan's oak is cut down, Islam driven out and Pépin crowned king.

94

Empress was taking command, Europe, united from the Ebro to the Oder under the sceptre of Charles, was acquiring a personality. The world looked on in wonder. The powerful Caliph of Baghdad, Haroun al-Rachid loaded Charles with gifts and the Patriarch of Jerusalem sent him the keys of the Holy Sepulchre.

With Charlemagne master of Christian Europe, one could hope for the end of the chaos in which the West had been blundering for the past three centuries. It looked as if order and unity had been secured for ever. That was the central hope and wish of the Church, who realised that without them she could not hope to accomplish her mission of salvation and civilisation. In Rome Pope Leo III spoke of that century, enriched with the memory of great men, in which the West became Christian in the midst of the Pax Romana, under the pro-

That son was Charlemagne—not the Emperor with the white flowing beard of the legend, but the stalwart Frank with short hair, shaven chin and
94 full moustache we see upon his coins. He soon extended his kingdom from Aquitaine to Bavaria, dispossessed the Lombard kings in Italy and dealt a death-blow to Saxon paganism. Thus he became master of Italy, Gaul and Germany, old and illustrious countries in which European civilisation was for the first time to enjoy its diverse inheritance.

In order to contain the Slavs and the Avars he created 'marches', or frontier districts in the regions which later became Brandenburg and Austria, while, to keep out the Saracens, he created the Spanish 'march'. He established the seat of his power between the Meuse and the Rhine in that district flanked by the Moselle which had been the most romanised part of Germany and in which survived a true balance between the Latin and Nordic genius. Charles set up his capital in a simple rural domain where in 794 at Aix-la-Chapelle he built a palace and a fine basilica
95 dedicated to the Virgin.

This Frankish monarch made no attempt to copy Roman or Byzantine organisation. Better as an administrator than as a general, he preserved the framework of the Merovingian administration and inspired it with new life. Twice a year he convened his military and civil chiefs and his ecclesiastics, to draft laws at the autumn session and promulgate them in the spring. In the three hundred counties which constituted his kingdom he kept a permanent staff of inspectors, the *missi dominici*, who gathered information and conveyed the king's commands as well as acting as judges and administrators guided by a code of very precise and detailed instructions. While at Byzantium the

95

Charlemagne, Emperor of Christian Europe, makes his capital at Aix-la-

tection of Constantine and his successors. The heir of St Peter still hoped to be defended by Caesar. The future, it is true, was to show that this was not the right road for the Church, nor yet for Europe. But at that moment everything conspired to encourage such a design. Like his father, Charles protected the Church, respected the spiritual authority of the Holy See and assigned to the Pope a territory of his own in order to guarantee his independence. Inevitably, Charles became

Caesar. At Christmas in the year 800 he received the imperial diadem from the hands of Leo III. The Pope prostrated himself before the Emperor in accordance with ancient usage and henceforth he was known by the style of Emperor and August.

96

The resurrection of the Western Empire encouraged the rebirth of letters and the arts from which the whole of mediaeval culture was to derive, as well as to preserve for us the literary treasures of pagan and Christian Antiquity.

Chapelle, in the country where the Latin genius is balanced by the Nordic.

Charlemagne encouraged the literary renaissance which was aided by new, simple and effective measures : the first was to perfect the Carolingian small letters which now displaced the illegible Merovingian scripts; next came the creation of schools where monks and clerks taught a pure Latin, the only language then available for intellectual intercourse and which became the great international language of the Middle Ages. In the Frankish countries experts were few, so "foreigners" were imported : Italians, Pietro of Pisa, Spaniards, like Elipand of Toledo, Scots, as the Irish were called, and the great Alcuin, an Englishman from the school of York. The writer, hitherto shut up in a monastery and anonymous, began to command general respect.

This cultural fever overspread the boundaries of Charlemagne's empire and secured the conquest of several new provinces. The conversion of North Germany took place when, in the year 1000, the Prussians, pagans and strangers to Europe, found in St. Adalbert a truly Christian apostle.

Charlemagne's empire barely survived its emperor. The Verdun treaty of 843 separated France from Germany and dismembered the continent irremediably. A new flood of invaders now submerged the West, as if they had been waiting for the break-up to take place.

A great era of peace not destined to survive its great man.

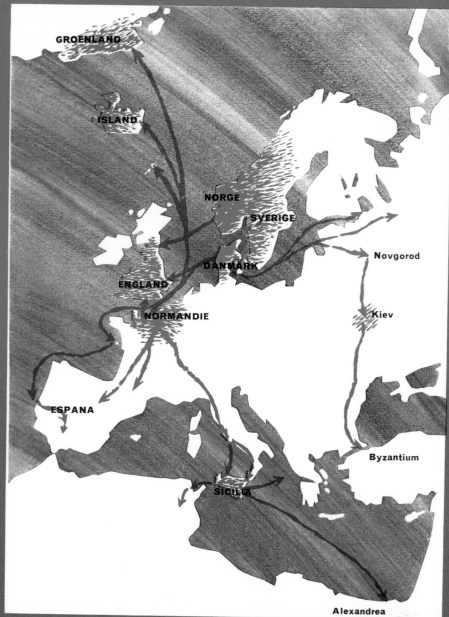

The Norwegian wooden church at Borgund, typical of Scandinavian architecture.

them by treaty in 911. (2) Eastwards: Varangian Norsemen entered Russia and marched southward via Novgorod and Kiev as far as Constantinople (865).

B (11th century). Normandy became the centre of diffusion. Expeditions against the Moors in Spain (1020); conquest of England by Duke William (1066); conquest of southern Italy and Sicily (end of 11th century); raids on Tunis and Egypt. Settlements in Greece.

Detail from the ceiling of the Palatine Chapel at Palermo. The Norman art of Sicily was influenced by Moslem art.

Norsemen, or men of the North, and Vikings, or kings of the sea, Danes: these were the names given to this race of fearless seamen and formidable fighters, whose expansion covered two phases.

A (end of 8th to beginning of 11th century). Expeditions from Scandinavia and Denmark: (1) Westwards. Raids on England (790–1016), which became subject to Canute, King of Denmark (1017–1035). Expeditions up the Seine (840), the Loire (843), the Tagus and the Guadalquivir (capture of Lisbon and Seville, 844). Paris besieged 845 and 866. Settlement on the lower Seine, ceded to

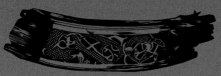

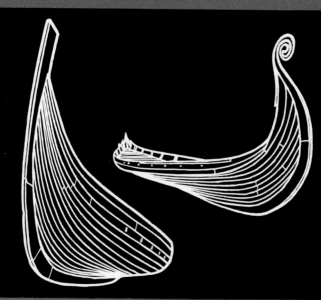

The 'Drakers' or Norse dragon-ships from a rock-carving in Sweden: a piece of carved wood originally part of a dragon-ship: design of prow and poop of a dragon-ship.

100

101

The great plains of Eastern Europe were alternately dominated by the mounted hordes from Asia and the fluctuating power of Byzantium. The Bulgars, who had settled in 679 in the lower reaches of the Danube valley, were converted to Christianity in the 9th century and occupied themselves with raiding in all directions. They even fought against Byzantium, but in the great conflict between the two halves of the Christian world, they decided, in 870, to embrace the Greco-Byzantine Faith.

At the same time the Magyars or Hungarians, who had been driven out of Central Asia by the Petchenegs, crossed the Carpathians and settled in the middle reaches of the Danube. From there they launched sanguinary attacks on Germany and Italy and even penetrated as far as France. In the year 1000, their chieftain Waik decided to be baptised into the Roman Church. He took the

name of Stephen, under which he was later canonised. The Emperor Otho III, his godfather, made him king. His successors on the throne of Hungary always wore his crown on the day of their coronation.

Convulsions in the East and in the West effactually shattered the edifice built up by Charlemagne. Even without these new invasions it could not have survived as a united empire. Economic conditions thrown into disorder by the first waves of the barbarian invasions made it impossible to maintain any centralised system of government. The only way of remunerating generals was to make generous grants of land over which they would, in fact, exercise sovereign power. The feudal system which was now taking shape differed little from anarchy. Chaos reigned.

101

102

The Imperial Crown is shattered.   Anarchy prevails.

104

The chaos was worse than in the years before Pippin and Charlemagne. It engulfed even the Papal power on which the Roman feudal lords had laid hands. The fearful lessons of experience confirmed the intuitive warning of Gregory the Great: 'St Peter's heir can no longer count on Caesar's aid!'

Was the world coming to an end? As the fateful thousandth year approached, the hearts of men were wrung with anguish and confused apprehension. More poignantly than the painters who adorned the walls of churches or illuminated prayer-books a miniaturist of Cologne expresses 103 the sadness of humanity in this illustration. A tempest is rocking the boat in which Jesus and his terrified disciples are sailing. Is Christ asleep? What could bring salvation to a Europe irrevocably and intentionally split in two? Nothing but the heavenly order dreamed of by St Augustine in his 'City of God', a work widely read and commented. And this order could only be achieved by the efforts of believing Christians.

In 910 the monks of Cluny set out to restore the reign of the Lamb 'who taketh away the sins of the world', in homage to whom this scene was 104 carved on one of the capitals in their abbey.

A burning fever of piety spread throughout the monasteries of France, finally reaching Rome.

The example of holiness offered by the monks and the hope of heaven they entertained came as balm to peoples crushed by tyranny and accustomed only to violence. The conscience of many a bishop was awakened and even politicians became aware of the rôle of invisible forces.

The naïve chronicles of Brother Glaber were filled with lamentations, wars, deeds of violence, famines, plagues and invasions, but in reality the dawn was already breaking before the clock had struck the first hour of the year one thousand.

103

The year 1000 - is the world at an end? All that men can do is pray.

In this new atmosphere the actions of rulers recovered a certain breadth, which had been denied them as long as the jungle conditions of barbarism prevailed. Now Germany reconstituted herself under Henry the Fowler, Duke of Saxony. His son, Otho the Great, extended his rule to Italy, precariously enough, it is true, but sufficiently to enable him to secure for his own person the crown
105 of Empire. On February 2nd, 962, Otho was crowned 'Emperor and August' at St Peter's in Rome, as Charlemagne had been. The Germanic Holy Roman Empire was only to enjoy sporadic periods of greatness at long intervals during the centuries and it was seldom that its effective powers extended beyond the frontiers of Germany. Nevertheless the Emperor never ceased to affirm his right to rule over the whole of Western Europe. The gospel-book of Otho III, who was Emperor in 1000, has an illustration showing Italy, Germany,
106 Gaul and Slavonia paying him loyal homage.

Just at this time, however, Gaul was being transformed into France. Emerging from the ruins of Charlemagne's empire the 'Frankish Kingdom of the West', *Francia occidentalis*, had been the last country to keep its Carolingian kings, who were understandably hostile to the new Imperial House of Otho. In 987 a prelate, affected to the German Court, succeeded by his intrigues in

ousting the king in favour of Hugh Capet. Nevertheless this new dynasty showed itself no more favourable to the pretentions of the Emperor than did the descendants of Charlemagne. Hugh,
107 Robert, Henry I were, as a matter of fact, needy monarchs, possessing little authority, but their descendants were destined to pull France together and make her one of the great nations of Europe.

History's cards are dealt, Germany to the Othos, France to the Capets...

Meantime a new European country had started in a career that led to greatness. That was England. Integrated by Canute the Dane in an ephemeral Nordic Empire, England had lived peacefully in the reign of Edward the Confessor.

But the Normans of France, who in 911 had succeeded in colonising the lower Seine and creating Normandy, were casting their eyes on England. Their Duke William had persuaded Edward to name him as his successor. On Edward's death he claimed the succession, which was disputed by Harold. This gave rise to the epic struggle commemorated by Duchess Matilda in the famous piece of embroidery known as the Bayeux Tapestry. Here are portrayed the skill of
108 the Normans in capturing strongholds, their
109 talents as horsemen, the landing of their forces at
110 Pevensey on September 28th, 1066, and the battle of Hastings on October 14th, where Harold, ill
111 served by the halberds of his house-carls, was mortally wounded by an arrow in the eye.

William was crowned at Westminster on Christmas Day 1066. While in Normandy he remained a vassal of the King of France, in England he was king. He gave his kingdom a social and juridical organisation which made it the best governed state in Europe. The English character was to retain traces of the vigorous manner in which William set the country in order, the impress of which helped to create the civic spirit allied with respect for the law, and a strong sense of individual liberty and the rights of the subject.

... and England to William, whose epic is unfurled in the Bayeux tapestry.

112

114

Islam by excluding Western Christendom from Africa and interfering with the traffic of the Mediterranean had hastened the awakening of a European conscience. Actually the presence of the Moslems in Spain created a civilisation which was to exercise a profound influence over all the West. Cordoba, 'the city of sixty thousand palaces', was the capital of the Moslem west as Baghdad was of the east. Its Blue Mosque was one of the wonders of the world. For two hundred years each Caliph had contributed to its embellishment. Its 1,293 columns of jasper, porphyry, marble and alabaster give the visitor a disconcerting impression of
112 infinite space. Islam's contribution to Europe combined barbarity with refinement. If the Moslems made a wilderness of regions which in classical times were famous for their fertility, they also gave to the Middle Ages their greatest agriculturist, Ibn el Awan of Seville. Moreover they introduced from Asia and cultivated in Spain rice, peaches, pomegranates, apricots and oranges. Settling down after generations of nomadic life they assimilated with an astonishing speed the sciences and techniques of the Oriental civilisations with which they had been in contact. They served as hinges between two worlds. They also conveyed to the West a great stock of intellectual riches accumulated over centuries. The numerals we call arabic are of Indian origin. The Baghdad school of astronomy owed much to the Chaldean astronomers. Arab geography had Ptolemy for its father. The techniques and mechanical devices

of irrigation, such as the bucket-wheel which the 113 Moslems brought into Spain, originated in China and found their way to the West via Persia and Syria. The 'horseshoe arch' used by their architects is Vizigothic.

The Moslems were not only capable of absorbing and propagating this wealth of scientific knowledge, but they succeeded in utilising it in new fields of progress. Their extremely original love-poems influenced the lyric poetry of Europe in striking fashion. They were famous lute-players and the lessons which this Moorish lutenist is giving to his Christian pupil set vibrating notes of 114 music which still echo round the Mediterranean.

113

Islam, with one foot in Baghdad, the other in Cordoba, inherits the legacy of

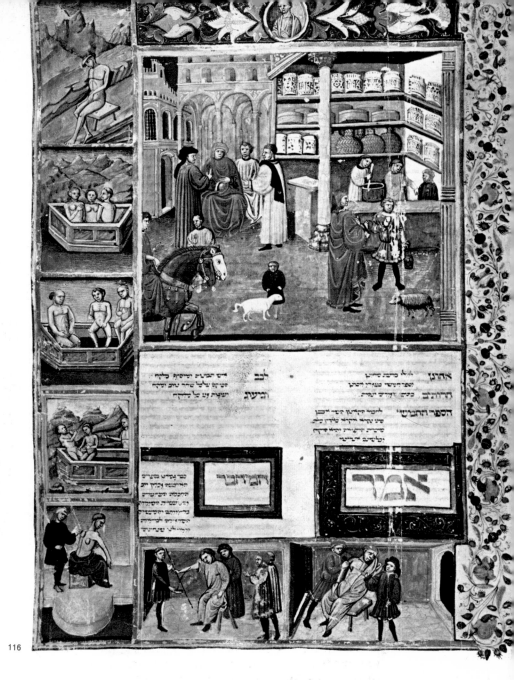

The Arab also excels as a story-teller—an art which he has inherited from the earliest times. During the 11th and 12th centuries Arab philosophy and science enjoyed immense prestige. But in these fields the Arabs were, in fact, perpetuating the traditions of Hellenistic and Alexandrine civilisation. In 830 they started systematically to make translations of ancient Greek works. They took pleasure in their inheritance from the Ancients, whose works they studied profoundly and even enriched. In philosophy they rediscovered Aristotle and studied him with passion. They made advances in mathematics and medicine and laid the foundations of modern chemistry. After the 13th century this great intellectual effort, which had more than once aroused the suspicion of the Moslem religious authorities, seemed to have spent itself. However, it had lasted long enough to permit the Christian countries of Europe to benefit from its achievements. Spain, where the Moslem, Christian and Jewish populations mingled freely, became the chosen bridge for the happy transfer of Moslem learning to Christian scholars. The champions of Allah and those of Christ who, since the 11th century, had been trying to regain a footing in the peninsula, made unexpected contacts with one another. In the intervals of fighting we see them sometimes playing chess together. 115

The Jewish intellectuals served as a kind of cement between Latin Christianity and the Moslem world and it seems quite normal that the Milanese doctors of the 14th century should have been reading the works of Avicenna, the great Arab physician, in a Hebrew translation illustrated by an Italian miniaturist with pictures of operations or consultations. 116

Thus Europe took advantage of the achievements of the past and the present to give them a new aspect and a fresh impetus.

Alexandria. From her, Europe derives mathematics, medecine, and the orange.

117

119

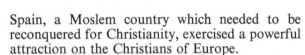

Spain, a Moslem country which needed to be reconquered for Christianity, exercised a powerful attraction on the Christians of Europe.

117   Under Charlemagne, a region round Barcelona was declared a Spanish 'march'. After the disaster of Roncesvalles, the Emperor captured Pamplona, an important base for the reconquest of the whole northern coast of Spain. In Galicia, at the end of the coastline, stood Compostella, famous for its cathedral, which housed the remains of St James, the brother of St John. Pilgrims to the number, it is said, of half a million yearly crowded to this holy place. Their costume, consisting of a broad-brimmed hat adorned with shells, the beggars'

118 sack and a staff, is familiar to all. The French and German sculptors attired their statues of St

James in similar garb.   119 120

    On the long roads to Compostella, which, starting from all parts of Europe, cross France by way of Paris, Vezelay, Clermont or Arles, the Song of Roland was often heard and brought distraction and spiritual comfort to anxious wayfarers. The death of Charlemagne's handsome nephew became the symbol of Christian heroism matched against the Saracen. There are miniatures which tell the story and stained-glass windows like those in Chartres Cathedral. Soon the knights of the First   121 Crusade would be inspired by the epic, the prelude to reconquest. And what an audience the Song of Roland had. The first manuscript is Anglo-Norman, two others are Venetian and in Bavaria the Ruolandsliet was current in 1130.

121

118

120

Our early literature tells of war against the Saracens.

56

An elegant church tower of the 11th century at Cluny displays a revolutionary change of style. Its polygonal structure and double row of windows were soon to be copied in the 1400 Cluniac foundations throughout all the countries of the West as far as Halberstadt in Germany.

The period which gave birth to the Song of Roland saw the beginnings of literature written in national languages, and, with Romanesque art, laid the foundations of a style proper to the genius of the young continent.

It is true that this style is not original but it blends in a harmonious and original synthesis the different Mediterranean, Oriental and Lombard traditions with which European culture is linked and adds to it the fire of its inventive genius.

The art of building, which had recorded little progress since the days of the Carolingian masons, made a great leap forward towards the end of the 11th century.

Admittedly the great abbey-church of Cluny was the largest and the most imitated church in the world until the reconstruction of St Peter's in the 16th century. But the variety of Romanesque styles was great, as was to be expected among the countless buildings being constructed from Portugal to the Baltic and from Scotland to Sicily.

Every region developed its own style, having regard to the materials available and the great historical currents experienced. Only the style of the churches built in Normandy and England from the time of William was homogeneous. Were we not aware of the constant exchanges of monks between the English and the Continental abbeys, we should be inclined to see in the church architecture of England a certain insularity.

Throughout the West new, curious bell-towers heralded Romanesque art.

From the Elbe to the Pyrenees stone spoke, and colour sang in unison.

125

It is a community of ideals that makes for the essential unity of Romanesque art. Imagination and feeling together with pictorial language for the eye are there to vitalise the sacred texts of scripture.

In the Words of Christ Glorified graven on the tympanum of the portico at Vezelay, St Matthew reminds the twelve Apostles of their duty to go and teach all nations. Pygmies, men with dogs' heads and all the peoples who cluster round them are worthy to receive their message. The fabulous beasts on this pillar-head at Canterbury, the devil devouring a wicked rich man from a capital at Autun also have their origin in the Scriptures. The Saxon bishop, Bernward, himself an ironfounder and goldsmith, produced scenes to illustrate the New Testament in bronze. The dance of Salomé with which he has decorated the cathedral at Hildesheim is executed with such fidelity that we can well comprehend the emotion of Herod. One of Bernward's rivals was responsible for the doors of St Sophia at Novgorod. Distance was clearly no obstacle to the expansion of Romanesque art with its genius for movement and space.

The dynamism of this art was nowhere more evident than in painting. Examples of this are found even in little country churches. At St Martin of Fenollar in the southern Pyrenees, where Arab, Latin and Nordic influences are allied, an anonymous artist has confided to the old men of the Apocalypse the task of asserting his devotion to Christ. Note the passionate faith with which they are brandishing their cups and their zithers.

For several centuries, despite the religious struggle between Rome and Byzantium, their painters spoke the same language—that of the Faith they held in common. Between the 12th-century frescoes at Berzé-la-Ville and the 13th-century Russian frescoes at Wladimir, between a Spanish 'Christ the King' and one from Novgorod two centuries later, there were closer affinities than there are between Gainsborough and Reynolds.

125

126

127

128

129

The Romanesque cathedral was the measure of the faith and devotion of the citizens who built it, often over a period of several generations. It could be regarded as the image of the city in which it stood, a reflection of its economic and political power. Take for example Tournai. The town was the seat of the first diocese of Belgium, the capital city of the Merovingian kings and the birthplace of Clovis. Although systematically pillaged by the Normans in 881 and depopulated by the plague in 1090, Tournai, with its rich quarries of blue stone and its prosperous commercial life, erected at the end of the 11th century the superb building shown here. 130 Its cluster of five towers with their numerous belfries is the precursor of the majestic style which, from Laon onwards, was to mark the future of the Gothic cathedrals. The proportions of Tournai cathedral were so vast (nearly 150 yards long by 72 broad at the transept) that it took centuries to complete the work. The Romanesque nave and towers date from the 12th century, the Gothic choir from the 13th and the main door from the 14th while the rood-screen was only finished in 1572.

The inhabitants of Pisa, for their part, were able to undertake the construction of their cathedral 131 out of the proceeds of their naval captures. Additions to their cathedral kept pace with the development of their fleet. Enlivened by polychromic effects the building follows the general principles of the Northern Italian Romanesque school. Its façade is sober but complex and it has a single campanile standing apart, which has stood up without flinching to the subsidences which have made it into the famous Leaning Tower.

Romanesque art, even though it reached its climax in a city, was the fruit of monasticism.

130

131

In the cities faith raised mountains of stone, the cathedrals.

132

136

The rule of St Benedict insists upon intellectual and manual labour as well as on prayer. Many monks were occupied in reading or copying manuscripts. The most erudite illuminated chronicles or wrote commentaries on the texts of Holy Writ or drafted sermons. The untiring labour of others brought great areas under cultivation and we can count in thousands the number of villages brought into being by this truly civilising activity.

132
133
134

There were periodic reactions against the forces of corruption which threatened the monastic order from within. In 1098 Robert de Molesme founded Citeaux and there restored the pure Benedictine rule. His successor was the illustrious St Bernard, whose strenuous and missionary vocation did not debar him, as a man of action, from various incursions into secular life.

135

The bastion and headquarters of the Order was the Abbey of Monte-Cassino, founded in 529, by St Benedict on the site of one of the temples of Jupiter between Rome and Naples. The foundations of the Order were legion. In 1415 Europe could count 15,000 Benedictine abbeys. Every European country could boast of rich foundations belonging to all the monastic orders, some dating from the early days of the missionaries, and others founded during the later progress of Christianity. A summary list would contain the names of Reichenau, Fulda, Bremen, Magdeburg and Ratisbon in Germany; Canterbury, York, Yarrow and Melrose in England; Lérins, Jumièges, Saint Denis, Saint Michel and Fleury in France; Saint Gall, Saint Maurice and Einsiedeln in Switzerland; Bobbio in Italy; Velchrad and Prague in Czecho-Slovakia; Salzburg in Austria and Martinzberg in Hungary.

134

135

133

The Benedictine abbeys, 15,000 strong, work with quills and scythes.

Cum domibus multos plures preter accipe libros.

The Pope wields the highest power, and the Emperor kneels to the abbot.

137

138

It was not long before the sovereignty of the Pope came to overshadow the spiritual powers of the greatest monastic orders and their greatest foundations. In 1059 the papal election was conducted independently of the Emperor. Peter was, henceforth, to be no man's servant, though Caesar could not be anointed without him. A theocracy was thus created whose principles Gregory VII hastened to proclaim. One of his chief aims was to deprive the Emperor of his power to nominate bishops and preside over their investiture. However, in Germany particularly the bishops were often feudal lords and the Emperor refused to give up his right to select them. This resulted in the War of the Investitures between Henry IV and

Gregory. At the outset the Emperor, shattered by a papal decree excommunicating and deposing him, journeyed to Canossa to humble himself before the Pope. Our illustration shows with what humility he bent the knee before an abbot and the Countess Matilda, the lady of the place. He was to retaliate later, but in vain. The first blow to his supremacy had been dealt. The dispute was to be settled on a reasonable basis in 1122. But a hundred years after Henry IV, Frederick Barbarossa challenged Pope Alexander III. Yet he too had to give way, and the Pope gave him his blessing. The scene is highly symbolic of the commencement of the great epoch of the Papacy and the powerlessness of the Emperor to hold the Pope in check.

137

138

139

139

136

Magna Carta asserts, for the first time, the nation in face of the king.

140

between Henry II and his sons, all of which gave Louis VII of France a certain breathing-space. His successor Philippe Auguste had more worries but was more capable of dealing with them. 141

A cunning diplomatist and a prudent soldier, he exploited to the full the mediocrity of Richard Cœur-de-Lion and the incoherent blunderings of John. Normandy and other English possessions in France were wrested from the Plantagenets and the division of Europe into stable nations began to take shape. The internal history of England was of no less importance. Magna Carta, which John was forced to sign in 1215 was the first European document to assert the rights of the people *vis-à-vis* their king. Eighty years later Edward I was to 142 organise a system of parliamentary representation on principles which would assure its constant future development.

The conflict between the spiritual and temporal powers had influenced the political struggle being waged between England and France. Already in possession of Normandy, the English monarchy now held the whole of western France since the accession of Henry Plantagenet, Count of Anjou and husband of Eleanor of Aquitaine to boot. In respect of his French territories the English sovereign was a vassal of the King of France—a paradoxical situation which could only be solved by the expulsion from France of the Plantagenet or the disappearance of the Capet.

In the 12th century English politics largely consisted of disputes between the Crown and the Church, the most famous of which ended in the 140 murder of Thomas à Becket, and the struggles

141

142

143

Disputes and political innovations continued to arise within the framework of a society which remained feudal. The land lord—and every piece of land belonged to some local lord—held his property from the paramount lord to whom he had sworn homage and whose vassal he was in respect to this 'fief'. In his turn the paramount lord was expected to do homage to his superior and so on, up to the king. The vassal was bound to give military aid to his lord as justification for the enjoyment of his 'fief'. But, as a matter of fact, at any rate during the centuries immediately after Charlemagne, the local lords did what they liked. They usually built on their lands a castle that was well-nigh impregnable. In a short time Europe bristled with these castles, which have imprinted on their surroundings a certain physiognomy that still survives in many places. The builders of these strongholds made rapid progress in the art of

146

145

144

defensive architecture. Towers, at first square built, became round in order to eliminate useless space, as at Caerphilly Castle in Wales, which dates from   143
the 12th century, or Château Gaillard, a formidable   144
stronghold on the Seine erected by Richard Cœur-de-Lion and soon afterwards dismantled by Philippe Auguste. There was great competition for the highest perch, the most impregnable castle, the most suitable site. Regions traversed by high roads and great rivers like the Rhine and the Danube teemed with fortresses, of which the Markburg,   145
near Braubach, is a solid example.

In the Middle Ages life in these bleak barracks was lacking in comfort. The lords were glad to leave them and go off on hunting or other less   146
innocent expeditions.

The feudal landscape is commemorated by what will be romantic ruins.

147

149

Sometimes a whole town occupied a strategic position, like Mantua in Italy, which for long was one of the finest fortresses in Europe. The lord of the place had constructed there an enormous
147 building with square towers, which conformed more nearly than the round towers to the traditions inherited from the Etruscans.

Strong in the possession of such a powerful fortress, the lord of Mantua could give himself the airs of a king of Italy rather than conduct himself like the lord of a mere city.
148 The castle of Guimaraes, where the first king of Portugal was born in 1110, possesses all the characteristic features of an Arab casbah, and in the great cities of the Iberian peninsula such as Cordoba, Segovia, Toledo and Seville we find splendid palace-fortresses—the alcazars.

It may be that the pleasures of the table, hunting
149 on horseback or with falcons, not to mention warfare, sufficed to preserve the seigneurs of these castles from boredom, but their wives, more closely confined in their great houses, needed distraction. It was to the women that we owe the evolution of social life and secular literature. Such writings are doubtless not the first that appeared in these young national languages. They were preceded by what are called *les chansons de geste*, the chronicles in verse of heroic exploits. But their tone differs greatly from that of those untutored epics. In the social life which sprang up round the ladies of the castles, and in the literature dedicated to them, we are not surprised to find a great preoccupation with sentiment and courtly love. The castles were soon to receive visits from troupes of entertainers who sang songs to the lute, performed acrobatics or
150 danced to divert the ladies and their lords.

148

The lord's citadel is the lady's bower : here courtly love is born.

The Quest of the Grail is Europe's childhood memory.

150

151

In course of time the lords themselves took to poetry and singing. Called troubadours in England and south of the Loire, trouvères in France and Minnesänger in Germany, they would sometimes commemorate the wartime exploits of the barons, but more often their love for the lady of their choice.

151 What female heart could resist the shaft of this pure love, unselfish and chivalrous, expressed in such terms: 'I love only her, I can fear only her. No pain is pain to me if she finds pleasure in it. When she deigns to accord me a glance from her bright, lovely, eloquent eyes, I feel as if it were Christmas Day. But she keeps me waiting so long for this pleasure, that a single day seems to me as long as a hundred.' Thus sang Bernard de Ventadour. Thousands of lyrics with highly developed versification have survived. They treat of every imaginable amorous theme. In the 'Courts of Love' romantic subjects were debated in verse before a jury of ladies who awarded prizes and garlands.

This new literature of love has its roots in Arab poetry, but it also bears the imprint of Christian mysticism. Many of the poets must have practised it in order to be in the fashion and few from the promptings of a sincere emotion. Nevertheless its symbolism invaded the whole of European literature and its echoes can still be heard. Nowhere is it better represented than in the polite romance, where tales of real or imaginary adventures are mingled with the ancient Celtic traditions and given a Christian flavour. The Quest of the Grail is the masterpiece of this school. One of the episodes deals with the story of a virgin who brings the precious vessel, in which Joseph of Arimathaea 152 received the blood of Christ, to the table of the Fisher King. The legend of King Arthur and the Knights of the Round Table—Galahad, Lancelot and the rest—brought enchantment to French and German readers. Christian of Troyes, Wolfram von Eschenbach and in modern times Richard Wagner have all paid homage to the heroes of the Grail.

152

Before being accoutred by his lord, who girt on his belt, while his squires fastened his golden spurs, and before being placed in the saddle for his first joust and receiving his helmet from his lady, the young knight received Communion after a night spent in prayer.

The perfect Christian knight is represented by the armoured figure in the cathedral at Rheims, whom the sculptor showed standing erect and receiving Communion.

Such men were in love with fighting and they knew no keener pleasure than charging the foe on horseback, with drawn sword, in the quest for glory and renown.

But the knight knew that his sword must not be used without good reason and that it should only be drawn in his lord's defence and for the cause of Christ.

The Knights of the Round Table were obedient in all things to the wishes of their 'ladies', braving mortal danger and the most galling ridicule to please them. But the knight who was the backbone of the Christian West was a very different person from these heroes of literature. He was a tough fighting-man, whose faith made him loyal and upright. But too often the seigneur took advantage of his right to make war in order to provoke a fight. He would challenge his neighbour and do battle with him on the slightest pretext. From the 10th century onwards the Church made efforts to soften these rough manners. Churchmen evolved a conception which they called the Truce of God, which enjoined on combatants to spare the weak and forbade all fighting at certain seasons.

Soon they did more by introducing Christian principles into the ceremony of initiation by which, among the Germanic peoples, young men were admitted to the degree of knight-at-arms. The dubbing of the knight took on the aspect of a sacrament.

The warriors of Christ pass from literature into life.

And in this latter cause thousands of knights had, since the end of the 11th century, given up their fratricidal wars, which had for long drenched Europe in blood, and enrolled in the Crusades, the great offensive against Islam.

The Pope, whose authority at this time was immense, gave the signal, when on November 28th, 1095, Urban II, speaking from Clermont in France, called upon Christians to deliver the tomb
157 of Christ from the hands of the infidels. To the cry of *Dieu le veut* the knights marked their tabards with a cross. A well organised expedition was in preparation, but crowds of common people no less ardent and more impatient wished to leave at once for the Holy Land. Among these was Peter the Hermit, a mystic, who claimed to have had a
158 vision of Christ and who felt himself appointed by God to lead them to the sacred tomb. The heroic mob of pilgrims set out, taking wives and children with them, without order and in ignorance of the route and the dangers of travel. Under the casual guidance of Peter, the German knight Gautier the Landless and Gottschalk the priest, they wandered through central Europe. Sometimes they mal-treated the inhabitants of the regions through which they passed and often, as in Hungary, they
159 were slaughtered in large numbers.

At last the remains of this host reached Asia Minor, where it was almost entirely destroyed by the Turks. This lamentable expedition at least testifies to a popular urge which simultaneously stirred all the peoples of Europe. In this exceptional moment of history one feels that a common faith created in Europeans a common spirit.

157

158

159

Christendom unites under the banner of the Cross.

160

The four armies which made up the Barons' Crusade—Southern Frenchmen, Northern Frenchmen, Lorrainers and Germans, as well as Normans from Italy—also represent a European force. None of the kings went with them. Their supreme chief was the Papal Legate, Adhémar de Monteil, Bishop of Puy. Marching by four different routes, they met at Constantinople, where they caused some misgivings to the Emperor Alexis. From there they crossed into Asia Minor, where a long bloody and harassing campaign began. At last on July 15th, 1099, the Crusaders, now led by Godfrey de Bouillon, broke through the formidable Turkish defences and captured Jerusalem. Palestine now became the Latin kingdom of Jerusalem, which included the County of Tripoli and the Principalities of Edessa and Antioch. The Syrian people, a mixture of races of different creeds, was enriched with new elements by the arrival of a host of knights, merchants and peasants from the Latin countries. Foucher of Chartres says: 'We who were Westerners have been changed into Orientals: the man who at home was a Roman or a Frank has become a Galilean or a Palestinian out here. This man has married a foreign wife—a Syrian or Armenian or even a Saracen (but a Saracen redeemed by baptism). One man has a vineyard, another cornfields and all have got into the way of speaking several languages.'

A few years as neighbours taught the Arabs and the Europeans to respect each other and to recognise what they had in common. But the spirit of the holy wars subsisted in both camps.

The recapture of Edessa by the Turks in 1144 was the signal for the Second Crusade. St Bernard started the movement at Vezelay and devoted all his energies to a campaign of preaching. The King of France, Louis VII, and the Emperor Conrad took part in this crusade, which met with deplorable reverses. Forty-three years later Saladin reconquered Jerusalem.

The Emperor Frederick Barbarossa constituted himself champion and leader of a Third Crusade, to which he was followed without enthusiasm by Richard Cœur-de-Lion and Philippe Auguste, who sailed from Genoa. On arriving in the East they were greeted by the news of the Emperor's sudden death. They succeeded in capturing Acre but not Jerusalem. Richard, who remained alone in Palestine, ended by coming to terms with Saladin, whom Christendom would recognise as one of the best monarchs known to history.

Barbarossa, Richard, Philippe-Auguste strive for one goal : Jerusalem.

162

Emissaries sent out over the whole of Europe continued to preach the Crusade. In Iceland a host of the faithful enrolled themselves, but, when the moment came to leave, they refused to go. In future, whenever there was talk of a crusade, there was no intention of putting it into effect. There were always plenty of arguments against it: the dangers of sea travel, the epidemics prevalent in eastern lands, love of the homeland, ill-health, family ties and what not. Most people felt the uselessness of embarking on an enterprise which never succeeded. Nevertheless the mysticism of Louis IX and his authority as King of France were powerful enough to induce the knights on two more occasions to march with him against the Infidel. Louis planned to strike at Islam in Egypt. In 1248 he crossed the Mediterranean and landed before Damietta, which fell immediately. But soon his forces were beaten and he was taken prisoner. Eighteen years later, when Acre was the last foothold of the Christians in Palestine, he resumed the enterprise. He died of the plague while besieging Tunis. His death removed not only the last of the Crusaders but a great king whose moral prestige had made him on more than one occasion the arbiter and peacemaker of Christian Europe.

163
164

Soon Acre fell and not an inch remained of the territory conquered by the Crusaders. Nevertheless Palestine retained many traces of their occupation. Among these were the great fortresses constructed by the religious orders of knighthood, the Templars and the Hospitallers—Tortose, Chastel-Blanc, Chastel-Rouge and Le Krak des Chevaliers, the most famous of them all. On a deeper level the century-old coexistence had woven manifold links between Westerners and Orientals. The Moslems of Syria could no longer treat the 'Franks' as foreigners.

165

163

The enthusiasm which inspired Peter the Hermit and his companions now seemed dim and distant. The fourth overseas expedition stresses the decline with melancholy emphasis. The Crusaders forgot the real object of their quest and now attacked Constantinople, the Christian capital of the Orient. Successful in their assault, they founded the Latin Empire of the East, which once more became Greek after less than sixty years.

162

The Emperor Frederick II, a clever and sceptical man, who was excommunicated early in his reign, saw in the sixth crusade, in 1228, merely an excuse for interfering in the affairs of the Orient. He was the first Western leader to come to an agreement with the Turks—in this case for the partition of Jerusalem between Christians and Moslems. Needless to say, the arrangement proved ephemeral.

164

St Louis dies of the plague; so passes the knighthood of the Crusades.

165

These three centuries, marked by expeditions and adventures, gave Europe a new look. The men who came back from Palestine brought with them memories which enlarged their horizon and enriched the literature of poem and chronicle, story and song. They also brought back with them hygienic habits, a taste for luxury, recipes for the doctor and the cook, new fabrics like muslin and camlet (woven from camel's hair), new decorative techniques, such as the damascening of weapons, new seasonings such as saffron and shallot. Singly these items seem insignificant, but when multiplied they change the complexion of life.

During the Crusades Europeans conquered, occupied and colonised regions outside their continent and this they were not to forget.

Another consequence of these wars was the blow they struck at feudalism. If one Count of Vaudémont returned safe and sound to his loving wife how many nobles never came back! Relieved of the turbulence of her feudal lords Europe could breathe again, produce goods and develop her economy. Their absence permitted the kings to replace the feudal organisation by a sketchy system of centralised administration. Finally, the Crusaders gave a great impulse to international commerce. The great Mediterranean ports of Venice, Marseilles, Genoa and Pisa enjoyed an ever-increasing trade. New gold coins were minted—the florin in 1252, the ducat or sequin in 1284, both to enjoy a wide currency.

The increased liberties of rural communities, favoured by the absence of their feudal masters, encouraged the towns to emulate them. A new wind was beginning to blow over feudal Europe.

166

166

Many barons met their end at the Holy Sepulchre, before the new dawn.

The renascence and emancipation of towns formerly subject to feudal authorities, whether lords, bishops or abbots, was a feature of these great changes.

In France progressive seigneurs created in their lands new towns to which they granted immediate freedom. The oft-repeated names of Ville Neuve and Ville Franche commemorate this practice. In Castile the kings made free towns of the cities which they recovered from the Moors, and entrusted them with the defence of their own territory, as witness the formidable ramparts of Avila. Meantime the older towns faced up to their feudal lords and obtained from them by negotiation or by force a charter in which their rights and liberties were set forth. The seigneur who compounded with the citizens of his town found the arrangement profitable. The town paid a capital

sum for the charter or guaranteed him a comfortable annual rent, while the prosperity arising from free conditions of life and trade enabled the community to meet its expenses without difficulty.

There was no stopping the spread of the communal movement, but each community evolved a constitution suitable to its particular requirements. Hence there was a great diversity in the nature of the charters.

However, some of these served as models to others. The charter of Beaumont-en-Argonne, for example, entitled the citizens to elect annually a mayor and a jury of twelve to govern the town and administer justice. An identical charter was adopted by more than five hundred towns or villages in Champagne, Lorraine, the Ile-de-France and Belgium. This miniature of the 15th century shows a Belgian town receiving its charter.

Civic liberties can be purchased; municipal life is renewed.

The cities govern themselves now through their elected rulers.

In Italy feudalism was always kept in check by two great forces, the Papacy and the Empire, and in consequence the towns, in quite early days, achieved their freedom and became great commercial cities governed by powerful merchants. These became regular overlords in their own quarters and used the sword to impose their authority. They fought one another savagely to achieve supremacy and signalised their importance by constructing high towers, of which spectacular examples are still to be found in 169 Bologna.

The communities in other European towns had a stronger communal spirit. The burgesses in combination took the place of the feudal lord. Their clock-tower had the same significance as the keep in the castles—it implied protection, but also authority. The communal seal of Ypres symbolises 170 this collective lordship.

The municipal magistrates, called *échevins* in the 171 northern towns and *consuls* in the south, conceived of social relations as being based on common interest and believed they could be better regulated by friendly agreements than by fighting.

169

170

171

The bare-footed friars bring religion out into the streets and squares.

172

173

The new society had to have its new saints. The people who swarmed in the towns needed eloquent preachers who would come and find them in their own quarters and offer them an example of true evangelical poverty rather than the prayers of Benedictines, ardent no doubt, but entrenched behind the walls of huge and wealthy abbeys. To these fresh needs St Francis of Assisi first responded. The Saint chose to possess nothing, to be homeless, and was ready to preach anywhere, and regarded all nature as a house of prayer. With the twelve companions whom he presented in 1210 to Innocent III he founded the Order of the Friars 172 Minor—a mendicant order—whose preaching transported the crowds and filled the highways with flocks of fresh apostles.

The Castilian, Saint Dominic, less of a poet and more of a theologian than St Francis, set himself to put an end to the Albigensian heresy, which was rife in Southern France and which had hitherto been combated only by force of arms. With this end in view, in 1205 he embraced poverty in order that the poor might believe him. One day fire miraculously took up his cause against the Albigensians. A conflagration broke out, destroying their books but sparing St Dominic's work condemning them, which floated undamaged over the flames. The 173 Dominicans or Friars Preacher constituted themselves as the oral champions of orthodoxy. Even

174

though they were at the bottom of the indefensible Inquisition, which employed torture to stamp out heresy, we must remember that the Dominicans had first produced St Thomas Aquinas, the great 174 philosopher who planted Christian thought in the sturdy framework of the Aristotelian system and has remained the beacon of Catholic theology. The two Orders, Franciscan and Dominican, were to spread throughout Europe.

175

The same decline in the influence of the Benedictines and the same insistence on an open-air religion, practised in the sunlight, began to manifest itself in the second half of the 12th century by the appearance of a new architectural style, which in modern times has acquired the name of Gothic.

175　Yet what is there in common between a cathedral like that of Laon, for instance, and the barbarous Goths whom we saw in the 4th century sweeping like a flood over the Roman Empire? It may have been in England, though it was more probably in other countries directly subject to the King of France, that the first experiments were made (initially in small sanctuaries), with the ogival vault, which in conjunction with the use of flying buttresses enabled the builders to raise the level of the roof to great heights, virtually without the support of walls. In place of horizontality and the

The Gothic arch points upward like a pair of hands joined in prayer.

Europe learns the Gothic idiom first from the French.

opus francigenum. Outside France only England showed a natural taste for the Gothic, though the English builders employed a style essentially their own, to which Salisbury Cathedral with its single 177 spire and windows with triple arcature bears striking witness. In other countries it was the diffusion of French culture, one of the remarkable phenomena of the Middle Ages, which introduced new architectural conceptions—usually executed with certain reservations which stamped the Gothic buildings in those countries with a certain local individuality.

contemplative obscurity of the Romanesque churches, we now have pillars rising vertically and floods of light pouring into the Gothic naves. This art, which favoured great spaces, soon gave birth in the Ile-de-France and the neighbouring regions to vast cathedrals capable of containing the entire population of a town. Noyon, 1151, was the first of these. Then came Laon, constructed soon afterwards, which retained a robust Romanesque bell-tower. This cathedral shows traces of a certain timidity in respect to its height, but its architects had clearly mastered the perpendicularity of the new style, and its proportions were to influence numerous German cathedrals. Notre-Dame de Paris, Chartres, Amiens and Rheims are the great masterpieces of the period and the time spent in erecting them covered the whole of the 13th century. Planned by master-builders whose great knowledge of architecture is evident, built by 176 skilful masons sometimes helped by enthusiastic volunteers, and paid for by the generosity of princes, dignitaries of the Church, nobles, burgesses and the faithful of lesser degree, these cathedrals are the true expression of the faith of a whole people and of their creative power. They reveal with signal force the aspiration of the people towards spaciousness and height, which, as expressed in these great edifices, has no utilitarian basis and is purely concerned to satisfy the needs of the human spirit.

Gothic architecture, unlike Romanesque, was limited to a well defined section of Europe outside which it was rarely found. In the eyes of the people it was essentially a product of the French genius:

177

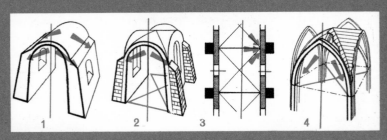

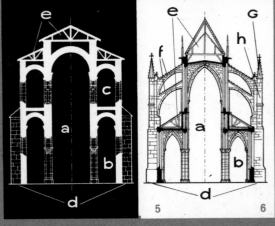

Above: *gradual enlargement of openings*. On the left, *bay formation of Notre-Dame de Paris* (*left half shows early treatment of high openings: œil-de-bœuf, little windows; right half, single large window*). On the right, *bay formation of Beauvais*.

The *Romanesque* (*Norman*) *vault* (1) thrusts the side walls outwards. They have therefore to be thick, with modest openings. This thrust is often counteracted by lateral *aisles* (5 b) surmounted by *galleries* (5 c); *buttresses* are also placed against the external walls. The *cross-vault* (2 and 3), formed by the intersection of two barrel vaults, distributes the load on to the four supporting corner piers; but it is heavy and, in spite of the buttresses, the wall has to be solid. The windows cannot therefore be much enlarged. The vault formed by the intersection of continuous pointed arches (4) is a cross-vault in which the only operative elements are the ribs where the curved surfaces meet; the stresses, concentrated entirely on the four pillars from which the pointed arches spring, permit walls with very wide openings; but they subject the pillars to severe compression stresses. *Flying buttresses* (6 f) provide the answer to this: whilst doing away with the galleries which darkened the nave, they link the top of the pillars to the buttresses (6 h) which, forming a single structure (monolith) with the sides of the aisles (6 b) lower down, stand up high and away from the nave, being held in position by the weight of the *pinnacles* (6 g). This technique is adapted to achieving vertical effects. It leads particularly to the near-elimination of walls, which could now be lit with great windows.

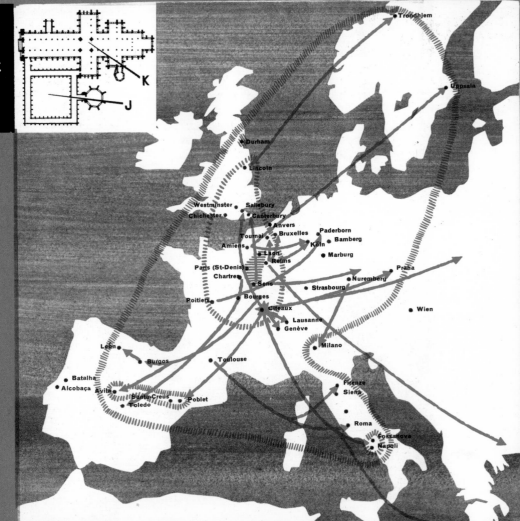

Above: left, plan of cathedral of French type. A, West portal; B, nave; C, crossing; D, north transept; E, choir; F, ambulatory; G, apse chapel; H, chevet chapels; H[1], side chapels. Right, plan of cathedral of English type, characterised by a tower surmounting the crossing (K) and cloisters communicating with the nave (J).

Right: spread of Gothic cathedrals. Their influence was widely scattered, but blended at times. We have tried to indicate this by arrows. It was principally transmitted by French master-masons. Etienne de Bonneuil built the chapel of Upsala in Sweden. Other Frenchmen worked at Toledo, Burgos, Leon. Gérard (from Picardy) started work on Cologne cathedral in 1248. Guillaume de Sens began the abbey church of Canterbury in 1192.

In contrast to the Romanesque artist who un-hesitatingly did violence to natural forms, the Gothic artist respected them. He regarded, as St Francis did, the members of the animal kingdom as witnesses to the glory of God. He would not even portray in stylised form the various plants with which he decorated the capitals of columns. But his realism did not extend to the human subject. He preferred to perpetuate in stone human forms approaching as nearly as possible his idea of perfection. He copied reality, but clothed his subjects with an immortal beauty, evoking the masterpieces of Greece. There is nothing more noble than the face of the 'Beau Dieu' in the 178 cathedral at Amiens and nothing more harmonious than the posture and drapery of the fabulous Abbess Uta in Naumburg Cathedral. In the 179 animated groups such as 'The Resurrection of the Dead' at Bourges, the artist tells his story in 180 detail and with truth. Nothing is forced, nothing superfluous. The Gothic sculptors sought above 181 to record the dignity of man created in the image of God.

In the Gothic churches the stained-glass window takes the place of the fresco and its object is to present a poem in coloured light. This mission is nowhere better fulfilled than in the 2000 square metres of glass in the 173 windows at Chartres. In 182 them one can read transcriptions from the Bible in coloured letters traced on broad glass pages.

The Cathedral gave life to other arts beside architecture and sculpture, containing as it did wood-carvings on the choir-stalls, rood-screens and so on, ironwork on the grilles and doors, enamel-work and jewelry on the reliquaries, and tapestries, extending its influence to music and even the drama.

The cathedral is a chorus of light

A church with all the refinements of Gothic art was centuries a-building.

Many variations of the original Norman-Gothic are to be found in Europe. Toledo drew its inspiration from Bourges, whose cathedral, like that of Coutance, provided a model for Burgos. Léon has an affinity with Chartres and the architecture of Champagne. The monastery of Alcobaça in Portugal reflects the austerity of Cistercian art. The Abbey of Saint Mary of the Victories at Batalha is without question the most poetic expression of 'Southern Gothic', but do we not detect in it the secret influence of York and Canterbury? This admirable diversity in the midst of similarities is a sign of richness and originality and nowhere justifies the reproach of weakness or plagiarism. Only Italy, faithful to the Byzantine tradition, held out against the Gothic. At a late date the cathedral of Milan yielded to Gothic influence, but that was because the architects were German and French. Siena adopted triangle arches for its windows, but horizontal lines interrupt the heavenward flight of the columns. The basilica of Padua is covered with cupolas. The name of *duomo*, which the Italians soon afterwards gave to all their cathedrals, shows clearly enough their antipathy towards ogival vaults and soaring spires.

Germany, on the other hand, although she called her cathedrals *Dom* became unreservedly Gothic. In the 13th century the cathedrals of Magdeburg, Our Lady of Trèves and the vast and towering collegiate church at Marburg were constructed and Cologne Cathedral was begun.

The Gothic edifice was even more ambitious than the Romanesque, aspiring as it did to such heights that it needed generations of builders to complete it. Striking examples of this are Milan Cathedral, finished by order of Napoleon I, and Cologne Cathedral, only completed in 1880 by the help of funds collected throughout Germany.

183

184

185

An enquiring mind can discover China or harness the wind.

The impulse which drove the builders of cathedrals to invade the skies urged seamen and traders to traverse seas and continents. In 1241 Europe was shaken by the blows of the Mongol invasion. The Tartars had already reached the gates of Vienna, when a dynastic crisis caused them to withdraw. As early as 1245 the Pope sent an Italian Franciscan, a certain Giovanni di Plano Carpini, to Karakorum in the heart of the Chinese continent, in order to assist at the enthronement of the Great Khan.

In 1254 Louis IX, King of France, despatched a Flemish Franciscan, William of Rubrouck, to the Mongolian capital. The most famous of these explorers of unknown regions was a young Venetian merchant called Marco Polo. Attracted by the fabulous prosperity of Kublai Khan, he spent twenty-five years in Asia. His memoirs reveal his view that in China everything was on a greater scale than in Europe. But he also reported that the Chinese dug out of the earth a black stone which burnt like wood charcoal, and told of numerous techniques still unknown to Europe. He vaunted the prodigious wealth of the trading cities of the Middle Empire and praised the use of paper money as a convenient medium of exchange. He had watched the peasants harvesting
186 pepper, the principal import from the Eastern world.

The lessons brought back from Asia were not wasted. In the 14th century Europe began to mine coal and to use gunpowder. But such inventions, which had remained static in Asia for centuries, were to accelerate in remarkable fashion the material progress of Europe.

'Accelerate' is the correct term, for since the early Middle Ages Europeans had not ceased to increase their control over nature. About the year 1000 the working capacity of draught animals had
187 been tripled by the use of the collar, which in no way interferes with the animal's ability to pull. In 1105 windmills began to be used, first in Mediter-
188 ranean countries and later in the plains of Holland. The water-mill was employed by the Romans and after the 6th century became common in Europe, where it was used, *inter alia*, to create the
189 draught in foundries. Nor was mechanical ingenuity backward. The improvement in the
190 spinning-frame contributed refined variations of taste and colour to European dress fashions.

188

190

189

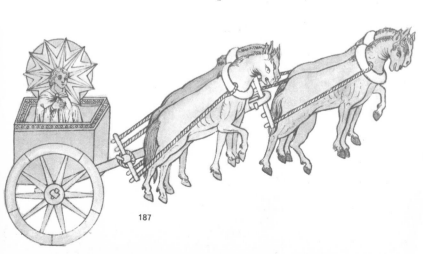

187

The merchants of Venice and of the Hansa trade at the big fairs.

192

Spices were conveyed on camel-back by the
caravans of Arab merchants as far as Alexandria,
where they were loaded on to Genoese and
Venetian ships and carried to Europe. The same
methods of transport were used for other Arab
products such as handworked leather, dates, figs
and oranges.

The Genoese, who controlled the route from
one end to the other, used to collect furs and
amber from the Black Sea coast. Venice imported
what she needed directly from Syria. These two
powerful states also sold to the rest of Europe the
products of their own particular industries—velvet
from Genoa and glassware from Venice. Commerce which was developing simultaneously in the
North Sea dealt in commoner but more indispensable products: cloth from Flanders, wines
from Aquitaine, salt from Brittany, fish from the
Baltic, Scandinavian timber and Swedish steel. The
German Hansa derived ever-increasing property
from these trades. Before long no less than ninety
trading cities, the most active being Lübeck,
Hamburg, Brunswick, Dantzig and Cologne, were
incorporated in the League. Their ships established
communications with the whole world.

Mediterranean and Germano-Baltic traffic, using
land or sea routes, met together in the numerous
markets and trade-fairs. London, Bruges, Troyes,
Chalons-sur-Saône, Frankfurt-am-Main, Zursach,
Friedberg and Geneva were the great mercantile
centres. Certain markets had their own special-
ities, such as the fair of Lendit, near Paris, which
had no equal for the requirements of universities—
a class of goods held in high esteem.

191

193

191

192

193

The universities

194

all teach in Latin.

In the 13th century a growing thirst for knowledge created in Europe powerful and well-organised centres of culture. The schools, hitherto maintained and controlled by bishops, had grown in numbers and size since the 11th century and had freed themselves from their former guardians. Following the example of the burgesses in the towns, masters and pupils combined to claim the right of self-government for their 'university'. The Pope approved their aim and in 1221 the University of Paris was granted its charter.

There was nothing less national or more European than these intellectual centres, whose dons and students from all countries rubbed shoulders; Latin was their common tongue. The main difference between universities was in the nature of their specialisation. In Italy, the University of Bologna, where Master Rolandino taught, made a special study of Roman law, using the great works of Justinian discovered at Pisa in the 12th century.

In England, the Universities of Oxford and Cambridge grew to the stature of regular towns.

194

195

Theological studies would soon bring Oxford into conflict with Rome. The teachings of Wycliffe paved the way in the 14th century for the rupture with Rome two hundred years later.

The University of Paris taught letters, that is to say, the 'Arts', Canon Law and, above all, Theology.

The ideas of Aristotle, widely disseminated in the West, dominated the intellectual life of the 13th century and greatly stimulated the universities. In the previous century a physician in the service of the Caliph at Cordoba, Averroes, had written a treatise on Aristotle, a translation of which had been read by many. The apparent contradictions between the Aristotelian philosophy as presented by Averroes and Christian dogma disturbed Christians so much that two Dominicans, both of whom contributed much to the effectiveness of the University of Paris, the German St Albert the Great and the Italian St Thomas Aquinas, set themselves to appropriating Aristotelian philosophy for the benefit of Christian thought while eliminating its inherent dangers to the Faith.

195

196

197

While the University of Montpellier concentrated on medicine, that of Toulouse, founded by the Pope in 1229, had for its principal aim the conversion of the Albigensians to orthodoxy. The University of Naples was founded by Frederick II of Hohenstaufen for the training of officials.

In Spain Salamanca soon possessed a flourishing university whose superb buildings make the town a regular treasure house of architecture. The liberal King Diniz of Portugal founded in 1290 the University of Lisbon, later transferred to a picturesque site on a hill-top at Coimbre, where it still flourishes. Both of these centres were devoted to the arts and were at the outset strongly influenced by Languedoc literature. 196

Germany, led by the Othos, was from the end of the 10th century the first country of Europe to renew its ties with the Carolingian revival, but its universities came much later, owing, perhaps, to the political instability which reigned throughout the 12th and 13th centuries. The Universities of Heidelberg and Leipzig were not founded until 1386 and 1409 respectively. The latter was destined to become a great intellectual centre in which the science of medicine was not neglected. 197

In this way was evolved an admirable framework for intellectual life in which tradition served as a springboard rather than an obstacle to the incessant progress of the human spirit.

Centres of higher learning spring up on all sides.

Byzantium declines, Poland gains her great king and Switzerland her liberty.

198

The spread of intellectual progress was barred in the East by the conquests of the Ottoman Turks.

The Byzantine Empire, after shaking off the Crusaders and their Latin Empire of Constantinople, remained feeble and exposed. After their victory at Kossovo in 1389 the Turks had subjugated first the Serbs and then the Bulgars. With its western flank turned, Byzantium defended itself hopelessly for another half century. In 1453 it surrendered in its turn. Round the Church of St Sophia, now a mosque, four tall minarets stood as guardians of the Islamic faith.

198

Further to the north the Slavonic peoples were in a continual state of movement and disturbance due to the incursions of the Teutonic knights; Poland, however, formerly Christianised by Byzantium but converted to Catholicism before the year 1000, had its moments of greatness. In the 14th and 15th centuries King Casimir and after him the Jagiellos made Poland a great country. In Cracow the famous royal palace of Vavel was erected and there, too, was founded that university from which a truly Western culture radiated throughout Eastern Europe.

199

200

Poland even took her place in the vanguard of social progress by establishing the liberty of the peasants and their right to own property by legislation which, unfortunately, did not long survive.

On the other side of the Empire the Swiss people achieved their independence in the 14th century and founded the Confederation of Helvetic Cantons, Europe's first democratic state.

Was the world at the dawn of a new age?

199

200

In the midst of strife and bloodshed, Italy disclosed Dante and Giotto.

201

202

At the opening of the 14th century the Florentine
201 Dante Alighieri awakened Italian letters with his
Divine Comedy, written in the Tuscan dialect, a
poetic masterpiece unequalled till then in any
language. The accent was fresh and the intensity of
the writing was something quite new, but Dante's
theological faith and his political conceptions,
which made him a partisan of the Emperor—a
Ghibelline—stamped him as a man of the Middle
Ages.

Soon after him arose another Florentine,
202 Petrarch, the author of sonnets and odes which
added greatly to the youthful glory of Italian
poetry. These, together with his works in Latin,
much more voluminous and the result of long
familiarity with the classics, justify us in consider-
ing him as the initiator of the coming Renaissance.

At this time the genius of Giotto endowed

Italian painting with an entirely new depth of
expression. Looking at his scenes from the life of
St Francis in the upper church at Assisi or in the 203
Scrovegni Chapel at Padua, one feels that he was
the first artist to portray men and not the image of
men. We have to wait till the *quattrocento* to find
artists worthy of comparison with him. In con-
sidering Giotto we do not feel, any more than we
do in the case of Dante, any tendency towards
the classic. Nascence, not renascence, is the term
to apply to the pictorial art of the period.

Only Italy, which had already supplied Europe
with the better part of her culture, was affected by
this impulse towards scholarship and creative art.
Cruel times were coming. The forces of France
and England were to be exhausted by an intermin-
able war. The crossbowman was to become more 204
important than poet, monk or knight.

203

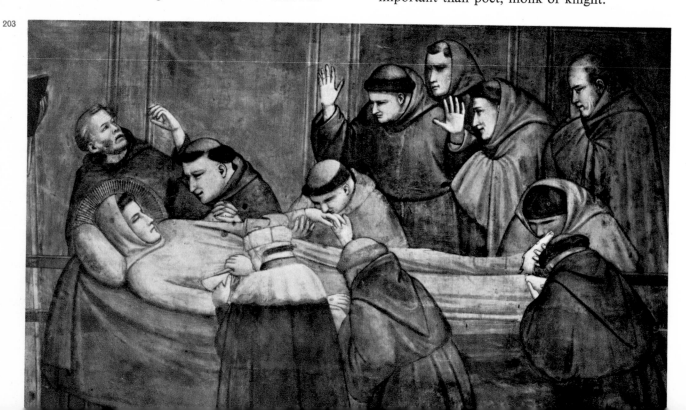

204

205 At Crécy in August 1346 the Welsh archers easily decimated the French knights, too heavy for their horses, with their light arrows. The Hundred Years' War, originally a dynastic and feudal conflict, became a national struggle. It was no longer a question of deciding whether Edward III of England had a better title to reign over France than Philippe de Valois. The crucial question was whether France was to remain independent. French patriotism crystallised round the dynasty of St Louis. The English nobles, whose language and mode of living had been French since the time of William the Conqueror, learnt English, which, instead of remaining a people's dialect, developed into a great national language. The nobles became merged with the Anglo-Saxon population and the English nation was born. With this change all thought of union between England and France had to disappear.

The English army won Crécy and the Black Prince, son of Edward III, was victorious at 206 Poitiers, but Charles V reconquered the lost provinces. The madness of Charles VI delivered France into the hands of Henry V of England, but Joan of Arc appeared, aroused the French people 207 and drove the 'Goddams' out of France. Perhaps her ambition was to save, more even than France, the idea of a Christian monarchy sanctified by the rite of coronation, but her niche in history is that of the heroine of French independence.

Halfway through the 15th century one might well have asked where was Europe? Nowhere. In Germany although the House of Hapsburg wore the crown of the Holy Roman Empire, the Imperial Idea was now simply a memory. The Hundred Years' War had done more than destroy one of the vital principles of Western unity. It had dealt a shrewd blow to civilised thought.

England and France rise from the ashes of the Hundred Years' War.

Spain, up in arms under the Cid, drives the Moors from the Alhambra.

209

210

which the Cid made an epic contribution.

By the end of the 13th century Andalusia with the Kingdom of Granada was the sole remaining foothold of Islam in Spain. There the Hispano-Moorish civilisation, more attractive than great, survived for a few generations. Its genius is accurately portrayed by the architecture of the Palace at Grenada, the famous Alhambra.   208

The epilogue for which Europe had to wait for two hundred years coincided with the creation of a united Spain through the marriage of Ferdinand of Aragon and Isabella of Castile—the Catholic   209 210
Monarchs. Spain now, after France and England, the third in chronological order of the European nations, dealt a mortal blow to Islam by seizing Grenada from the Moors.   211

Artillery had made a shattering entry on to the French scene. With cannons spitting fire and lead, Europe would no longer have to fear the invasion of nomadic hordes. Better still, she would be mistress of the destinies of the world. But was that a gain?

The Hundred Years' War was fought at the expense of the unity into which the Crusades had induced Europe. The new nationalism of France and England was a negation of mediaeval Christendom. Nevertheless about the same time another great Christian nation came into being under the banner of a Christian mission—namely the recovery of Spain from the Moors.

At first, during the 11th century, there were the expeditions of the French, Normans and Burgundian barons. Then when Castile, her frontiers extended, had become a kingdom under Ferdinand I, there followed a period of victorious wars to

211

208

With the passing of the Middle Ages man's fate sets a new course.

212

The retreat of Christendom in the East before the Turkish assaults, compensated in the West by the Spanish *reconquista*, established the shape of Europe which was to last until modern times.

The emergence of three great nations, which made a more powerful appeal to the hearts of their citizens than did the conception of Christian solidarity, opened a new era. The Middle Ages were coming to an end, but in the ten centuries of their duration they had done much for the good of Europe. This continent had evolved a conception of man unexampled in any other civilisation. Like the Orientals, Europeans had come to know that true reality is something spiritual, not temporal, and had learnt, as the Greeks had, that man's destiny depends much on himself. From Rome they had derived a high respect for the rights of the State, but from their Celtic, Germanic and Scandinavian forbears they inherited a powerful sense of individual liberty. Their Christianity welded these divers tendencies into a harmonious synthesis. The Son of God, in becoming a man, had bridged the gulf between the temporal and the eternal. Life on earth was only a journey, but one during which man, by doing good to his fellows for the love of God, had to fit himself for the life to come. Life was an adventure with a meaning. It had a beginning and an end. Time existed, according to the Judeo-Christian perspective, and it was for men to use it for the best purposes, for progress. Hence the slow but continuous improvement of the human condition in Europe. Slavery disappeared, serfdom became rare, citizens acquired liberties and intellectual life became free.

213

214

became haunted by the fear of death. The fresco of the Camposanto in Pisa, where a brilliant procession of princes and ladies halts in terror before three open coffins, the *danse macabre* on the bridge at Lucerne or in the Church of the Chaise-Dieu echo the same sinister dirge. The visionary Last Judgment of David Bouts is only one of many works inspired by the fear of eternal punishment. Hitherto art had sought for calm and simple forms, but now it turned to the complicated and tortured. This tendency in sculpture became so exaggerated as to inspire a 16th-century German sculptor to mould this fantastic head of God the Father.

In architecture sinuosity became a universal fashion, lending alike to the main doors of churches and to their smallest windows this flame-like form which makes the church of Caudebec the most perfect example of the flamboyant style. Was this a fresh proof of religious decadence? At this epoch secular buildings could compete in splendour with sanctuaries. The Town Hall at Brussels, for example, seemed to proclaim that the power of the citizens was comparable to that of God.

213
214
215
216
217

Nevertheless, such great efforts in the cause of progress, pursued in spite of the devastating conflicts of the Hundred Years' War and the ravages of the Black Death of 1347–1349, may in some ways have overstrained the strength and determination of men; during the decline of the Middle Ages it may be asked if the vain quest of the unattainable did not discourage mankind.

Abandoning illumination, Jan van Eyck not only invented easel painting, but excelled in oil painting. This technique enabled him to reproduce atmosphere and light effects, and the relations between the infinitely small and the totality of the universe. His picture 'The Virgin reading' expresses rather the love of the fireside and of a well-kept home than a mood of mystical ecstasy.

212

As a result of excessive concentration on the details of life here on earth, the minds of men became dismayed at its transitoriness. Europe

Europe becomes haunted by the fear of death.

Charles the Bold takes to his grave the dream of empire in Europe.

219

The Princes continued to cherish the ideal of chivalry which their ancestors had realised. They never grew tired of their palaces and castles. The Duke of Berry built no less than nineteen. These provided the setting for pageants which satisfied the taste for the fictions of polite romances. King René made a set of rules governing the conduct of the ideal tournament and illustrated his text with 218 splendid miniatures.

If the chivalry of the Chansons de Gestes was dead, the golden age of the princes was only beginning. The new generations, in search of other reasons for belief and hope, began to turn their back on God and to attribute an enhanced rôle to the power of man: and who was better equipped to wield that power than the princes?

The end of the 15th century was remarkable for a duel on which the future of Europe was to 219 depend—that between Louis XI, King of France, 220 and Charles the Bold, Duke of Burgundy. Charles, who was heir to the Duchy and County of Burgundy as well as to Flanders, the Low Countries and Luxembourg, dreamed of uniting all these regions by the conquest of Alsace, and creating a great western Duchy which might enable him, with a foot in Germany and a foot in France, to reconstitute the Empire of Charlemagne. This was by no means an idle dream. But no great purpose can be achieved without prudence, perseverance and political foresight—three gifts in which Charles was lacking, but not Louis. Beaten at 221 Grandson and Morat by the Swiss, defeated and killed by the Lorrains at Nancy, Charles the Bold carried into his grave the last hopes of a European empire. Was it by pure caprice that history chose to entrust Burgundy to a hot-head and France to a great statesman? Then it was a caprice to which History would remain committed.

221

220

8

97

222

223

By the end of the 15th century a hare-brained prince had no chance of success. The Feudal Age had given opportunities to men with more energy than brains, but now there were cannon, which only the princes could afford, to keep the feudal barons in check. But it was not only cannon that they needed. In their constant grappling at close quarters, they needed foresight, tenacity, imagination and cunning—in short all those talents, consecrated by a serene absence of scruples, which 222 were recommended by Machiavelli in a work known to posterity as *The Prince*.

Clearly the scope of this famous treatise of political philosophy was vast, but its practical lessons were effective in small-scale examples, drawn from recent history. Louis XI practised Machiavellism before *The Prince* was written. In Italy where, for lack of any national unity, several good-sized states had come into existence, a complex game of grab was played pitilessly and stubbornly between the invading princes and the princelings struggling to retain their territory.

One can guess from his thin, compressed lips how well this game was played by Frederick of Montefeltro, Duke of Urbino, the famous 'man 223 with the broken nose'—a man of high culture and a tough negotiator. Similar inferences may be drawn from the portrait of Lorenzo the Magnificent, who 224 stimulated in Florence a wonderful intellectual and artistic revival, and of whom Machiavelli was the servant, if not precisely the counsellor. Leonardo Loredano, Doge of Venice, had the same tight- 225 lipped look and we feel that such men knew well how to keep their secrets.

224

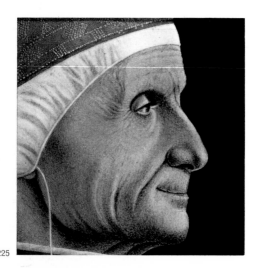

225

In Machiavelli's world there is little room for chivalry.

Men looked westward, across the Ocean, for a second route to the Indies.

The Italians concentrated on their internal quarrels the more keenly because the Mediterranean, then infested by Barbary corsairs, was more or less closed to their merchant ships. The advance of Turkey and the capture of Constantinople entailed the withdrawal of Europe towards the West. The continent was now more than ever a promontory jutting out into the Atlantic. Ptolemy's maps, brought from Constantinople to Florence early in the 15th century and printed at Vicenza in about 1464, were completed by the German Martin Behaim. They set the explorers dreaming. If it were true that the earth was round, one should be able to find the coast of Asia on the other side of the Atlantic. This would open a new route to India which would conveniently replace the one closed by the Turks. But methods of navigation which are adequate for the Mediterranean would not serve to cross an ocean. The European mariners of those days depended largely on two contrivances familiar to them since the 13th century: the first of these was the hinged rudder, which had replaced steering by oar and which pivoted on the stern-post, thus enabling the vessel to turn much more easily; the second was the compass, consisting of a magnetised needle mounted on a pivot, which made it possible to keep the ship on course. Besides these the astrolabe and chronometer of improved design provided a greater element of accuracy in navigation. With the astrolabe the seaman verifies his latitude by the stars, while the chronometer enables him to calculate more exactly his longitudinal position: he notes the difference between the time of day at the point he has reached and the time of day on the meridian from which he has sailed.

226

226
227

228

226

227

228

229 The altar-piece of Nuño Gonzalves, with its princes and monks, knights and fishermen grouped around St Vincent, causes us to ask what the Portuguese were doing at this time. It has been said of this astonishing, many-panelled picture that it marks the triumph of individualism in society and raises for the first time in the West 'the song of human solitude'. The men pictured here, each imprisoned in his own personality, are occupied with other things than prayer. They bear witness to the strength of Portuguese society and celebrate the conquerors of the ocean. Alphonso V, his son John and his uncle Henry the Navigator are the giants of the group, not the handsome St Vincent. It was the Portuguese who first dreamed of reaching India across the ocean, in search of spices and precious metals and, no doubt, to carry the Gospel to the benighted heathen. With the Pope as arbiter, they signed a treaty at Tordesilla in June 1494, whereby they should become possessors of all territories to be discovered in the Eastern Hemisphere, while the Spaniards should be entitled to the same rights in

234 the Western. Henry the Navigator established at Cape Sagres, the most westerly point of the continent, an Institute of Navigation which prepared the way for the methodical exploration of the coasts of Africa. His scientific work and new techniques reaped their reward when Vasco da Gama rounded the Cape of Good Hope and landed in May 1498 at Calicut—where he found an interpreter speaking Portuguese.

230

229

Christopher Columbus and Vasco da Gama set out to measure the globe. Their

However, six years previously Christopher
230 Columbus, a Genoese financed by Ferdinand and
Isabella of Spain, had sailed his caravels across the
Atlantic and, thinking he had reached the East
234 Indies, discovered America on 11th October, 1492.
He returned thither three times and died in 1506
without realising that he had opened up for
Europe a new and unknown world.

The following year Martin Waldseemüller, a
topographer living at St Dié in Lorraine, confirmed the existence of the new continent and
named it America, after another transatlantic
231 explorer, the Florentine Amerigo Vespucci, who
had recently landed in the future Venezuela. When,
in 1513, the Spaniard Balboa had crossed the
Isthmus of Panama and seen the Pacific, the
existence of the American Continent could no
longer be doubted.

Nothing more important had ever happened to
Europeans. They were the first human beings to
measure the globe, which they found much larger
than anyone had ever imagined. Wherever they
landed, they felt they were doing so as conquerors.
They concluded that, if their own domain was
small in comparison with the unguessed immensity
of the world, few races were strong enough to
refuse them a place in their country. On every
coast the European imposed himself on the
indigenous inhabitants, whether they were wel-
coming, reserved or hostile. His face, dress and
arms aroused curiosity, surprise or admiration. At
Benin in the Gulf of Guinea skilled bronze-

231

workers modelled the Portuguese mariners with a
keen observation of costume, attitude and physiognomy. This face is at once realistic and hieratic. 232

Conquest and discovery went hand in hand. In
1503 Vasco da Gama drove the Moslems from
the coast of Malabar and secured for Portugal the
monopoly of spices, to the detriment of Alexandria
and Venice. Other Portuguese, led by Albuquerque, 234
fortified the stopping-places on the route to India.
They established themselves at Aden, the gateway
of the Red Sea, and at Ormuz, the entrance to the
Persian Gulf. They also occupied Malacca,
Macao and Goa. Lisbon became the centre of
international commerce. Every spring a flotilla put
out with cargoes of glassware, textiles and wines
and returned eighteen months later loaded with
spices, lacquer, silk, pearls and diamonds.

232

discoveries opened to Europe unlimited vistas of exploration and of conquest.

233

234

The Portuguese explorer Magellan suggested to 233 his sovereign a voyage to the spice-markets of the Moluccas by the western route. Discouraged at Lisbon, he offered his plan to the King of Spain, who agreed to assist him. On this voyage Magellan's ships sailed round South America, passing through the narrows, still called the Straits of Magellan. The tireless explorer died on the voyage, but his second-in-command, Sebastiano del Cano, returned three years later, 1522, in the first ship to have sailed round the world. 234

In America the Portuguese made but slow progress in developing Brazil, which they had discovered by chance in 1500. The Spaniards on

235

the other hand carved out for themselves a great empire. Cortez in Mexico and Pizarro in Peru, each 235 accompanied by a band of, at the most, a few hundred adventurers, overthrew two great kingdoms. Their exploits were hateful but heroic. These conquistadors, inhuman and superhuman figures, were stimulated at once by a sincere desire to spread the Gospel and an insatiable thirst for gold. They pillaged, massacred and enslaved. But among them right-minded Christians appeared who stood up effectively against their atrocities. Bartolomeo de las Casas crossed the Ocean twelve times to plead in Madrid the cause of the oppressed, and Francisco de Vitoria was the first champion of anti-colonialism.

Inhuman, superhuman, the adventurers preach the Gospel but seize the gold.

This was certainly a new feature in the history of conquest. Hitherto no conquering peoples had ever produced their own critics.

In point of fact, in spite of much injustice and unpardonable violence, which later recoiled on their own heads, the conquerors raised the level of civilisation in America. The Aztecs of Mexico oppressed their subject peoples with blood-thirsty violence, they worshipped savage gods never satiated with human sacrifices. The Incas of Peru knew nothing of iron, the wheel, or writing, and their society was formed of slaves commanded by a small ruling class.

On the ruins of these two kingdoms, the Spanish dominion, greater than that of Alexander or Genghis Khan, was established over a length of 6000 miles. New explorations and new campaigns were to extend the European conquests to the whole of South America, transforming it into a second Europe on the far side of the Atlantic. The first towns sprang up: Rio de Janeiro and Bahia, 236 Portuguese, and Buenos Aires, Spanish. Europeans introduced wheat, acclimatised the olive tree and the vine, replaced porterage by wheeled haulage

and increased the number of horses and pigs. In return they brought back much from America: logwood for dyeing, tobacco, sugar and later the potato. These seemingly small contributions were destined to have precious results. The potato proved a remedy for famine, tobacco enriched the exchequer and sugar improved the race.

North America, in which Cabot, an Englishman, Cartier, a Frenchman, and Alfinger, a German, left the first traces of European penetration, and the Arctic seas into which Berentz, a Dutchman, 237 pushed his way, developed a taste for furs on this side of the Atlantic, but, most important of all, the Peruvian mines flooded Europe with silver and 238 gold.

The conquered Americas provide tobacco, sugar, gold and the potato.

More history in a single century than in the preceding 4000 years.

240

In a century and a half 180 tons of fine gold were to cross the Atlantic and Spain was to receive 16,000 tons of silver. All these things produced a veritable revolution in the world of business. Famous old markets stagnated and new ones came to life. Bruges declined, but Antwerp became the Queen of the Atlantic and created in 1531 the first international currency exchange. The Counts of Thurn and Taxis organised the first European postal service in 1544. New demands were created and business exchanges intensified. 239

This great economic transformation was brought about mainly by the bankers, in the forefront of whom was Jacob Fugger, who was important enough to be able to write the following lines to Charles V: 'It is well known and clear to all that Your Majesty would not have obtained the Roman Crown without my help.' Times had changed and it seemed that wealth was now a passport to political power. 240

But on the whole Europe has always preferred intellectual and spiritual adventures to business and politics. At the opening of the 16th century Europe was astonished at her own transformation.

But the revolutions and changes were only beginning. The ambassadors and bishops whom Holbein painted in 1533, appear to be guarding with jealous and magical authority a globe, a collection of scientific and musical instruments and a pile of bulky manuscripts. The time was coming when these privileged persons would no longer be the guardians of man's intellectual treasures and when the human spirit, free and untrammelled, would set out to conquer new worlds. 241

239

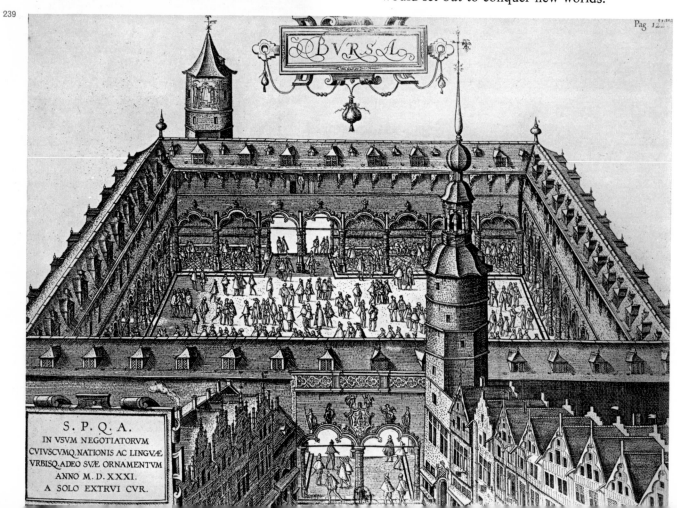

It seems to be a rule that no spiritual revolution can take place without material support, without some important technical innovation. And so the century which made way for the Renaissance was first of all the century of printing. Gutenberg, a goldsmith from Mainz, conceived the idea of making a stamp in hard metal at the end of which a character or sign is graven in relief. This stamp strikes a soft matrix in which the character is sunk. The matrix is then placed in a mould, which enables one to cast as many characters as one likes. In 1454 Gutenberg printed his first book, the Bible, in movable type. Imitators followed and his technique was improved on.

The lines of characters were placed in a frame enclosing a solid surface to put under a press. The idea came from the wine-press. After the type was inked, a sheet of paper was laid out on it and the whole frame was moved under the press. So the printed page was produced. Soon a flood of broadsheets, popular almanacs, religious and even technical books appeared. At Venice the Aldi produced first printed editions of the ancient manuscripts. In Paris the Estiennes published the first dictionary of classical Greek. At Antwerp, Christopher Plantin, a Frenchman by origin, was a notable printer, while at Basle the Amerbachs worked for the whole of Europe.

Thanks to the printed book, the spread of culture and its secularisation became a feature of European life.

Art, too, underwent a similar transformation. Religious inspiration was, to some degree, supplanted by profane themes, as when the Bavarian Altdorfer portrayed Susannah bathing. Purely biblical themes gave way to a taste for decoration, landscape printing and architectural display.

CHRISTOPHORVS PLANTINVS *Architypographus Regius,* vixit annos LXXV. obijtque Antuerpiæ CIƆ.IƆ.LXXXIX.

The wine press, adapted by Gutenberg the printer, became the letter-press.

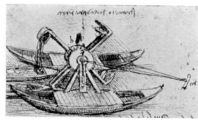

A girl with long hair has a flower springing from her mouth. Her young body is clothed with soft garments. Botticelli's *Primavera* heralds the triumph of the Renaissance.

The 16th century was to free Europeans from the yoke of feudalism as well as delivering them from their religious obsessions and dazzling them with the glittering attractions of individualism.

'You may fix the limits of your own nature according to your own free will which I have granted you. I have placed you in the centre of the universe so that you may the better see what goes on around you. Make of yourself what you will." Thus does God address man, in the words of Pico de la Mirandola. But where was the centre of the universe? The spirit of man had been dazed by a new discovery. Copernicus, the Pole, after studying first at Rome and then at Padua, disclosed to the world in 1512 that our planet is a mere unit of the solar system. Goethe said of this discovery 'Nothing ever had a greater influence on men's minds. As soon as it was established that the world was round and that it formed a complete entity in itself, Terra had to renounce the exorbitant privilege of being the centre of the universe.

This involved an unparalleled sacrifice on the part of human beings and dispelled, as mist and unreality, the manifold dreams that had so long comforted them—dreams of a second paradise, a world of innocence, of poesy and of piety, the evidence of the senses, the faith of the saint and the poet.' Now man had to create a new paradise cut down to his measure.

Leonardo da Vinci was the precursor of the new age, the father of the great Europeans with an insatiable appetite for creation. Astronomer, geologist, biologist, architect, anatomist, he was also the designer of fantastic mechanical devices. And what a painter! His mission was to show, and show he did, that man could be a demiurge capable of remodelling nature.

If Florence, with Donatello, della Robbia and Brunelleschi, and Venice, with Titian and Veronese provided glorious masterpieces of the efflorescence of art, Rome was, in fact, the leader of the artistic movement which was to overrun Europe during the coming centuries. In Rome painters, architects and sculptors manifested their genius. When Pope Julius II laid the foundation-stone of the basilica of St Peter on 18th April 1506, he turned the

Copernicus reduces the earth to a grain of dust and a human paradise disin-

Vatican into a workshop in which, for more than a century, the most wonderful creations were to be elaborated. The greatest artist of them all, Michelangelo, there created two of his masterpieces—the Sistine Chapel and the dome of St Peter's, which he derived from the Pantheon of ancient Rome. 247

Germany, on the other hand, was slow to abandon the aesthetic tradition of the Middle Ages. Cranach clung to the Gothic style and only Dürer attached himself to the Italian School, owing partly to his wide culture and partly to his powers of execution.

It was largely owing to its most obvious aspects that the art of the Italian Renaissance made such headway in Europe. One can detect many attempts to blend the two styles—the old and the new. The Town Hall at Antwerp, with its Florentine loggias 248 and Gothic roof, displays a synthesis of Italian and Flemish characteristics.

France readily admitted Italian artists; at Fontainebleau and in the Loire valley there flourished an original type of architecture.

If sometimes, as in the castle of Chambord, the 249 structure remained mediaeval, though the contours reflected the style of Italy, the heavy, clumsy houses of the 12th century and the Hundred Years' War had long passed into limbo.

248

249

tegrates. In the splendid Renaissance mankind is awakened to a new life.

251

Now everything was new and young. Raphael was just as ready to paint the charming mythological characters of the Farnesina or Galatea gracefully escaping from the jealous Cyclops, as to portray gently smiling madonnas or Popes on horseback. The moulds of the Middle Ages were broken and scrapped. Would the Roman Church be able to escape the current passion for innovation which was spreading over Europe?

250

A strange destiny was in store for Martin Luther. He did not wish to break with Rome, but he meant to reform the Church, with its insolent wealth, artistic preoccupations and political pretensions. A Bull of Condemnation was issued against him in 1520, but rather than submit he founded a new church. Uncompromisingly he declared to the Diet of Worms: 'Here I am: I cannot do otherwise.' Then with a massive gesture, he consigned the ecclesiastical hierarchy to hell.

251

Holding that the souls of all men were in the direct keeping of the Creator, he rendered to the secular ruler many of the privileges belonging to the Roman Church. In short, he set out to create a new order, in which the clergy played a minor part.

In Switzerland Zwingli introduced a practical application of the new dogma. Unlike Luther, who was an autocrat and a centraliser, he combined the salvation of individual souls with the democratic reorganisation of the Church and non-clerical society. He dreamt of a church formed of communes, in the tradition of his country.

251 bis

In 1555, thanks to Melancthon and his conciliatory spirit, Protestantism was granted legal status in Germany at the Diet of Augsburg.

251 ter

250

251 bis

251 ter

Religious thought is also in revolt, and stubborn Luther founds his church.

Several great humanists hesitated before siding with the Reformation, possibly because they were Europeans and unsectarian. Among them was 252 Erasmus. He had studied in Paris, England and Italy. He was a pensioner of Charles V in Holland, but he made his home in Basle in 1521. His movements in search of a centre are symbolic of his spirit. He found his central abode in a town on the cross-roads of Europe.

In Erasmus it was the intellect that triumphed. His faith grew fainter and his preoccupation with material things less and less. His influence was considerable and it contributed to overthrow the traditional defences of Catholicism. But in order to revolutionise not only men's souls but the epoch they lived in, more burning convictions and a livelier temperament were needed than Erasmus possessed.

253 Jean Calvin of Noyon, a lukewarm ecclesiastic, was quickly carried away by the new ideas. Following the example of Erasmus he fled to Basle where he could publish his works unhindered. The *Christian Institution* appeared in 1536, first in Latin, then in French.

Soon he was invited to Geneva. This town, which formerly belonged to Savoy, was fighting a long war of liberation with the Dukes of Savoy and the Kings of France, champions of Catholicism. Calvin reformed the city completely with his religious decrees. He founded a university which became the centre of a sort of Evangelical International aimed towards France. He was essentially a party man and, when he thought fit, he had his opponents burnt at the stake.

He wrote a work of 40,000 pages, as well as carrying on an enormous correspondence; he used to give up to 280 addresses in a year; he was tireless, inexhaustible, and as lucid as lightning. Eventually Calvin became the *de facto* dictator of Geneva, the Protestant Rome.

Galvanised by Calvin's exhortations missionaries set out from Geneva for all parts of Europe. They destroyed statues and paintings in the churches, deeming them idolatrous. The 254 agitation was only beginning.

Calvinism was, in fact, a political as much as a religious movement. Luther had recommended agreement with, if not complete submission to, the secular ruler, but Calvin, though he had strangled democratic tendencies in Geneva, proclaimed the individual's right of opposition. The idea was already favoured by certain thinkers of the Middle Ages and was to lead mankind to the modern conception of democracy.

253   254

enigh Predication   Das bildent furmen fiengen an   Kap Monfrantz, kilch, auch die altar   Zerbrochen all in kurtzer stunde

From Geneva Calvin throws his fire-brands onto the Protestant bonfire.

255

The ideas of the Reformation reached Sweden at a moment favourable for the plans of Gustav Erikson Vasa for national independence. Vasa, who had been held as a hostage in Denmark, escaped in 1519 and raised the peasants of Dalecarlia. In 1523 he had himself made king. Vasa 256 paid his debt to the Hansa by instituting a modern state. He introduced the Reformation into Sweden and used it to acquire control of the property of the Church. He established a permanent army and navy and was created a hereditary sovereign by his people.

Henry VIII of England, a headstrong giant, 257 reacted violently to the Pope's criticism of his matrimonial excesses. He was a great politician: in order to further his continental policy of alternately supporting France and the Emperor, he broke with Rome and initiated in 1533 an original form of Protestantism whereby ecclesiastical administration became an integral part of the Crown's prerogative—in fine the Anglican Church.

In France the affray at Wassy caused only 258 twenty-eight victims among the Protestants but it was enough to inaugurate a period of atrocity and ruin which lasted for thirty-six years and during which fire and the sword were adopted as the only means of bringing heresy to heel.

About this time a young Basque swashbuckler, Ignatius of Loyola, who had been wounded in a

The Reformation became more and more pregnant with fateful consequences. By admitting all persons to the priesthood and by the hope of a general revival which it fostered, it gave rise to many social and political convulsions and inaugurated a century of confused conflict—not only in the individual consciences of men but also between States and within them. Germany being the country in which the juridical aspect of Roman Law lent a certain stiffening to the social structure, it was there that the first disorders broke out, in 1524. The rebellion of the Baden peasants against
255 their landlords, based on an egalitarian ideology, produced heroes, tyrants and martyrs, but its constructive results were few. Fire, massacre and a blood-bath were its main features.

256

257

258

brawl, was visited by the grace of God on his
259 sick-bed. He founded the Society of Jesus, persuading the Pope to recognise the Order in 1539.
His Jesuits, churchmen in their dress and in their
vows, soldiers by virtue of their discipline, and
politicians in their chosen milieu, exercised an
immense influence on society. Their training in
political science and their ambition to promote the
glory of God fitted them to become the father-
confessors of princes and to provide the brains of
the Counter-Reformation.

After twenty years of work the Council of Trent
succeeded in laying the foundations of internal
reform and the revival of the Catholic Church, but
the Great Schism had nevertheless become a *fait
accompli*. The saying *cujus regio, ejus religio* had
become a common-place—'To every man the
religion of his country and his prince.' Henceforth,
Europe was shared by two religions: in the north
evangelical Protestantism and in the south traditional Catholicism. Germany suffered most from
the effects of this partition. Three faiths confronted
one another there—the Lutheran in the north, the
Calvinist in the west and the Catholic in the south.

259

Who would mend the riven fabric? A Reformist International made up of the people, the sovereigns and the intellectuals? Or a Catholic monarchy animated by the dream of Empire? A miracle of history placed the sceptre of world dominion within the reach of Charles V of Spain. No more ambitious motto had ever been devised than that of his great-grandfather, Frederick III of Hapsburg: A.E.I.O.U.: *Austriae est imperare orbi universo* (*Alles Erdreich ist Oesterreich unterthan*). The destiny of Austria is to rule over the whole world. . . . Doubtless the claims of the Hapsburgs to the Holy Roman Empire were consecrated by a long tradition, but should the Holy Roman Empire comprise the whole world or Europe only? Charles V might, with some reason, dream of an empire vaster than that of Tamburlaine and richer than that of Augustus. As the grandson of Ferdinand and Isabella his European patrimony included Austria, Aragon and Castile, Naples and Sicily. From his grandmother, Mary of Burgundy, he had inherited the Low Countries, Flanders, Artois and the Franche-Comté. But he was also master of America, that is to say of the gold and silver of Mexico and Peru. In his name Mendoza had founded Buenos Aires, Valdivia had conquered Chile and de Soto had reached the Mississippi.

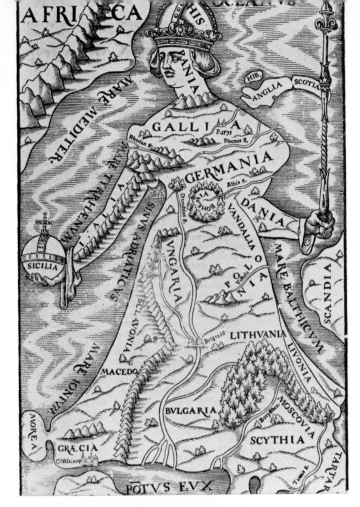

261

260

260 Charles was a complete European. He spoke five languages and travelled incessantly from one country to another. However, he had to cross swords with many adversaries. First with the King of France, whom he defeated and made prisoner in 1525; then with Pope Clement VII, who had to own defeat in 1527: At this moment the rebirth of Imperial Europe seemed imminent. This allegori-

261 cal figure portrays a Virgin, whose head and crown is Spain, whose navel is Bohemia, whose neck and breast are France and Germany and whose arms and hands are Denmark and Italy holding the globe and the sceptre.

The dream was too vast to be realised, but, in default of a European, Charles might have hoped to reign over a Mediterranean Empire.

In the south-east, along a permanent battle-front extending from Tunis to the Ukraine, cutting

Charles V dreams vainly of remodelling Europe with a Spanish profile.

The name of Philip II is carried even to the distant Pacific Islands.

262

through Malta, the Ionian Islands and the Hungarian plain, the Hapsburg Empire faced an adversary no less powerful than itself—the Ottoman Empire and the Sultan, reigning in Constantinople, in whom was vested all the political, military and religious authority of the state.

The Turks carried Belgrade by storm and, after crushing the Hungarians at Mohacs, threatened Vienna in 1529. Their fanatical troops, of whom the Janissaries formed the core, poured into the Danubian countries. Charles, the champion of Catholic Europe, found himself fighting on two fronts, for in 1536 the King of France had allied himself with the Grand Turk.

At last way-worn, old, crippled with gout and haunted by sombre and oppressive thoughts, he abdicated in 1556 and retired to the solitudes of Estremadura, where he died in the monastery of

263

Yuste. His Empire split into fragments and was divided among his successors.

While the Hapsburgs of Austria were facing the Protestants of Germany in the north-west and the Turks in the Balkans, the Spanish branch, strong in their threefold heritage of Spain, Southern Italy and Burgundy, to which the kingdom of Portugal was now to be added, pursued their quest for the hegemony of the Mediterranean. They made an alliance with the Pope and with Venice and it seemed as though a new Crusade were in preparation. The Turks were severely defeated at Lepanto, 7th October 1571, in a terrible naval battle. The prestige of Charles V's successor, Philip II, in whose name the battle had been won, was brilliantly enhanced by this great victory. The distant paradise of the Spice Islands took the name of Philippines to commemorate the monarch.

263

A great monument of the Faith and the realisation of a vow : the Escorial.

264

The Divine Right of Kings, personified in Philip II, was illumined and sustained by a mystic power, the Holy Faith, expressed through the medium of a rigorous etiquette and enforced by the discipline, at once religious and political, of the Inquisition. It was apparent that the victory of the Faith over Europe could not be won unless France were first encircled as a preliminary to being absorbed. In a brilliant campaign starting in the Low Countries, the Spanish armies fought their way to St Quentin in 1557. This signal success, not destined to be followed by others, was the origin of one of the most magnificent monuments of Spain, for during the bombardment of St Quentin the Spanish gunners had destroyed the Church of St Laurence. Philip determined that this crime must be expiated and, with this object, constructed at Escorial, on the bare plateau of Guadarrama, a vast monastery with 1100 windows, whose design recalled the gridiron on which St Laurence perished. This monument was typical of its century and, indeed, of the country of St John of the Cross and St Teresa of Avila.

264

265

265

The Invicible Armada sinks, carrying down with it the Spanish dream.

Philip's Empire, too diversified in its elements, was threatened from within. Centralisation of authority and excessive taxation exasperated the people of the Low Countries. The monarch very imprudently curtailed the freedom of the townships. Resentment grew and the Dutch nobles, appealing for justice, got no satisfaction. A counsellor of Margaret of Parma, Philip's sister, treated them like beggars. They took pride in the insult and vowed to be revenged.

They were represented in the liberation movement by three leaders, William of Nassau Prince of Orange, the Count of Egmont, and the Count of Hornes. In 1566 a national rising took place. The mob, goaded by poverty and by Calvinist preachers, sacked the churches. But the repression was fearful. The Duke of Alba and his 'Council of Blood' beheaded the leaders of the resistance. A war started that was to last for eight years. The 'Beggars of the Sea', brave and hardy privateers, won many fights against the ships of Spain. The 'Spanish Terror' might lay waste their towns, but the Dutch nation grew stronger day by day. In 1579 the United Provinces were proclaimed at Utrecht: none of the seven little republics forming the new federation felt strong enough to stand alone, and the need for solidarity was urgent. So the supreme authority, that of Statthouder or Lieutenant-General, was entrusted to a Prince of Nassau-Orange. In comparison with the other monarchies of the period, this one was undeniably civil and secular.

266

This remarkable evolution led to the creation in 1581 of the States General, who at a meeting at the Hague declared that Philip was deposed and proclaimed the independence of the United Provinces —an independence recognised in 1648. After Spain's golden century, it was Holland's turn. Spain, though she had lost the war with the Protestants of Holland, still retained Antwerp and the southern provinces, where the Catholics predominated. Antwerp, though ruined, was destined to be the cradle of the future Belgium.

Philip II now turned his attention to the heretical English He assembled at Cadiz an enormous invasion fleet. It was baptised the Invincible Armada, but the result belied the name. It consisted of 130 ships carrying 30,000 men. Harried by privateers and decimated by the scientific use of fire-ships, most of the Armada was sent to the bottom by the English fleet, or dispersed by storms, on 8th August 1588. Thus Philip, whose fleet could no longer operate in European waters, finally lost the initiative and England gloried in her well-won victory.

267

266

267

Queen Elizabeth founds the might of Britain on the grave of the Armada.

268 Elizabeth the Great was carried in a sumptuous litter to a thanksgiving service at Westminster. She could well be proud of this first manifestation of British sea-power.

Born a Protestant, Elizabeth had, till her majority, been kept in semi-confinement by Queen Mary, her Catholic sister, and had been forced to abjure her faith. On her accession she took her revenge by adopting the formulae of religious and political autonomy enunciated by Henry VIII in the Act of Supremacy of 1534.

She brought about the unification of her country by promoting its prosperity. Her expeditions to Ireland and the long-delayed execution of Mary Queen of Scots extended the influence of the English monarchy. The economic crisis, paradoxically enough, increased the prosperity of the country. The arrival of bullion in Europe caused a general rise of prices. The landed gentry, pledged to an unalterable currency, dismissed their tenants, who went to seek their fortunes in the ports. In this manner England first discovered her vocation for the sea. Her first national heroes were seamen.

269

GVALTHERVS RALEGH,
EXPVRGATA CIVITATE, HISPANVM
Gubernatorem captiuum abducit.

Among the great mariners of England, whom the bankers helped to prosperity, were Chancellor, who plotted the great northern route to Russia in 1553; Frobisher and Davis, who attempted the north-west passage; Hawkins, merchant and corsair, who started the traffic of African negroes to the Caribbean. As for Raleigh, sea-captain and 269 courtier and one of the most cultivated spirits of England, he founded a precariously sited colony in North America, which he called Virginia after Elizabeth, the Virgin Queen. He is said to have been the first European to smoke a pipe. In the following reign the tax on tobacco produced £5000.

Francis Drake sailed round the world by the 270 western route between 1578 and 1580, ravaging Spanish colonies on his way. The expeditions of explorers and cruises of privateers were accompanied or closely followed by the formation of shipping or trading companies. One of those, the Merchant Adventurers, obtained from the Crown the monopoly to trade in distant parts of Europe and countries outside Europe.

26

The contemporaries of Erasmus, Luther, Calvin and Rabelais were the first writers to profit by the discovery of printing. They were the Latinists, brought up in the bosom of the Church and preoccupied with matters of doctrine. Very different was the intellectual attitude of the generation which synchronised with the development of the wars of religion and the protracted arguments of the Council of Trent, and displayed its most brilliant luminaries in the second half of the 16th century. This generation wrote in the vulgar tongue. Spain, England and France simultaneously gave birth to an immortal trio—Cervantes, Shakespeare, Montaigne—each typical of his own country, but typical of Europe too.

271   *Don Quixote*, which Cervantes published in 1605, had an immense and immediate success. Was it a satire, or, under the guise of a satire, a lament for the departed world of the Middle Ages? Whatever the motive, the author has painted a full and living portrait of Spain the eternal, adventurous and proud, idealistic and suffering. Cervantes has given a philosophic turn to the fruitfulness of failure, which Europe could not misunderstand.

272   The power and grace with which Shakespeare wields the English language are unsurpassed even in his sonnets. But it is as a dramatist that he reveals the true measure of his genius: leaving his characters free to experience in their own lives the most urgent impulses to good and evil, he always places his conflicts within a framework of moral responsibility, and under the cope of a divine Providence.

Montaigne is even more modern and certainly 273 more European. There is only one character in his writings—himself; only one passionate desire—to see clearly, to see with the eyes of the mind. Montaigne was the father of the essay.

These three men, Cervantes, Shakespeare and Montaigne, have taught men to know themselves.

Was science to become a greater danger to religious faith than literature? One might think so to judge by the echoes of the bitter controversy of which Galileo, in 1632, was the unwilling hero.

Europe displays three immortals : Cervantes, Shakespeare and Montaigne.

274

An optical instrument with two superimposed lenses had been manufactured in Holland in order to observe ships more closely. In 1609 Galileo had transformed this spy-glass into a powerful apparatus to be used for observing the heavens. From his numerous observations he concluded that the earth was not the centre of the universe; that it was not static but moved, obviously, round the sun.

274

Monteverdi revolutionised the musical climate of his epoch. In Mantua, in 1567, the first masterpiece of opera, his *Orfeo*, was played. The innovations and the versatile genius of Monteverdi were

275

273

275

276   277

to make Italy dominate European music for generations.

Mankind's search for a new spirit and new dimensions was assisted by Mercator who conceived the idea of transforming the unmanageable globe into a plane surface. His Projection made it possible to print maps on which the navigator could conveniently plot his course.

276

Finally Francis Bacon, who was closely connected with affairs of state in England, appeared as the pioneer of scientific research. He put together a great encyclopedia of knowledge, was the initiator of experimental observation and invented the inductive method, which aimed ultimately at placing nature at the service of man.

277

Science keeps pace, opening to man the skies and the oceans.

Homage to a great European of wide accomplishments : the studio of Rubens.

278 This workroom of a Flemish amateur of the 16th century is, as the painter C. de Baellieur pictured it, nothing less than the studio of Rubens. Both through his art and his many voyages Rubens, a citizen of Antwerp, was a great European. He was born in Westphalia, where his father was living in exile, was employed by the ducal court at Mantua and lived for a time at Rome and Madrid. He made his home at Antwerp, but went to Paris to paint a series of sumptuous pictures portraying the life of Catherine de'Medici. Afterwards he was charged with various delicate diplomatic missions between Madrid, Paris and London.

With the object of reflecting the atmosphere, at once bourgeois and refined, of Rubens' dwelling, the painter has assembled here very imaginatively samples of his work particularly admired by the connoisseurs of this epoch, thus stressing the universality of the master's genius. It has been said that Rubens is supreme in all genres and branches of painting. In his religious and mythological works he is more eloquent than the preachers and more exact than the archaeologists. He is an annalist, an incomparable decorator, an artist capable of giving life both to his huge canvasses and to his smallest sketches.

278

279

The Europeans continued to spread over the world, but the French, for their part, quite content with the comfortable trade which their friendly relations with the Moslem world enabled them to maintain, at first had no inclination for adventure overseas. Their only foreign establishment was in North America, where Champlain founded Quebec, on the St Lawrence, in 1608.

The Protestant nations, more interested in trading than in proselytising, aimed above all at expanding their overseas possessions. Thus the United Provinces of Holland derived the bulk of their wealth from the trade in spices. The first Dutch colony in Indonesia was established in Sumatra, 1595. The East India Company not only obtained the monopoly of the Far Eastern trade, but also were granted the right to make war, to conclude alliances and to annex certain territories if they were minded to do so.

Wherever the absence of Portuguese competition permitted, this Company established trading posts, just distinguishable from fortresses, in

279 Bengal and other places. In 1619 the Dutch founded Batavia on the island of Java. In 1620 they appeared in Guiana and in the following year the West India Company (of America) was created. In 1623 the Walloons founded New Avesnes at the extremity of a peninsula first charted by Verajjamo in 1525 and later rediscovered by Hudson in 1609. This settlement was soon rechristened New

280 Amsterdam and changed its name once more— this time to New York—when the English occupied it in 1664.

The continuous increase in the strength of the

281 Dutch fleet made the Hague a keen competitor with London. These rivalries, even if their field of action was in distant lands, were not calculated to improve international relations in Europe.

280

281

The East and West India Companies trade in spices and girdle the earth.

282

The Mediterranean had lost something of its attraction. The spice road was no longer in fashion. But Venice, after numerous vicissitudes, remained the great entrepôt where, according to ancient custom, the German traders came to get their supplies. The Hostelry of the Germans overflowed with activity. Like the Asiatic caravanserais it was at once a hotel, a bank, a warehouse and a trading centre.

Nevertheless, for the 17th century European the western routes were still the most attractive. The French developed the province of New France around Quebec, and at the same time obtained footholds in the Antilles, in black Africa and even in remote Madagascar.

North America was the queen of what were called the Virgin Lands. Danes, Hollanders, Swedes and the Elector of Brandenburg himself

were constantly exploring these vast regions, but the English were the master-adventurers.

The newcomers took little interest in precious metals though imports of these into Spain had greatly diminished. From the northern territories they got furs and from the tropics sugar, rum and tobacco. To balance these imports the Europeans exported manufactured goods, especially textiles. New homelands were growing up overseas.

The famous *Mayflower* carried across the ocean a group of puritan dissenters, who in 1620 landed in America and founded a colony in New England. Soon afterwards Massachusetts came into being, and in 1632 Maryland. America could soon boast of its first university, Harvard, founded in 1636. Austerity and hard work were the watchwords of the new colonists.

283

To the new colonies overseas the Mayflower is a symbol.

In an upsurge of the Wars of Religion Bavaria and Sweden come to grips.

The passions aroused by the Reformation were still alive in Europe. In Germany, since the Peace of Augsburg in 1555, fire had been smouldering under the ashes. The Catholics, thanks to the Emperor and the Jesuits, had little by little been gaining ground from the Protestants. After having taken two of the advisers of the King of Bohemia, a Hapsburg whose Catholicism was too zealous for their taste, and thrown them from the palace windows, the Czech Protestants placed a German prince on the throne, the Elector Palatine Frederick V. A Catholic alliance crushed them at the battle of the White Hill and the Palatinate fell into the hands of the Duke of Bavaria, a Catholic prince. This German war spread to other parts of Europe when the Protestants, alive to their danger, appealed for aid to Christian IV, King of Denmark. This new ally proved ineffective, and in 1629 he was forced by Count Tilly and by Wallenstein, a Czech soldier of fortune loyal to the Emperor, to come to terms.

The crown of the Holy Roman Empire almost seemed to become a hereditary possession of the House of Hapsburg, but Gustavus Adolphus of Sweden, a convinced Lutheran, intervened, supported by France, who was equally mistrustful of the Imperial ambitions. In 1632 his new-model army, which comprised a mobile force of light artillery, invaded Bavaria, after winning the battle of the Lech, at which Tilly fell mortally wounded.

284

285

The whole European family fêted the Peace of Westphalia in 1648.

286 Gustavus Adolphus was killed in the hour of victory at Lützen. Wallenstein seemed ambitious for power, but the Emperor had him murdered in 1634. It now seemed possible that the war would end. Henry IV of France and his minister Sully had dreamed of an alliance between France and Germany as the basis of a European Republic composed of fifteen nations, administered by an international council of sixty members and possessed of a powerful army. This plan for peace had been swept away by the quarrel between France and the Hapsburgs. And the quarrel had its repercussions, the initiative passing from the Swedish to the French king. The war which had already lasted for more than fifteen years recommenced and swept over Germany like a tornado. Thousands of villages disappeared with two-thirds of their houses and nine-tenths of their livestock. In the market square at Wiesbaden a wood had grown up, sheltering rabbits and roebuck. The population of Württemberg fell from four hundred

286

thousand to forty thousand. The Hanseatic League was dissolved. Meanwhile Germany gave a most cordial welcome to Simplex Simplicissimus, the 287 popular character created by the author Grimmelhausen, who personified the ingenuity of the German peasant, anxious to see justice and mercy, but at grips with all these social, economic and moral disasters.

The Treaty of Westphalia, in 1648, put an end to hostilities. There was widespread rejoicing. 288 Was this to herald the birth of a new order in Europe? The Treaty, even though lacking the signatures of both Spain and England, was none the less an event of capital importance in the history of the Germanic Empire. In future the Emperor would have nothing but his title. His authority was controlled by the Diet of Ratisbon, to which the princes and the free cities sent their delegates. Meanwhile Germany, dispersed and dissected, became a mosaic of about two thousand

287

288

distinct territories, some of which had an area of only a few square miles. A mob of dukes, counts, landgraves, rhinegraves, wildgraves, bishops and abbots presented themselves before the Emperor demanding the right of absolute power in their territories. The Westphalian Treaty laid down that the princes should impose their own religion on their subjects but that Calvinists and Lutherans should enjoy equal rights. The treaty finally established the independence of Switzerland.

Throughout the Thirty Years' War England, grappling with her internal problems which had grown up since Elizabethan times, was absent from the European stage. The claims of the Stuarts to absolute power finally roused the people of London in 1642. Charles I would doubtless have won the day and the civil war would have dragged on indefinitely, kept alive by religious animosity, had not the rebels found the best
289 possible leader in Oliver Cromwell. In 1645 the Royalists were beaten at Naseby and in 1648 Cromwell proclaimed the Commonwealth. Charles
290 I was brought to justice, condemned and executed.

289

290

Cromwell, having thus demolished the royal power, felt himself strong enough to impose his will on Parliament, Scotland and Ireland.

While England was evolving in the direction of a liberal monarchy, which for long was to be regarded as a model, France entrusted herself to
291 an absolute monarchy. Cardinal Richelieu set himself to quell the turbulence of the nobles. He razed castles to the ground and decapitated their rebellious owners. He besieged La Rochelle and smashed the Protestant party. And he extended the frontiers of France to the north, the east and the south. His successor Mazarin contrived, in alliance with Cromwell, to keep Spain within bounds.

291

In England the Crown falls to Cromwell, in France it rises with Richelieu.

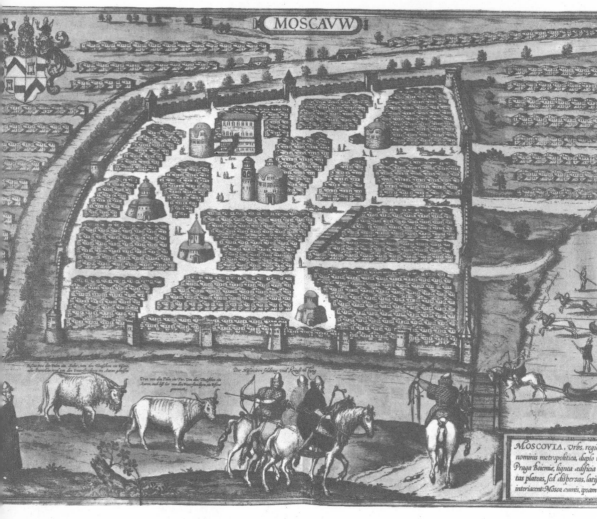

Now it was the turn of Eastern Europe to become restless. The Russians, who in the 13th century had fallen under the domination of the Mongols, had been isolated from the West for two hundred years. Then a local prince from the Moscow region, Ivan III, managed to drive out the Mongols and establish the first Russian monarchy in the lands round Moscow. His grandson, Ivan IV, surnamed 'the Terrible', the first ruler to take the title of Tsar, succeeded in capturing the Don region from the Tartars. But Muscovy was beset by a series of disasters and difficulties until the accession in 1613 of Michael Romanoff. By the end of the reign of Alexis Romanoff (1645–1676) his country occupied such a strong position in Northern Europe that no international problem could be settled without its participation. Moscow, half a town and half a military encampment, was raised to the status of a capital city. Suburban quarters surrounding the Kremlin were aligned with geometrical precision, testifying to the ruler's will towards orderly expansion.

While Russia was thus establishing herself, all the east of Europe was in a ferment. Charles X of Sweden succeeded in converting the Baltic into a Swedish lake, fulfilling the dream of Gustavus Adolphus. At the same time a small princely family in South Germany, the Hohenzollerns, favoured by fortunate inheritances and clever diplomatic manipulations, forged for themselves a substantial kingdom. The head of the family took, at first, the title of 'The Great Elector', but in 1701 he was solemnly crowned King of Prussia at Königsberg.

The Orthodox Cossacks, semi-nomadic horsemen who inhabited the Muscovite marches, had plentiful occasions for quarrelling with their Catholic neighbours, the Poles. King John-Casimir succeeded in containing the Swedes on the north, and the Turks, Tartars and Cossacks on the south-east. But this new balance of power in Northern Europe seemed precarious in comparison with the imposing might and glory of Louis XIV in the West.

This century sees Moscow become the capital of eastern Europe.

296

Louis XIV, war-lord and art-patron.

What a gulf there is between the splendid tapestry which portrays Louis XIV solemnly receiving the ambassadors of the Swiss cantons before the altar in Notre-Dame de Paris, and this Dutch caricature of the 'Sun-King,' covered with surrendered towns and fortresses!

The fact is that there are very few peaceful landmarks in the reign of Louis XIV. He is a war-maker. Whether power, security or prestige was the goal of his policy, we see him everywhere, north, south and east, in quest of natural frontiers. The War of Devolution gained for him part of Flanders: by the Dutch war he acquired the Franche-Comté. But by revoking the Edict of Nantes, which tolerated the Protestant religion in France, he united Europe against him. After the war of the League of Augsburg, which dragged on indecisively for nine years, came the War of the Spanish Succession, which terminated after thirteen years in the treaties of Utrecht and of Rastadt. The king's dominions were consolidated but French ascendancy in Europe was declining. No matter!

295

296

297

From Rome, the other hearth of the Grand Siècle, stems the Baroque style.

Grouped round the Great King we see the Court, in which the great nobles had been reduced to the status of harmless courtiers and the high officials participated in the daily display of royal majesty, the City—Paris, that is—the burgesses, France and Europe itself. Religious unity was assured and the life of the spirit had acquired a national colour. 'The dream of the 16th century had at last been realised—the creation of a French civilisation comparable with that of classical antiquity and setting up no less criteria for the world.' Louis' policy was to use the arts as the instruments of his power and glory. Charles Le Brun made Ver-
297 sailles the centre of French art. The leading architects, sculptors, painters and decorators gave of their best to this end. The interior decoration of Versailles and the gardens owe much to Italian art. The age of Louis XIV is indebted to painters like Poussin or Claude Lorrain, who were already mature artists under Louis XIII, but it was through the inspiration of the Great King that classic French art reached its culmination.

The whole of Europe took as models the noble proportions and prospects of Versailles and imitated them more or less successfully. Examples are provided by Peterhof and Kovskovo in Russia, la Granja in Spain, Caserta in Italy, Hampton Court in England, and the palaces of Stockholm, Potsdam, Schönbrunn, Würzburg and others.

But there was too much talent in Europe and too much originality for Paris and Versailles to be the only light-diffusing centres. Rome began to shine with a new brilliance. Already at the end of the 16th century, Vignola and della Porta had turned their backs on the Gothic and with the Gesù and Saint Louis des Français had created a new style of church architecture whose severity and solid compactness did not exclude ornamented façades. This style was to be adopted almost everywhere by the different religious orders.

From 1623 to 1667 three Popes, Urban VIII, Innocent X and Alexander VII, gave a new look to the Eternal City. St Peter's was completed by Maderno, who prolonged the nave and added to this most spacious of all churches a two-storeyed façade of loggias and galleries. Later, Bernini built
298 the magnificent colonnade that encircles the piazza. Bernini applied the painter's art to his sculptures, introducing movement and vivacity. With his curved, twisted, coiled and tormented figures, the baroque was born. Borromini pushed this form of art to its extreme. It became the principal artistic medium of the Church and had an immense success at Versailles and later in Central Europe, Russia and even as far afield as Brazil.

298

300

But European art of the 17th century was by no means confined to the grandeur of Versailles or St Peter's, the lofty austerity of the Gesù, Bernini's baroque sculpture, or the mythological and allegorical canvases of Poussin and Claude.

Velasquez, official painter to the Court of Spain from 1623, aimed to portray man exactly as he is. Thus in his 'Surrender of Breda', the culminating episode of the long struggle between the United Provinces and Spain, the garments, the lances, the movements of the crowd, the burning city, the faces of the people all combine to record a true picture devoid of grandiloquence.

Holland, free at last and rich, produced a host of great artists anxious to convey in their treatment of faces as well as in the objects of daily life

a higher order of thought and feeling. Rembrandt is the greatest of these men of genius. Along with his religious compositions, where his use of chiaroscuro penetrates the recesses of the human soul, he does honour to the spirit of association so dear to the people of Holland. His 'Syndics of the Cloth Hall', 'The Anatomy Lesson', and 'The Night Watch' are as rich in art as they are in social history. Vermeer of Delft devoted himself to intimate Dutch interiors and to the imperturbable calm of canal landscapes. Caravaggio used light and shade to portray the secrets of the human face. Less inclined towards grandeur in the classic sense European painting of the 17th century sought for peace and truth. Le Nain's 'Rose Gardener' is typical of this spirit.

299

300

301

301

Painters use chiaroscuro to search the recesses of the soul.

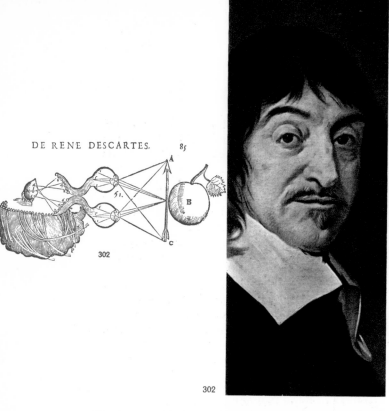

DE RENE DESCARTES. 85

302

303

302

302

The great thinkers of the 17th century produced masterpieces on which European culture was to be based in the coming centuries. Thanks to them the different European languages reached such a level of perfection as to become established in permanent form. Breaking away from scholasticism and theology, the thought of mankind aspired to new heights. Descartes, feeling himself cramped in France, made his home in Holland and, in 1637, published his 'Discourse on Method', the first philosophical work not written in Latin 'in order that even women may be able to understand something of it'. His influence on all the intellectuals of his time was important, even decisive. He laid down general principles applicable to all forms of research and thus became one of the founders of modern science.

303 Holland was also the chosen home of Baruch Spinoza, who was descended from Portuguese

Jews. His 'Ethics', completed in 1675, are designed to show how human reason and the mathematical spirit contribute to our knowledge of God. Spinoza appears in this work as a reformer of traditional philosophy and religion and as the first modern writer to theorise on the subject of liberty.

Every country of Europe contributed something important to the cause of progress and the enrichment of the human spirit.

The German Leibnitz by his conception of the 304 Infinitesimal Calculus doubled the power of mathematics. His curiosity and his thirst for discovery led him to visit capitals and courts. His mind was full of projects, all tending to enlarge the world of thought. In 1700 he was responsible for the creation of an Academy in Berlin. Disunion in Germany and discord in Europe, which he longed to see at peace, caused him to seek, with

304

305

A vital spirit breathes on the mill-vanes of Holland and revives Europe.

306

307

Bossuet as an ally, to bring about the union of the churches. He suggested to Louis XIV a federation of European kingdoms which should divert its superfluous warlike energies to other continents.

In 1657 a Dutchman named Huyghens, by inventing the pendulum clock, made a valuable contribution to the measurement of time. Meanwhile the English mathematician Newton, by establishing the universal principles of gravity and attraction, reinforced men's confidence in the power and truth of science.

In literature France, to use the words of Macaulay, 'was legislating for the whole world'. At the beginning of the classical era Corneille's dramas, *The Cid* (1636), then *Horace, Cinna* and *Polyeucte* were put on the stage. In them men found the very laws of noble conduct. In 1667, when its author was twenty-eight years old, Racine's first masterpiece, *Andromaque*, was played. In the course of ten years this work was followed by six other tragedies. Racine's language possesses an unequalled clearness and purity, but he is not less great as a keen analyst of human motives. Between 1659 and 1673 Molière wrote and produced more than thirty plays in which he shows up with forceful derision the defects and absurdities of human society. The Florentine Lulli was appointed Master of the Ballet at the court of France, and collaborated with Molière in numerous productions.

The age of Louis XIV sought for unity in diversity, greatness combined with a sense of proportion, power without illusion. It fell to Bossuet to remind the great men of his epoch that they were but dust and that the fate of empires did not depend on them alone.

Society, influenced by these master-minds, acquired discipline, shape and countenance. Thus the famous French *politesse* came into existence, based on a tender respect for women, courtesy to others, ease of deportment and tasteful simplicity.

305

306

307

308

309

308

309

On the French stage words and music orchestrate the classical ideal.

If France was the source of elegance and Rome the school of taste, England suddenly found herself promoted to the position of political educator of Europe. The restoration of the monarchy which, in 1660, followed the Commonwealth, did not take place without some serious reactions. The inclination of the Stuart kings towards Catholicism disturbed public opinion to such an extent that in 1679 the first law was passed guaranteeing the freedom of the individual. This was the Habeas Corpus Act. In 1688 William of Orange, a Protestant prince, Statthouder of Holland and son-in-law of James II, intervened to uphold the right of

312

311

governments are nothing but the delegates of the sovereign people.

The blind poet Milton, drawing inspiration from the Bible, from Virgil and Dante, wrote an immense Christian epic *Paradise Lost*. He was also a pamphleteer, who called for the abolition of all censorship. 310

To this period belonged the greatest and most original of English musicians, Purcell, organist of the Chapel Royal and a versatile genius. 311

Early in the 18th century the implacable Swift emerged and devoted his irresistible powers to satire and polemics. Unsatisfied and a rebel, Swift is a typically European author, for Europe, now more than ever, appeared at the dawn of modern history as an unsatisfied spirit bent on two adventures—the search for happiness and for truth. 312

Originating in England, the spread of this new and restless spirit was to be greatly facilitated by the progress of urbanisation, which offered an ever-increasing scope for the propagation of ideas.

the English to have a Protestant king. Followed the Declaration of Rights which proclaimed the principle of constitutional sovereignty and parliamentary government. At the very moment when the principle of the divine right of kings was triumphing in France, the condemnation of this principle in England was urging thinkers and writers in new directions. In 1690 John Locke published his 'Essay concerning Human Understanding', which was for long to be a text-book for philosophers of all countries. His 'Essay on Civil Government' had no less widespread repercussions. The author asserts that man has certain natural rights: to freedom and property. Government is the result of a social contract, that is to say a tacit agreement between the different categories of citizens in their common interest, and accordingly

310

The key-words of individual liberty are of English extraction.

On the shores of Europe the true face of a civilisation is seen.

313

The development of urban civilisation, of which the Middle Ages had seen the beginnings, was a feature of the 17th century. Town builders were attracted by the banks of rivers and canals and sea-coast sites, rather than by high-roads and strategic points. And this development harmonised with the true aspect of Europe with its immense coast-line and its countless rivers.

313 Stockholm replaced Upsala as the capital of Sweden. It had always been a great meeting place for merchants and seamen since, in 1252, Birger Jarl had fortified the three main islands of the channel through which the waters of Lake Maelar flow into the Baltic. And now the greater importance of the Baltic in international politics and the constant increase of maritime traffic made Stock-

holm the first of the cities of Sweden.

London, the Roman Londinium, owes its prosperity to the Thames and the neighbouring sea. Since, in 1566, Sir Thomas Gresham founded the Royal Exchange on the model of the Bourse at Antwerp, the city's economic and political influence had not ceased to grow. Under the Tudors London became a world market. London Bridge, 314 dating from 1209, almost rivals in fame the Tower, the stronghold built by William the Conqueror. The bridge originally carried in mediaeval style two parallel rows of wooden houses and in the centre a chapel dedicated to St Thomas à Becket. At each end was a gate bristling with spikes on the ends of which were exposed the heads of persons executed for high treason.

314

316 b

315

316

316 a

315 Our illustration shows a gallant yacht sailing by the proud tower of Belem built by King Manuel of Portugal in 1521. His capital, Lisbon, mistress of the first European colonial empire, was disproportionately large in respect of its hinterland, but it matched the scale of its oversea commitments. The Portuguese called their city the Queen of the Tagus, which is more than five miles wide at its mouth. Although the immense prosperity which Lisbon enjoyed in the 16th century had somewhat declined, the city remained active and rich until . . . in 1755 an earthquake transformed it in six seconds into a heap of rubble with 30,000 dead and 9000 wrecked houses. It all had to be rebuilt.

316 The smooth and peaceful canals and the quiet gabled houses of Amsterdam masked an ardent zeal for life. Amsterdam was the mushroom-city of the 17th century. It had outstripped Antwerp in importance and in it was concentrated all the maritime and financial power of the new republic of the United Provinces. The Bank, founded in 1609, was a municipal institution housed in the Town Hall. All the merchants kept their accounts there. At this time Amsterdam was the greatest business centre in the world with an unequalled gold and silver reserve, alimented by vessels arriving from Cadiz with cargoes of bar gold and ingots of silver.

Three great towns of Eastern Europe, Prague, Budapest and Vienna, owed their importance as

The seas, rivers and canals reflect the grandeur and charm of the cities.

317

much to the rivers on which they stand as to their strategic position and their royal past.

Prague, which lies in the heart of Bohemia, was, no less than Vienna, a nerve-centre of the Hapsburg Empire. The Vltava runs through the city, passing under the bridge of St Charles, each of whose piers

317

is surmounted by the statue of a saint. Both the Old City, dating from the 9th century, and the New Town, founded in 1348, as well as the Jewish quarter are dominated by the Hradschin, the Royal and later Imperial Citadel and Palace.

A chain of high hills running from west to east plunges steeply into the Danube. This is the site of Buda, while opposite on the flat left bank lies the suburb of Pest. In the 16th century the Turk was reigning here. The Pasha in embroidered robes, wearing a majestic turban and carrying a marshal's baton, is giving orders to a Magyar shepherd in a horseman's cloak, girt with a curved scimitar and carrying an iron staff. The town was surrounded with a curtain-wall and fortifications, and the illustration shows the minarets of ten mosques. Buda was only six days' march from Vienna.

It was from the Danube, too, that Vienna derived its prosperity. Vienna stands on the crossroads, where the Western world had for centuries been meeting traders coming from Venice or Constantinople. But standing as the city did on the confines of the Ottoman Empire, the menace of the Turk was never absent. In 1529 it had already resisted the attacks of Sultan Soliman. As the capital of an ill-assorted Empire comprising Bohemia, Hungary and Austria, Vienna owed her political power to the Hapsburgs.

On the other side of Europe Frenchmen were adorning Paris with rich monuments, though the kings of France had left her for Versailles. The Place Royale and the Pont Neuf were the work of Henri IV, and more splendid edifices were constructed under Louis XIV, which were soon to find imitators in Europe. The palace of the Louvre was adorned with a great colonnade which supplied it with a worthy entrance.

318 a

318 b

318

Budapest, the shield of Islam, lies astride the Danube.

SWEDEN

VIBORG

KRONSTADT

PETERSBURG

REVAL • NARVA

PERNOV

RIGA

SMOLENSK

KAZAN

URAL

VOLGA

MOSCOW

NOVGOROD

POLTAVA

DON

DNIEPER

ASTRAKAN

AZOV

CAUCASUS

DANUBE

TURKISH EMPIRE

When his half-sister Sophie made herself Regent, the young Tsar Peter retired to the suburbs of Moscow where his neighbours—foreigners from Holland, Germany and Switzerland—introduced him to western methods of doing things. On coming to power in 1689 he resolved to impose the civilisation of the West on his still half-Asiatic empire. To this end he had to breach the walls erected by Sweden, Poland and Turkey round his country, which separated him from the West. This self-taught giant, six feet six in height, an astounding mixture of genius and barbarity, was never still and lost no occasion to show his activity. His first campaign was against the Turks from whom he captured Azov, at the mouth of the Don, in 1696.

But Peter found the Baltic, as being more European, more attractive than the Black Sea. In 1697 he declared war against the boy king Charles XII of Sweden and occupied the Baltic provinces. He nearly lost the war when in 1708 the Swedes marched to the aid of the Cossack rebel Mazeppa, who was fomenting an insurrection in the Ukraine. However Peter crushed Charles XII at Poltava, 1709, and Russia became the first power in the North. Charles XII lost all his Baltic territories and was eventually killed fighting the Danes. In 1721 the supremacy of Russia in the Baltic was recognised at the Peace of Nystad and the Tsar assumed the title of Peter the Great, Emperor of All the Russias.

In 1703 Peter founded on the Neva the capital of the new Russia, St Petersburg, planned by a Frenchman. Stone buildings were obligatory. All confessions were entitled to their place of worship on the Nevski Prospect, later nicknamed Tolerance Prospect. Two thirds of Russian exports were shipped from the port of St Petersburg, which was open to international trade. Peter also laid the foundations of Russian industry. At first he employed German engineers and technicians in developing the metallurgical resources of the Urals. There was great activity in the mines, the naval dockyards and the cloth factories. The Government did everything to encourage the creation of factories and mills and conferred on manufacturers some of the privileges of the nobility.

The Tsar spent 1697 and 1698 in the West, to see about the building of a fleet to overawe the Turks. He visited Germany, Holland and England and studied ship-building techniques at Woolwich Arsenal. On his return, he banned the wearing of long robes and of beards, both eastern customs, in favour of shorter dress and shaven chins. With accrued prestige Peter returned to Holland, 1716, and later visited Paris where he displayed his interest in science, letters and the arts.

The Tsar had given up the idea of slicing deeply into the Ottoman Empire, finding that the Turks did not constitute an immediate threat to Russia. The Hapsburgs, however, thought otherwise with the Crescent at their gates. The Ottoman power was most definitely formidable. The Sultan launched, during this century, two great offensives at the heart of Europe. In 1663 more than 100,000 Turks invaded Hungary and twenty years later the Grand Vizier led an army of 200,000 men with artillery and camels up to the walls of Vienna. The citizens defended the town like heroes, but all seemed to be lost, until a German army, and the squadrons of the Polish king Jan Sobieski defeated the Turkish army at Kahlenberg.

The Venetians and later the Russians joined in the struggle; the Turks were crushed at Mohacz in 1687 and lost much territory in Europe. By now the Hapsburgs had reconquered the whole of Hungary, but the Hungarians submitted with ill grace to an Austrian administration, their patriotism being now awakened.

In face of the continual menace of hostilities which overhung Europe men began to ask themselves if there was any means of putting an end to war once for all. A Frenchman, the Abbé de Saint-Pierre, started a movement to create a federation of European states. He proposed 'the foundation of a permanent association of all the sovereign Christian states' with a European Senate and, for purposes of war against any nation infringing the pact, an army under a single supreme command.

The threat from the East inspires Europe's first federalist, a churchman.

But Europe, so far from adopting the plan proposed by the Abbé de Saint-Pierre, sank ever deeper in the slough of discord and jealousy. Never have ideas been less fruitful of results. The characteristic of international politics in the 18th century was a progressive entanglement of interests and ambitions. Since the treaties of Utrecht and of Rastadt which in 1713 created a certain European equilibrium under the aegis of France and England, the power of Austria had been continually growing. The head of the Hapsburg House, alone in Europe, had the right to be called Emperor. But in 1740 this empire, a patchwork of different nations, fell under the sway of a woman—Maria Theresa. And now began the twenty-five years of struggle for the Austrian succession. Maria Theresa, vivacious and good-humoured and the mother of sixteen children, was not a woman readily to own defeat. Austria, attacked by France, Prussia, Bavaria, Saxony and Spain, lost Silesia to Prussia, but held her own everywhere else. Her artillery was soon to be the best in Europe. The French troops were surrounded in Prague and forced to retire. The Austrians threatened Alsace and the war became a duel between the French and Austrian monarchies. The generals of Louis XV conquered the Netherlands, but the Treaty of Aix-la-Chapelle in 1748 showed special favour to the claims of the King of Prussia, the ally of France.

In the previous centuries Europe had already witnessed what the historians have thought fit to call the Portuguese Adventure and the Swedish Adventure. Now once more we see a quite small state raise itself by persevering efforts to the level of the great powers. But while the Portuguese and Swedish Adventures came to a comparatively sudden end, the Prussian Adventure had consequences which were to last till its dénouement in the middle of the 20th century.

But the king of Prussia destroys Europe's equilibrium.

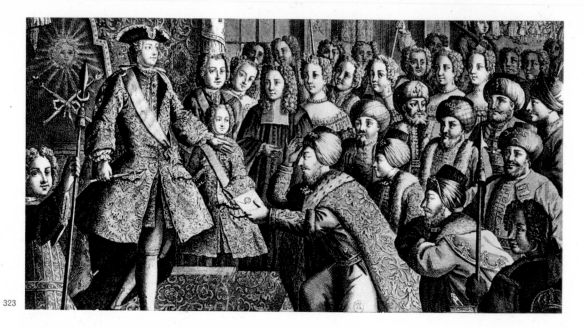

The ill-feeling between Austria and Prussia was too strong to allow of a peaceful solution. Taking advantage of the fact that England was casting a covetous eye on the colonial possessions of France, Prussia deserted her ally and joined forces with the English. From that moment France was forced to abandon a policy she had pursued for two centuries and to ally herself with Austria. She was soon joined by Russia, Sweden and the principal German states. The Seven Years' War began. What was at stake was not the future of Silesia—which was the direct object of the conflict between Austria and Prussia—but the whole future of Germanic Europe. The question was whether the Hohenzollerns were going to revert to their former status of small German princes. Their English allies, busy fighting in Canada and India, were of little use to them. Prussia, attacked on all sides, was on the verge of disaster. The Russians, even more than the French, had inflicted some terrible defeats on her, but she was saved by the Coalition's lack of cohesion and by the tactical faults of its leaders. In 1763 a peace was negotiated. England issued victorious from her distant campaigns, while France, for lack of good statesmen and good generals, had lost Canada and India, two hundred thousand men killed on the battlefields of Germany and many millions of money. Her old friendship with the Ottomans which Louis XV wished to maintain was severed. Prussia not only kept 323 Silesia but came out of the war with enhanced prestige.

Frederick II, not content with making his 324 country's army the best in Europe, was the first ruler to advocate compulsory primary education. He colonised uncultivated or depopulated territories, suppressed torture, improved justice and practised religious tolerance.

France, for lack of good leaders, loses her battles and her colonies.

326

327

On Sunday, 23rd September 1762, Catherine II, Empress of Russia, assumed the crown of the Tsars in the Church of the Annunciation in Moscow. Energetic in aspect, unusually strong-willed and industrious, she was determined to continue the work of Peter the Great and to prove that Russia was quite able to 'go it alone'. Seeing that France, Poland's traditional ally, and England were exclusively occupied in fighting one another, her hands were free. Poland had long been weakened by internal dissensions, and Catherine's armed intervention was successful. The Turks seized the opportunity to declare war on Russia and had their fleet destroyed at Cheshmeh. At this point Frederick II and Maria Theresa, disturbed by the weakening of Turkey, came to an agreement with Catherine for the partition of Poland. This operation, which today is universally regarded as a crime against the law of nations, was fraught with danger for the peace of Europe. In spite of this the greatest thinkers of the time, notably Voltaire and Diderot, prejudiced by their admiration for Frederick and Catherine, both friends and patrons of philosophers, uttered no word of protest.

325 326

327

In 1774 Catherine signed a treaty with the Turks by which Russia became the official protector of the Christian peoples of the Balkans. This gave her the right to intervene in the affairs of Turkey. Here was another potential source of trouble. Yet during this period the world of art and letters, never since the Middle Ages so sincerely imbued with a consciousness of its European ideals, indefatigably preached to the world the gospel of freedom, justice and concord.

Foremost admirers of Catherine were thinkers like Voltaire and Diderot.

THE TROELFTH | LE GÂTEAU
CAKE. | DES ROIS.

In the age of the Encyclopedia no house is complete without a library.

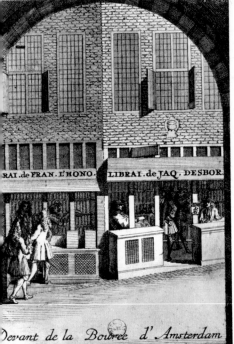

By a cruel but consoling paradox Europe, while indulging in wars as barbarous as those of the remote Middle Ages, displayed a strong desire for intellectual progress, a real thirst for enlightenment. Culture was no longer in the exclusive possession of certain great monarchs like Frederick the Great or Catherine of Russia: it was becoming more and more the common property of the middle and upper classes. Though books were proscribed by the ruler from time to time (especially in France) the number published continued to increase. It became the custom even in religious houses such as the convent of St Gall to build up a library full of scientific, literary, philosophical and technical works. 328

In 1737, the Masonic Order, which had taken root in England and which from there radiated light as far as the court of old King Joseph II of Austria, claimed that knowledge should be shared by all. In 1741 a plan was prepared for publishing

Rousseau preaches to Europe the sovereignty of the people.

a universal dictionary to be paid for by the subscriptions of European freemasons. The dictionary was never published but, basing themselves on Chambers' Cyclopedia, d'Alembert and Diderot, assisted by a group of intellectuals, engaged upon the preparation of an 'Encyclopaedia or Descriptive Dictionary of the Arts, Sciences and Professions'; the first volume appeared in 1751.

329   At the very moment when France was suffering such severe reverses in the field of international politics, the whole of Europe had fallen under the influence of the French language, now become that of princes, diplomats, philosophers and scientists. French artists were favourites in every capital. Castles reminiscent of Versailles abounded in the principalities of Germany. French architects were all the rage at St Petersburg, where Falconet executed his majestic statue of Peter the Great.

330   Voltaire, an idol in Paris, was the favourite author of Potsdam and Moscow. This continent, irradiated by the luminaries of thought, was a world without frontiers, in which the great capitals like Paris and London were beacons of universal culture. All nations gathered in Mme Geoffrin's salon. When a lone wolf, a fugitive from society, 331 like Rousseau made himself the apostle of the 332 sovereignty of the people, his words did not find an echo in one country alone; they were quoted and commented on through the length and breadth of Europe. His *Contrat Social*, published in 1762, proclaimed that all men were free and equal and that the proper aim of every social and political organisation was to safeguard the rights of the individual, who in his turn should submit himself to the wishes and study the interests of the majority. The people alone were sovereign. His ideas, which developed those of Locke, caused men's minds to ferment in preparation for the explosion of 1789.

332

Cook discovers the "good" savage, Wincklemann the buried city of Pompeii.

335

Society took no less interest in men of science. Academies of science were founded everywhere— the Royal Society of London received its charter in 1662, and the *Académie des Sciences* of Paris was founded in 1666; similar institutions grew up later in Bologna, Berlin, Upsala, St Petersburg and Stockholm. A network of regional scientific societies combined with the major academies to create a European Republic of Savants. The mathematicians had their hours of triumph. D'Alembert enunciated the principle of the conservation of energy; Euler discoursed on inertia. In 1781 Herschel discovered the planet Uranus. Linnaeus laid the foundations of scientific botany and zoology. French expeditions simultaneously measured a meridian in Lapland and in Peru in 1743.

334

333

The stories brought back by enthusiastic travellers taught Europe lessons in relative values. From them Europe learnt that the Chinese were virtuous though they had never heard of the Old or the New Testament, that 'good' savages existed, that the girls who danced for Captain Cook at Tahiti were 333 no less graceful than the ballerinas of London.

The German Winckelmann uncovered the ruins 334 of Herculaneum and Pompeii. His 'History of Ancient Art' showed by countless examples that daily life in ancient times was characterised by at least as much comfort, luxury, good taste and inventive genius as life in his own age. Two other great adventures by rationalists in quest of truth may be mentioned: in 1796 Laplace reconstructed the world as an expression of thought without the intervention of God, and Kant evolved a philo- 335 sophy in which God is declared unknowable.

The power of steam and of electricity makes its entry into human history.

And now came new creatures, if one can apply the name to machines. In 1735 Abraham Derby succeeded in smelting pig-iron with coke as fuel. This operation promoted coal to the leading rôle in industrial development, but it also raised in acute form the question of pumping water out of the galleries in the coal mines. It was known that atmospheric pressure was the great obstacle to the lifting of liquids and, to overcome it, means had to be found to create a vacuum. An Englishman, Savery, searching for a solution, invented the first steam-pump. Then Papin, a French professor in Germany, constructed a steamboat at Cassel which carried him to Munden in 1707, while Newcomen, another Englishman, produced in 1712 the first
336 pump possessing real industrial value. In 1763 a French military engineer thought of fitting such a machine on to a three-wheeled truck. This first automobile actually worked.

337

336

More sensational inventions were forthcoming. The brothers Montgolfier, after studying the list of gases prepared in 1772 by Priestley, conceived the idea of filling a cloth balloon with hot air, which would cause it to rise. In an early *entente cordiale* Blanchard and Jeffries crossed the Channel by air
337 for the first time in 1785. Other surprising experiments were carried out. In 1746 three Dutch scientists invented the first Leyden jar, capable, it was claimed, of atomising a whole company of French Guards. Meanwhile, in Paris, the Abbé Nollet was administering shocks to the charming *marquises* with his electrostatic machines and in
338 Florence Galvani was studying the effects of electricity on the nervous system of frogs. Who could have imagined, at this stage, that such a prodigious source of power was within reach?

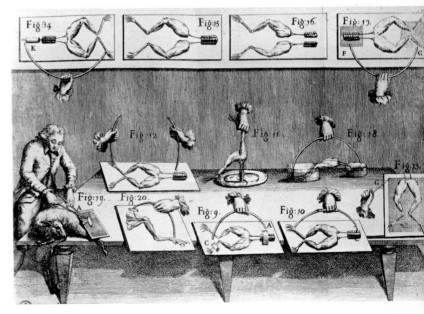

338

151

Grand balls and *fêtes champêtres* entertain Europe's aristocracy.

339

The taste for science and the success in that field of men from the lower middle class brought about a lowering of the old social barriers. But the aristocracy, who continued to enjoy the privileges of birth and wealth, for the most part gave little time to the pursuit of culture and learning. If certain noblemen devoted themselves as patrons to science and the arts, read the classics or, as in England, were actively engaged in business and in rural development, others, far more numerous, hardly knew how to spell. The German princes treated their territories as apanages of their court and the landowners as courtiers. A daily sequence of ceremonies took place in their theatre-like
339 palaces. The castle of Schoenbrunn in the outskirts of Vienna offered a luxurious setting to the courtiers of Maria-Theresa, who herself led a life of the utmost simplicity.

The splendid but futile distractions of the upper classes consisted of hunting and shooting, cardplaying, gambling, horse-racing, drinking, music, the theatre, and love-making—innocent or wanton. Throughout Europe dancing had never been indulged in with such passion. Dancers with or without masks disported themselves on the high-

ways, in the palaces and under the trees. Sometimes it was the formal minuet, the same dance at Versailles and in Venice, which, well performed, 340 was regarded as such a masterpiece that the couple whose turn it was to dance was surrounded by the other dancers in a ring. Sometimes it was country dances performed 'in familiar and playful style but at a tempo which made the dancers very hot'.

Society worshipped the opera, on which enormous sums of money were lavished. Charles Eugene, whose dukedom of Württemberg, with its capital at Stuttgart, numbered less than 600,000 subjects, kept a stable of 800 horses and possessed the finest opera in German Europe, the best orchestra and corps de ballet, and a French comedy troupe ranking second only to Paris. He used to give displays of unimaginable splendour of which he alone bore the cost.

The pleasures of the table now began to rank with those of the spirit, making a fourth with music, dress and reading. A cup of tea, oysters for luncheon, or ham, a cold collation for the 341 shooting-party, all these supplied Boucher, de Troy, Lancret and Van Loo with subjects for pictures.

340

341

Beer, happy Produce of our Isle
Can sinewy Strength impart
And wearied with Fatigue and Toil
Can cheer each manly Heart

Labour and Art upheld by Thee
Successfully advance,
We quaff Thy balmy Juice with Glee
And Water leave to France.

Genius of Health, thy grateful Taste
Rivals the Cup of Jove,
And warms each English generous Breast
with Liberty and Love

But the aristocracy much preferred the greater brilliance of town life to life in their castles and estates. In capital cities such as Rome, Paris, Venice, London, Dresden, Stuttgart, Munich, Vienna, Madrid, an ever-increasing number of great family houses was springing up.

In the 18th century, with the memory of destructive wars fresh in men's minds, the tendency was for towns to remain within their encircling ramparts and not to venture outside the area intersected by their main streets. The constant growths of the population flooded the streets with noisy, bustling life. Street vendors, knife-grinders, water-carriers, sedan-chairmen, criers and porters composed an astonishing miscellany best reproduced by the English painter Hogarth.

This artist, robust in health and rich in humour, deliberately broke away from all the schools. Whether he was painting the world of rakes and prostitutes, of drinking booths or pawnbrokers, he succeeded in debunking the glitter and affectation of high society by revealing the squalor of life behind the scenes. He enjoyed an enormous success in London, comparable with that of the *Beggar's Opera*. This work, which provides an astringent contrast to the antique gods and mellifluous heroes of the Italian opera, is full of graceful airs and old folk tunes, and, while claiming to depict typical characters from the London underworld, reveals the baseness of the human heart whether plebeian or aristocratic.

In this world of superficialities, one superficial aspect, the fashion in dress for men and women, reigned supreme. In Paris there were 1,702 dressmakers and 1,884 men's and women's tailors. The Empress Elizabeth of Russia used to await with impatience the arrival of the models from the Rue Saint Honoré bringing to St Petersburg the latest Paris fashions, from which she claimed the right to make first choice for herself.

Venice, in spite of its ruthless political police, became the Mecca of people in search of pleasure and gracious living. The city boasted of three newspapers, seven theatres, numerous gaming

The town house is preferred to the castle and the country estate.

clubs, and a Carnival which lasted nearly six weeks. Intellectuals and artists flocked thither from all parts. Addison, Montesquieu, Young, Voltaire, Mozart and Handel came to Venice to collect their thoughts and to work. Goldoni, himself a Venetian, revived Italian comedy by drawing for his subjects on the episodes and personages of daily life in the city, which Tiepolo depicted with brilliant good humour. The wearing of masks was permitted for the great festivals, for the duration of the Carnival and from October 5 to December 16, and in the streets many revellers completed their incognito by assuming some disguise. Harlequin, Pantaloon

345

and Isabel jostled among the crowd that surrounded the mountebank king. The original genius of Venice was well represented by its painters. Longhi depicts the frivolous and carefree society, while Canaletto perpetuates the aspect of the city and its lagoons. Guardi commemorates in twelve pictures the coronation of the Doge Alvise IV Mocenigo. In this series Ascension Day marks the culmination of the ceremonies, when the Doge, carried in his festal galley the *Bucentaur*, proceeds to the Lido, there to celebrate the marriage of Venice with the Adriatic. He throws a ring into the sea proclaiming, 'We take thee in marriage, O sea of ours, to mark our true and unending sovereignty'.

346

Venice, with its masques and festivals, is a gay and brilliant capital.

346

baroque. At Melk Jacob Prandtauer was the architect of a Benedictine abbey whose outlines, following a winding reach of the Danube, represent the most successful piece of monastic architecture since the Middle Ages. The architects of this epoch learnt to combine the mediaeval tradition of two towers, which they crowned with onion-shaped cupolas, with domes copied from Saint Peter's in Rome and the inspired frontage of the Gesù, modified according to the rules of baroque art. This composite style characterised a great number of churches in many different places, such as the cathedral at Fulda completed in 1712 by Johann Dienzenhofer or the churches of Vierzehnheiligen and Neresheim built by J. B. Neumann. The latter was also responsible for the Bishop's Palace at Würzburg, strongly influenced by Versailles, with decorations by Tiepolo

Architecture and the decorative arts acquired a new idiom in the 18th century, which in spite of the extreme diversity of its realisations and often of its conceptions bore witness to the common ideals of European civilisation. Baroque art, which made rapid progress in Italy during the early 17th century thanks to the work of Bernini and Borromini, became the fashion in France, where its massive and powerful character made way under Louis XV for the rococo style with its flamelike undulations. Conventionalised Celtic patterns, Roman grotesques, the interlaced designs of the steppes, Moslem arabesque, flamboyant Gothic, the Italianate grottos of the Renaissance and even the shell-collectors' specimens and the fashionable cult of Chinese curios all contributed to this new phenomenon.

At the very moment when the art of France was triumphantly traversing Germany on its way to Moscow, the baroque style, which the miseries of the Thirty Years' War had held up on the German frontier, invaded Southern Germany and the Austrian Empire. The blending of the two styles was to bring about the birth and the rapid development of the rococo in the east of Europe. The baroque and the rococo, which borrow so much from idealism and dreams, are particularly appropriate to countries aspiring to a rebirth after emerging from a stormy period. Baroque art flourished until 1740 in Bohemia. At Vienna Fischer von Erlach, who had studied in Rome with the pupils of Bernini, built the church of St Charles Borromæus in 1716. The façade of this building is framed between two allegorical columns and is classed among the finest examples of Austrian

348

The rococo, born of the baroque, flourishes in central Europe.

and a staircase which is in itself a masterpiece. At Dresden, between 1711 and 1722 Poppelmann designed the astonishing Zwinger Palace with its pavilions, terraces and galleries lined with statues all built around an open space admirably suited for public fêtes.

While façades were often stiff and formal, the decorators allowed themselves a free hand in treating interiors with all the opulence of rococo forms and colours. Referring to such buildings it was said 'One no longer knows where the walls are'. This comment could be true of the church at 348 Birnau, nicknamed 'the Good Lord's ballroom', or that of St Gall in Switzerland or the little church at Wies in South Baden; and here we have an illustration of the old chapel at Ratisbon, dating from 1000, now overlaid with oratories, loggias 349 and stalls in the rococo style.

349

But it was through the medium of much smaller objects that this truly oecumenical style was destined to become fashionable. In 1709 Bottger, jeweller to King Augustus the Strong, of Saxony, discovered the secret of making Chinese porcelain. The first European porcelain factory was erected at Meissen, where it has prospered ever since. Rival works were established at Nymphenburg in 1747, and later in France at Sèvres. England and Austria followed suit and before long very many homes throughout Europe were decorated by those charming china figurines in which the 350 Rococo achieved its most perfect expression.

350

Porcelain figures, from Meissen and Sèvres, grace fashionable salons.

The spirit of the age finds its voice in the music of Bach and Handel.

352

353

351 Here we see all the great ones of Rome assembled in the palace of Cardinal Melchior de Polignac, with its sumptuous *décor* of gold, blue and purple, to witness a performance of *La Contesa de' Numi* (The Contest of the Gods). Opera continued to be enthusiastically supported throughout the continent by the courts and the people alike. Nevertheless music, in this 18th century, was to express itself in other forms and achieve its greatest triumphs in very diverse genres.

Protestant church music found its chosen home in Germany. Its greatest master was undoubtedly Johann Sebastian Bach. Born in Thuringia in 1685, Bach sprang from a long line of fine musicians which can be traced back to 1550. Organist at Arnstadt and later at the Ducal Chapel at Weimar, he became Choirmaster at the Church of St Thomas at Leipzig, where he had constant difficulties with the civil and ecclesiastical authorities. 352 His portrait reveals his frankness and strength of will and in it we recognise that complete integrity, both in his art and in the conduct of his life, which enabled him to resist the pressure of the different influences which threatened the free expansion of his genius. In his own lifetime Bach was considered rather as a first-rate organist than as a great composer; nevertheless he left sixty huge volumes of music, religious and secular. His sacred works utilised all the current musical forms: chorales to be sung in choir, organ chorales, motets, cantatas with a great variety in their vocal and instrumental composition, oratorios, the Passions —two oratorios celebrating the death of Christ— and finally the Mass in B minor which followed the text of the Latin mass. Bach's music, drawing inspiration from the Reformation and from Lutheranism and blending the German with the Latin genius, occupies an important if not the

central place in the history of European culture.

Handel was born at Halle in Saxony in the same 353 year as Bach. He made his début as a musician at Hamburg, after which he took the road to Italy. He resided at Venice, Florence and Rome, and then established himself at Naples, where Alessandro Scarlatti, composer of 115 operas, and 354 his School reigned as dictator over the world of music. Handel also composed operas, which obtained a great success in London. However, finding himself hampered by all sorts of intrigues, he turned from opera to oratorio. The first performance of his *Messiah*, which took place in Dublin, 1742, was a triumph, and his subsequent career was unbrokenly successful.

While music won passionate appreciation from the public in the 18th century, some of the most gifted composers died early in its service. Pergolesi

354

To beloved music Gluck gives his Orpheus, Haydn his grace, Mozart his life.

355

the Austrian prince to whose court he was attached and peacefully climbed the ladder of fame. He was enthusiastically received in London in 1791. A new era was opening for music. The sonata, the concerto with a solo instrumentalist, the string quartet and the symphony had begun to take the place of the older forms—the fugue, the concerto grosso and the instrumental suite. The salons of the great and even public concert halls, taking the place of the churches, became the real temples of music. Haydn, with a style that could not fail to delight elegant and distinguished audiences, was the perfect precursor of this new era.

At the same time Gluck revolutionised grand opera, discarding the pompous and affected conventions of the past. More even than Vienna, it was Paris which, by its warm reception of *Orpheus* in 1774, and then of *Iphigenia in Tauris*, consolidated Gluck's success and proved the worth of his theories.

357

died at 26 leaving a volume of work which defies the imagination. Mozart passed away at 35 bequeathing to the world an imperishable monument.

An infant prodigy, Mozart was born at Salzburg 355 in 1756. As a child he astounded all the important persons to whom his father made him play. But in spite of the splendid success which attended his operas from the moment they were produced, he never succeeded in earning a comfortable income which would have enabled him to develop his genius free from the handicap of penury. He died in 1791 in poverty, before he had reached the prime of life. His seven operas, forty-one symphonies, and the mass of chamber and piano music which he composed (the piano had been invented in 1720), secured for him universal admiration. 356

356 Haydn (1732–1809) enjoyed the protection of

357

The countries of Europe were seething with life. Russia which under Peter the Great had contained fifteen million inhabitants had more than thirty by the end of the century. The population of France had gone up from twenty to twenty-six millions. Frederick's conquests had doubled the population of Prussia. Great Britain, including Scotland, had between five and six million inhabitants in 1700 and nine million by 1789. Populations thus increasing would require a great expansion of commerce to supply their needs.

358 In ship-design greater stability was achieved by broadening the beam near the water line; the area of the canvas was developed and a complicated network of lines made it possible to manœuvre with ease and precision. The perfecting of the chronometer greatly facilitated accuracy in course-plotting. Before long merchant vessels would require no escorts and no longer carry guns as the pirates who had infested the seas in the 17th century, were disappearing. A fever of commercial and financial activity swept over Europe.

In this movement France, to start with, lagged behind. Catholicism, the religion of the State, forbade the lending of money on interest as being a way of making profit without work or risk. It needed a Scotsman like Law or Swiss experts like Necker and Clavière to introduce the techniques of finance. In the German states the middle classes prospered. Fairs, like the wool fair of Breslau, 359 developed into specialised international markets.

Favoured by the south-west winds which brought the great sailing ships to her shores, England became the leading commercial nation in the world. The port of London had never been so 360 active. Faithful to her mercantile tradition, Britain sought to be self-sufficing, as far as was possible, by buying little and selling much.

358

359

360

Merchant vessels spread their canvas to catch the trade winds.

The European idea, crossing the Atlantic, will become the United States.

361

On the other side of the Atlantic the number of colonists from England, Germany and Holland was continually increasing and now totalled three million. These emigrants came from every kind of milieu. The most original among them were without doubt the Quakers, the enemies of the priestly hierarchy, the Church and of war. Persecuted in England, they left the country in 1681 under the leadership of William Penn, a warm-hearted idealist but a good man of business, to found a colony for themselves on the banks of the Delaware. It was in honour of Penn, 'the friend and brother' of mankind, that the state was named Pennsylvania and its capital Philadelphia. Penn concluded a treaty of friendship with the Indians which was to last 'as long as the sun and the moon shed their light'. And it was faithfully observed. 361 Scotsmen, Irishmen, Welsh, Germans, Swedes, men of every confession flocked to this liberal land. Philadelphia, with its Academy, its philosophic societies, its masonic lodges, which flourished under the inspiration of Benjamin Franklin, became a miniature European capital. The Constitution of Pennsylvania served as the basis for that of the United States. Better still, Penn conceived the idea of a European Federation with a parliament of ninety members.

The American Colonies, conscious of their maturity, began to chafe under the restrictions imposed on them by the British Government, who allowed them no liberty whatever in commercial matters and loaded them with taxes. The incidents which occurred at Boston on 16th December 1773 started a period of disorder which was in two years to culminate in open war. A remarkable series of events stood out as landmarks in the evolution of the new republic. In political assemblies the 'patriots'—soon to be called the party of the left— outvoted the conservative loyalists. In June 1776 Virginia adopted a constitution and declared itself a republic. Their new Charter was prefaced by a Declaration of Rights opening with the words 'All men are by nature free and independent and possess certain rights'—the right to live, the right to freedom, the right to property, the right to security—to which the authors optimistically added the right to seek for happiness here on earth. The government is the instrument of the nation, who have the right to improve or abolish it according to the will of the majority. These principles were solemnly reaffirmed by Congress, meeting at Philadelphia, on 4th July 1776, when the independence of the United States was proclaimed. 362

Europe showed enthusiasm for the cause. Distinguished volunteers flocked to the colours. Among them were Kosciusko, the Pole, Steuben,

366

363

The Declaration of the Bill of Rights recrosses the ocean with Lafayette.

362

the German tactician, and two French noblemen, Ségur and La Fayette. Contemporary pictures celebrate the benefits accruing from American independence.

The new state was lucky to find in its early days an outstanding military chief, George Washington, and an efficient diplomatist, the good-natured Benjamin Franklin. The former, a gentleman-planter of distinguished bearing, showed himself, if not a great leader, at least a great organiser, under whose cold but firm hands the militiamen became soldiers. Franklin, a typical self-made man, went to France, preceded by his reputation as the inventor of the lightning-conductor. With his spectacles and his fur coat, he became the fashion of the day. In 1778 Louis XVI recognised the United States and concluded a commercial treaty with them. Meantime Franklin succeeded in creating a League of Armed Neutrality embodying all the European Powers trading in the Atlantic.

La Fayette, who had won the friendship of Washington and been his guest at Mount Vernon, persuaded Louis XVI to send to America an expeditionary force under Rochambeau. The war, which might have ended very differently, turned in favour of the 'insurgents'. In 1775 the Massachusetts militia won the battle of Lexington; in 1777 General Burgoyne surrendered at Saratoga. Finally in 1781 the English admiral Cornwallis capitulated to Rochambeau, La Fayette and Washington in the square at Yorktown. On 3rd September 1783 the English recognised the independence of the United States at Versailles. The consequences of this step were important. England would henceforth look forward to the downfall of the French monarchy, and transfer her vital overseas interests to India. Furthermore, the success which attended democracy in America served to speed up the movement of radical and reformist ideas in France.

365

364

165

In compensation for the loss of America, Europe found a new world to explore—that of the imagination. Henceforward philosophers were everywhere to champion the life-force against convention, instinct against reason and nature against the artificialities of society. European literature had for centuries been analysing the nature of man and proclaiming his supremacy, but now external reality, hitherto forgotten, became the most absorbing theme for men of letters. 367 Young's 'Night Thoughts', the expression of a personal tragedy, written by a father who had just suffered a triple bereavement, had an immense vogue in Europe. Macpherson, a Scotsman, ascribed to Ossian, the Irish poet, a collection of his own verse, steeped in Celtic mist. The authenticity of his antique and barbarous heroes was discredited by Dr Johnson, but believed in by many readers who thought they were listening to

the genuine strains of the legendary bard echoing down from the dark ages. The paint brush of Ingres perpetuated the romantic illusion. 368

European taste soon veered from misty Scotland to Switzerland. Haller, the poet of the Alps, became popular in France about 1750. Ten years later the French acclaimed Gessner, a German-Swiss poet whose 'Idylls', purporting to describe the landscapes of ancient Greece, paint a smiling and sunny picture of the Zürich countryside. More than eighty translations of the 'Idylls' were published. The 'sixties of the eighteenth century present a new departure in European letters. The success of Gessner and Ossian is more than matched by that of *La Nouvelle Héloïse* and *Emile*, in which Rousseau aims to restore to mankind a taste for genuine pleasures and to convert them to the love of tranquillity and the beauties of nature. He extols, 'the Alpine air, so pure and health-giving, the gentle air of the Swiss homeland, sweeter than the perfumes of the Orient'.

A young German law student, Johann Wolfgang Goethe, born in 1749 at Frankfurt-on-Main, 369 devoted himself with passion to these new authors.

Rousseau and Ossian capture the imagination of Europe.

In 1774 he published 'The Sorrows of Werther', which derived its inspiration from an episode in his own life. His ill-starred hero is consumed by an incurable passion for Charlotte, the fiancée and later the wife of a friend, and in despair he kills himself. Werther had an immense and immediate success and through its pages the German middle-classes learnt a new way to feel and to love. The literary movement called *Sturm und Drang* was greatly stimulated by this work and this little novel, soon to be translated into all languages, contributed largely to Europe's Romantic Renascence. The *Sturm und Drang* movement revived the taste for Shakespeare and at the same time gave rise to a new literary form with a brilliant future, the historical drama. Frederick Schiller, even more than Goethe, can be considered as the creator of this new genre. His play *Die Räuber*, published in 1781, was his first essay in this form.

Everywhere the individual was in revolt against the pressure of society, which generally ended by crushing him. A typical example is Ludwig van Beethoven, born at Bonn in 1770. He profited by the achievements of Haydn and Mozart, but advanced still further than they. A brilliant era of musical invention was born with him. His nine symphonies are among the greatest treasures bequeathed to posterity. His thirty-two sonatas are regarded as a criterion for all music composed for the piano. His sixteen quartets enhance the versatility of this great composer.

'The gifts of liberal rationalism and of emotional sensitivity which Germany received from England and France, she repaid a hundred-fold,' wrote E. Vermeil, 'in a truly European framework, and in the form of a magnificent culture— one of the purest glories of the Continent.'

Goethe and Beethoven stand near the source of the Romantic movement.

Mechanics show progress, but it takes ideas to overthrow the Bastille.

372

The loss of the thirteen American colonies did not prevent England from remaining first state of Europe. The hero of fiction which she offered the world was a character far more intelligible than the shadowy Ossian, namely Robinson Crusoe, the resourceful and inventive castaway imagined by Defoe. Wesley and the Methodists gave new life to the Church of England. English liberals and philosophers met together in the lodges of freemasonry, whose light radiated throughout the Continent. Meantime the aristocrats, without 372 losing their elegance, turned their backs on the temptations of idleness. In a few years their control of Parliament enabled them to achieve an immense agrarian revolution. They redistributed agricultural property and, by adopting scientific methods of cultivation, secured an increased crop-yield. Simultaneously there was a decrease in the number of yeomen-farmers and the agricultural labourers flocked in multitudes towards the towns. But at the same time England, the first of the nations to do so, awoke to the possibilities of industry. In the textile industry the invention in 1733 of the flying shuttle greatly increased production in weaving and created a demand for thread. In 1785 Cartwright introduced the power loom and Wilkinson invented machine tools. Finally in 1785 James Watt made the first steam-engine. Meanwhile on the Continent it was imagined 373 that the new civilisation was to evolve through the progress of ideas rather than through that of mechanical invention. It was in the name of justice and liberty that a handful of Frenchmen, on 14th July 1789, captured the Bastille, the old prison 374 fortress and the symbol of autocratic government.

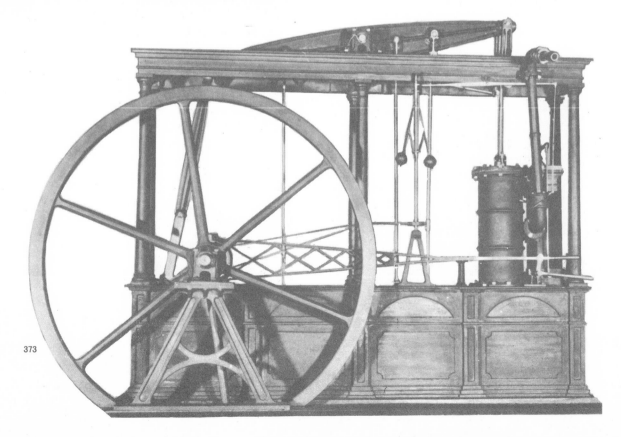

373

37

168

375

When he learnt at Königsberg the news of the storming of the Bastille, the philosopher Immanuel Kant prolonged his daily walk some distance further towards the west. He had divined that the revolution would affect all Europe.

The revolutionary movement started with the convening of an assembly of a traditional type—the States-General. This was the first admission of royal impotence. The primary object of the step was to relieve the financial crisis. Very good, thought the citizens, but we must still obtain the right of free enterprise and a share in the government. The assembling of the representatives of the different classes encouraged the expression of opinion.

375 The States-General at once declared themselves opposed to the authority of the king. They took an oath not to dissolve and proclaimed themselves a Constituent Assembly. The feudal system was abolished on August 4th. The Declaration of the

376

Kant foresees that the French Revolution will be a European Revolution.

world. On 20th April 1792, the Legislative Assembly took the initiative in declaring war against Austria, suspected of designs against the revolutionary movement. On September 20th, at Valmy, the volunteers of the Republic arrested, without serious bloodshed, the advance of the Prussian troops. This engagement had considerable psychological effects. Goethe, who witnessed the engagement, said prophetically 'In this place and on this day a new era in world-history is beginning'.

As soon as it was elected the Convention promised help and fraternal support to all the peoples desiring to recover their freedom. Rousseau had shown that sovereigns were in the nature of things imperialistic in their foreign and despotic in their home policy. And now we see the members of the Convention transferring to the sovereign nation the attributes of the former sovereigns which they had so fiercely condemned. The events opening a twenty-five year period of war and disorder in Europe were themselves to be linked in a chain of ruthless inevitability. The king was guillotined on 21st January 1793, and after him the queen, while the regime of purges became permanent in the new republic. A series of bad harvests, the inflation of paper money and the general insecurity added to the poverty and unrest of the nation and the guillotine pursued its task without respite in the Place de la Concorde.

War was the watchword of the day. War against Austria, Prussia, England, Spain: war against tyrants, *aristos*, traitors. The Revolution was in arms. Its leaders set the soldiers singing 'The battle song of the Army of the Rhine' soon to be called the *Marseillaise*, the theme of which Rude 379 was to engrave in imperishable stone.

376 Rights of Man and the Citizen proclaimed the equality of men, celebrated the accession of national sovereignty and enumerated the essential liberties—liberty of thought and of worship,
377 liberty of the press, the right to possess property, free access to all professions and occupations and the limitation of the powers of the state. In July 1790 the Constituent Assembly set out to reorganise the Church and to give it a secular constitution. And it was then that they entered into conflict with Louis XVI. The king attempted flight, but in vain. In August 1791 the Emperor Leopold of
378 Austria and the King of Prussia met at Pillnitz in Saxony and declared their interest in maintaining the throne of France. The Legislative Assembly, meeting in the autumn, was to take decisions as momentous for the future of France as for that of Europe.

By a decree of 22nd May 1790, the Constituent Assembly had declared France at peace with the

At Valmy Goethe predicts that this battle will open a new era.

Good and evil spring from it : the metric system and conscription.

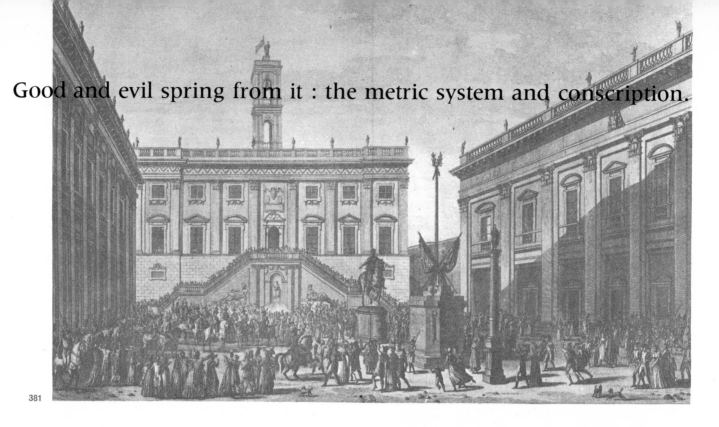

381

The Convention, ceaselessly agitated by violent intrigues and deadly convulsions, achieved, none the less, certain measures destined to last. Among these were the organisation of higher education and the construction of great schools and museums. The sale of the property of the Church and the *émigrés* gave rise to an immense transfer of possessions, which assured for the rural bourgeoisie a dominant place in French society during the 19th century. The Convention also modified family conditions by introducing divorce. The metric system, subsequently adopted by the whole of continental Europe, was also set up. But the most revolutionary of all the measures was the *levée en masse*; this mobilisation of the country's manpower for war had a profound effect on coming events. It produced an army which could identify itself completely with the nation. Since then war, instead of being the special concern of

princes, war ministers, and professional soldiers of indefinite nationality, inevitably has become that of the whole body of citizens and of public opinion.

In the east the adversaries of the Revolution were quarrelling over Poland, partitioned for the second time in 1793 and for the third time in 1795. Before long the armies of the Revolution were masters of the whole of the left bank of the Rhine including Dutch territory. In 1795 the Convention, after liquidating Robespierre, made terms at Bâle with Prussia and Spain, In order to conquer Austria, the new government of the Directory pushed the French armies across the Main and the Danube. To the general astonishment it was the   384
troops entrusted to Bonaparte, a general at 26,   383
who were intended to create a diversion in Italy, who forced a decision. The frontiers of France were now studded with 'sister republics' in which the tree of liberty was growing. After the Batavian   380

382

380

383

Republic of Holland came the Cisalpine Republic
381 of Milan, the Roman Republic proclaimed on the
Capitol, and the Parthenopean Republic of Naples.
These changes were not operated without violence,
especially in Italy. At Pavia, for example, the
382 troops had to use their sabres on the local militia.

A second coalition against France was easily
formed by the hostile powers, but the tide of war
ebbed and flowed. The French armies, successful
in containing the Russians in the Alps and the
Anglo-Russian forces in Holland, suffered serious
setbacks in Italy.

383 Bonaparte, returning from Egypt, persuaded
the Directory to confer on him dictatorial powers
in 1799. Thereupon he thrust an army into Bavaria,
hurled other forces upon Italy and routed the
Austrians at Marengo. The French Rhine army
marched on Vienna, but the Austrians made

peace at Lunéville in 1801 and the English at
Amiens the next year. In ten years the French
Republic, in the words of Mallet du Pan, 'had
eaten up Europe leaf by leaf like an artichoke'. But
in the process it had lost its republican constitution.
In May 1804 Bonaparte proclaimed himself
Emperor under the name of Napoleon I.

What were the ultimate ends of this prodigious
individual who for another eleven years was to stir
up the dust of battle in Europe, with a great
flourish of cannon and cavalry? Was it his main
ambition to crush England, instigator of the
coalitions, by closing the Continent to her? Or did
his insatiable lust for power tempt him to follow
Alexander's road to the Orient? Did he merely
desire the security of natural frontiers or did he
seek to realise the old Roman and Carolingian
dream of a Europe united under a single sceptre?

In ten years the Republic devours Europe and becomes an Empire.

384

On the day after his coronation Napoleon said, 'Europe will only know peace under a single chief.' And in 1805, after he had assumed at Milan the famous iron crown, he wrote: 'I am not the successor of Louis XIV but of Charlemagne. I am Charlemagne because, like him, I have united the crowns of France and Lombardy and because my empire is bounded by the Orient.' Representing, as he said himself, 'an alliance between philosophy and the sword', he underlined the absolute nature of his sovereignty by pointing out that he held his power not from God but from the Sovereign People. England was not inclined to leave him to realise his dreams and ambitions. With Russia and Austria she formed a third coalition against 384 him. The French fleet was annihilated by Nelson at Trafalgar, but on the Continent Napoleon struck like a thunderbolt. He captured Ulm on 12th October 1805, Vienna just a month later, and on 2nd December he inflicted a severe defeat on the Austro-Russian armies at Austerlitz. Negotiations opened at Pressburg, where Napoleon planned to organise the German mosaic under his own control. He founded the Confederation of the Rhine with Baden, Württemberg, Bavaria, Frankfurt and Berg as its components. The patriotism of the Prussians was alerted and soon a fourth coalition, with England and Russia as the other members, was formed. However, Prussia was heavily defeated at Jena and Auerstadt. Turning eastward Napoleon captured Warsaw and beat the Russians at Friedland in June 1807. Alexander I of 384 Russia, who contemplated an alliance, treated with Napoleon at Tilsit in July. Prussia was dis- 385 membered, and apparently annihilated. The Hapsburg Emperor was expelled from Germany and a Grand-Duchy of Warsaw was created as a sop to Polish nationalism. The Confederation of the Rhine was completed by the addition of the Kingdom of Westphalia. The French Empire, divided into 180 *départements*, was entering upon its most glorious

385

«I am Charlemagne», said Napoleon, and carved out an empire in Europe.

37

388

By a decree signed in Berlin the Emperor had ordained that Europe should be absolutely forbidden to trade with England. However, to ensure that the whole Continent observed the blockade he needed to control the entire coastline. Thus he had to make war on Portugal in 1807 and intimidate his ally, Spain. Madrid rose against the French troops and Goya recorded on canvas the terrible happenings of the *Dos de Mayo* (2nd May 1808). Napoleon's generals had to surrender at Bailem and Cintra. The Spanish example proved highly contagious. At Berlin, Fichte in his *Speeches to the German Nation* employed against the French their own doctrines of liberty and patriotism. Madame de Staël, the daughter of Louis XVI's minister Necker, conducted a furious campaign against the Napoleonic regime. Austria, thinking the moment ripe for a new attack on France, formed a fifth coalition, but Napoleon took Vienna for the second time and smashed the Austrian armies at Wagram. In the Treaty of Vienna, signed on 14th October 1809, Austria acknowledged her defeat.

386

337

388

age. Stretching from Lübeck to Rome, it embraced North-West Germany, the Netherlands, the Rhineland and Prussia and a third of Italy. Everywhere French prefects applied Napoleon's Code of Laws, while the satellite kingdoms were parcelled out among the members of the imperial family.

England, still intact, was pursuing a peripheric strategy. She stood firm in Malta and intervened at Copenhagen, at Constantinople, in Holland and in Portugal. Meanwhile she was mopping up, one after another, the French and Dutch colonies, which had been left to look after themselves. To palliate the effects of the blockade the English Government covered its expenses by bank credits.

386

An empire of 180 *départements,* but not including England.

At St Helena, when it was too late, he revealed the goal of his conquests.

389

Yet it was Russia that was destined to strike the decisive blow against the great empire. When the Tsar withdrew from the alliance concluded at Tilsit, Napoleon flung the 600,000 men he had massed in East Prussia across the Niemen, on 24th June 1812, and led them into the heart of Russia. The Russians laid waste the country before them. On 14th September, the *Grande Armée* reached 389 Moscow. The city was set on fire by the defenders and the Emperor decided to evacuate it. At this point he who has been well called 'General Winter' intervened. In December scarcely 30,000 men recrossed the Niemen. Napoleon's allies began to desert him. Once more Prussia became the Tsar's ally. In 1813 the Emperor campaigned in Saxony until he was defeated at Leipzig in 'the Battle of the Nations', which lasted from the 16th to the 19th October. The war was carried into France. Paris was taken and Cossacks bivouacked in the Champs-Elysées. Napoleon abdicated on 6th April 1814 and was exiled to Elba. In the following year be returned to France, but for a hundred days only. His defeat in Belgium admitted to history a resounding name, that of his last battle: Waterloo. The news brought rejoicing to every heart in England—as, for instance, to these Chelsea Pensioners.

390

Napoleon was sent to pass his declining years 391 and to die at St Helena. 'One of my grandest schemes', he wrote from exile, 'was to mould into a concentrated mass the geographic nations whom revolutions and politics have splintered and subdivided. . . . Then, maybe, the enlightenment brought about by the spread of the new and universal truths would have justified the hope that the great European family could combine into a system comparable to the American Congress or the Amphictyonic League'. But it was too late.

390

The Holy Alliance restores the façade of the old, monarchist Europe.

391

side but which claimed to be a sort of political expression of the divine will, aimed to place the thrones of monarchs beyond the reach of human aggression. It came into operation in France, where the regions evacuated by the allies were returned to the king, in Germany where the agitation among university students was suppressed, in Italy and in Spain where all attempts at rebellion were stifled.

In this so carefully safeguarded façade of the European Order, the lighted candles were already shining in the windows, but their fire was soon to set the whole building alight. For while seeking in art an escape from the injustices of life, the romantics revealed their longing for a new order.

392

Napoleon had in fact left the rulers confronted with peoples whom the turmoil of the Revolution had rendered extremely sensitive and umbrageous. New methods would have to be found to deal with this new situation. It fell to the Austrian chancellor Metternich to put forward these new methods at the

392 Congress of Vienna. The Quadruple Alliance of England, Austria, Prussia and Russia, an international consortium of victorious sovereigns, after dividing the spoils of Napoleon's empire, agreed on two courses of action. In the first place the Congress would decide on the solutions appropriate to questions of common interest, and in the second the great powers would be prepared for armed intervention in case of necessity. From 1818 France was a member of what was now called the Holy

393 Alliance. This mystic pact, which had its practical

393

395

Neither the French Revolution nor Napoleon's campaigns checked the great tidal wave of thought which swept over Europe thanks to *La Nouvelle Héloïse*, Ossian and Werther. England, more than any other country, became addicted to the romantic. British youth, chafing under the restraint of a society which had reacted firmly against the dangers of jacobinism, sought in painting and literature to express their rebellion against the political and social realities which cramped their

399

existence. The poets Wordsworth and Coleridge expressed in song their religious communion with nature. William Blake, painter and poet, committed to canvas or to verse his dazzling, mystical visions. Madame de Staël acted as an intermediary between the English and German Romantics and the French public. In 1813 her book on Germany acclaimed the 'literature of the north' and exhorted the French to study in the Germanic school in order to create a literature which would be at once modern, European and national. It was no doubt because he had left France early in life 394 and escaped the Napoleonic vortex that Chateaubriand did not await the promptings of Madame de Staël to appear as the herald of the new age. In his 'Genius of Christianity', written in a fascinating style which was long to serve as a model, he makes himself the advocate of a religion capable of

satisfying all the longings of the mind and heart. The sole occupation of his hero, René, was 'to procure happiness for himself by indulging the most exquisite emotions of melancholy and art, by travel, dreaming, isolation and communion with nature'.

Three English poets, all of whom were to die young as if they had been burnt up by their own genius, were typical of this fevered age. Byron 395 scandalised England by the irregularities of his private life, and his later years in Italy and Greece were no less stormy. *Childe Harold*, *Mazeppa* and *Manfred*, poems written in the perfection of classic style, describe the revolt of a man against a society riddled with hypocrisy and falsehood, shamelessly exploiting noble sentiments and dedicated to the suppression of truth, beauty and purity. To lay bare his inmost feelings Byron 'evokes the shades of the great dead cities, Athens, Venice and Rome. He reveals the beauties of the Moslem East, of Spain and Italy, the banks of the Rhine and the glaciers of Switzerland to satisfy the

394

The poems of Byron and Hugo express the general *mal du siècle*.

emotions of the new generation'. The poems of
Shelley and Keats are full of music, streams of
flowing crystal. At the same time Lamartine was
reviving the poetry of France and Victor Hugo
became the great interpreter of the eternal
mainstays of the human soul—love of the home,
love of nature, love of children, the joy of living in
the present and in the past, pity for the weak, the
humble and the unhappy.

National poets sprang up like banners among

400 401

396 397
the nations struggling for their existence—
Leopardi in Italy, Mickiewicz in Poland, Petöfi in
Hungary, Kollar in Slovakia, Lönnrot in Finland
and finally Eminescu in Roumania, the last of the
band. More than the expression of a private
anguish, these poets voiced the sufferings of a
whole nation.

The Romantics were destined not only to find
new ways of feeling and thinking; they also forged
a language for themselves. When Goethe in 1808
published the first part of his *Faust* he not only
flung a challenge at the whole traditional edifice
of religious and moral ideas, but also presented
romantic Europe with a new form of theatre—the
drama. While Shakespeare was coming back into
fashion, the romantic drama everywhere aroused
the enthusiasm of the young. Victor Hugo's
398 *Hernani*, first produced in 1830, made history in
the theatre. No less rich was the vein of the
399 historical novel of which *Ivanhoe* is the model.

From April to August 1822 a hundred and fifty
romances in the manner of Walter Scott appeared
in France. Balzac utilised this taste for the pictur- 400
esque, this scrupulous realism, not to bring back
to life the Middle Ages but to describe the manners
and morals of his own day. His 'Human Comedy'
promoted the romanesque, hitherto regarded as of
minor value, to be an essential element in European
literature.

Nor did painters lag behind. In England
Turner and Constable had discovered the art of
recording the finest nuances of light. In 1840
Eugène Delacroix first showed his famous 'Entry
of the Crusaders into Constantinople'. 'The play of 401
the lines, the shape of the bodies, the harmony
of the colours,' wrote Robert Rey, the art critic,
'make this painting into a sort of dream of leaden
desolation. It evokes the agony of a civilisation at
once precious and corroded, trodden down
beneath the hoofs of the great, weary horses of
the conquerors—knights who seem to be held in
the spell of sombre, afflicting dreams.'

396   397

A renewed admiration for the Medieval world distinguishes the Romantics.

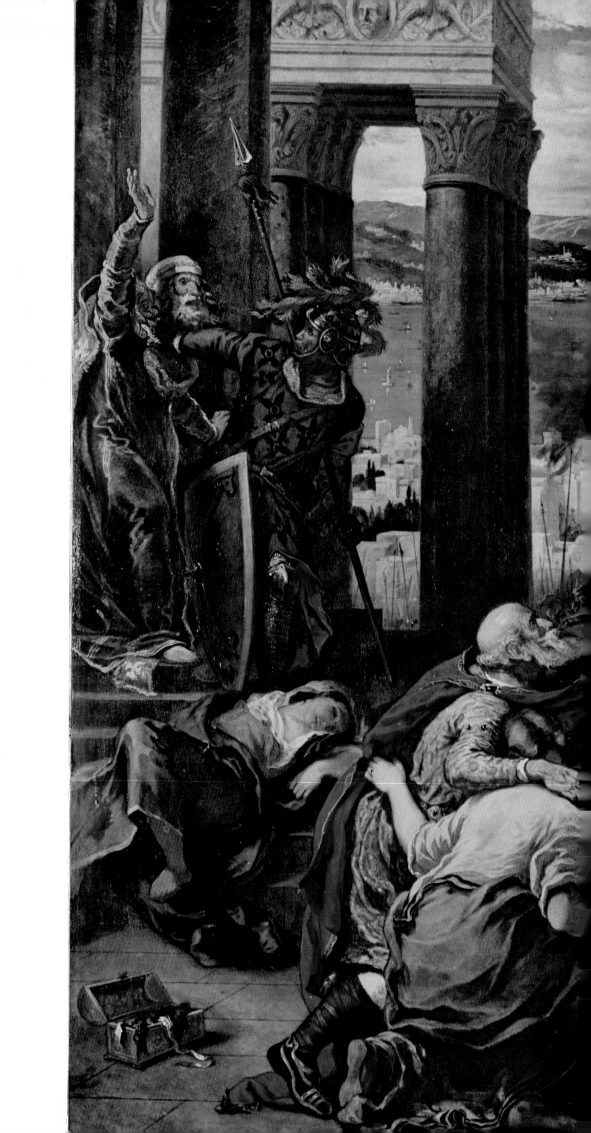

402

piano music, and a mass of songs in which his romantic settings accord perfectly with the text of the poems. In his *Gretchen am Spinnrad* he lends wonderful melodic variety to Goethe's verses, which he transforms into a touching drama. In all he composed more than six hundred songs, the best known of which are the *Erlkönig* and the *Schöne Müllerin* cycle.

Paganini, whose virtuosity was considered almost diabolic, made the violin the instrument *par excellence* of the romantic spirit. But the pianoforte, too, where the notes are struck instead of being plucked as in the harpsichord, was able to express every shade of feeling. The great master of the piano was Frédéric Chopin, born in Poland 403 in 1810 of a Polish mother and a French father. Leaving his native land at the age of twenty, he remained for the rest of his life homesick for his

Music is a universal language, knowing no frontiers and alone capable of expressing without translation the intensity of passion, the emotions of the heart and all the other variations of human sensibility.

402 Schubert was an initiator of romantic music. He wore his spectacles while sleeping in order not to lose time looking for them when he woke up. This trait is typical of his industry. Surrounded by faithful friends he composed at fantastic speed, almost without revision, a vast number of works. He was born in 1797 and died thirty years later with 1,250 pieces to his credit, most of which he had neglected to publish. These included symphonies— the Unfinished is one of the great treasures of musical literature—chamber music, church music,

404

403

Schubert, Chopin, Berlioz enrich the world of music with new strains.

405

406

tra. His contemporaries laughed at him, but he heeded them not. His *Symphonie Fantastique*, a genuine drama of amorous passion, is probably the most perfect example of romantic music.

But it was the waltz, a dance in three-four time descended from Viennese folk-tunes, which, more even than the slavonic polka and mazurka, infected all classes of society with the capricious rhythms of the romantic spirit. Johann Strauss the elder was acclaimed throughout Europe and his son, the second Johann, sent his Blue Danube lilting round the world. 405

Liszt, the Hungarian composer, a famous pianist who fell in love with one woman after another before ending as an abbé, was the most inconsistent of men. His striking personality and his incessant voyages made him the best-known musical figure of his day and the idol of the younger generation. As for Robert Schumann, whose varied genius was equally at home in symphonic music, in works for the piano and in lieder, of which he composed a large number, he must be considered a true servant of the movement which so greatly enriched the genius of Europe. 406 407

Disseminated though it was throughout the Continent and tinged with an international flavour by the itinerant lives of its foremost practitioners, the romantic school of music nevertheless possessed strong national features visible in the use it made of old folk-tunes, popular airs and ancestral rhythms. But there was one form of music, a really international form, that continued to flourish and that was opera. Rossini, a man of sparkling wit, who was born on leap year day and died on Friday the 13th, restored the glory of this form, lately in decline, and attracted immense audiences in every capital to hear the *Barber of Seville* and *William Tell*. 408

wounded country. The elegance and hypnotic melancholy of his music soon conquered Paris. An early sufferer from tuberculosis, his stormy liaison with George Sand hastened the progress of his illness and he died at thirty-nine. His ballades, études, scherzos, polonaises, waltzes, nocturnes and impromptus, in which he exploits with an elegant brilliance and an impeccable technique all the resources of the piano, soon won the hearts of all the world.

In contrast to Chopin, the Frenchman Hector Berlioz placed all the magic of the orchestra at the disposal of romanticism. In order to increase the volume and variety of his instrumentation, he made use of instruments rarely used in the orches- 404

407

408

Europe makes music her language and the Viennese waltz her dance.

183

409

In spite of all its avatars the French Revolution opened a new era. 'The former Crown Dominions, founded on the subservience of the people, had to give way to the emergence of nations conscious of themselves and of their right to be free.' By a paradox, this great precept was first put into practice in Latin America.

In the Portuguese and Spanish transatlantic empires the Creoles, the ruling caste of local-born whites, who had imbibed the lessons of European political philosophy, chafed against the tutelage of the mother-country. The difficulties encountered by Spain and Portugal in their struggle with Napoleon furnished the pretext dreamed of by the secessionists. In 1808 Bolivar, an officer educated in Europe, raised the standard of revolt in Venezuela with the aid of General Miranda who had already fought for American independence before taking part in the French Revolution. By 1810 the revolt

409

had become general. Argentine, Chile and Mexico had risen against their rulers. However, the loyalist forces succeeded in recovering Chile, suppressing the insurrection in Mexico led by the priest Hidalgo, capturing Miranda and driving Bolivar out of Caracas. The Creole General San Martin. who had managed to maintain the independence of Argentina, sent a force into Chile to liberate that country, which declared itself independent in 1818.

Meanwhile Bolivar came to life again. Returning to Venezuela, which served as his base, he marched on New Grenada and Peru, which surrendered successively to his arms. In 1819 he founded Colombia, while the highlands of Peru became independent under the name of Bolivia. Thus, everywhere, from what were formerly colonies, the Latin-American States were born.

Brazil was Portuguese, and the presence there of the legitimate sovereign of Portugal who had fled from Europe contributed to check agitation. But when in 1821 John VI returned to Lisbon the decisive step was taken. In October 1822 Dom Pedro, the king's son, was proclaimed constitutional emperor of independent Brazil amid the plaudits of the populace.

410

In 1823, President Monroe declared that the United States would oppose any attempt by the Old World to colonise the New or re-establish the old régime. Thus a page of European history was turned at the moment when a new and momentous chapter in the life of the Balkans was opening.

After the Serbs had become free, the Greeks rebelled against the Turks in 1820. Their efforts were maintained in spite of terrible difficulties for seven years. To block the expansion of Russia

410

But the hymn to liberty is not forgotten : Bolivar takes it up.

411

in the East the French and British governments embarked on a policy which, while securing the independence of Greece, would save Turkey. But at Navarino in October 1827, the admirals of the three fleets, without instructions from their governments, sent the Turco-Egyptian fleet to the bottom. Tsar Nicolas I gained the lion's share from the consequences of this action. Greece became independent, but the Holy Alliance was broken. In any case the time was past for diplomatic discussion. In July 1830, the young liberal bourgeoisie of Paris erected barricades and, joined by artisans and labourers, opened fire on the troops in their determination to replace an autocratic sovereign by a liberal one. This was the signal for Catholic and liberal Belgians to unite against the Dutch monarchy. In October they declared Belgium independent and Leopold I was proclaimed king with the support of France.

411

412

413

412

413

The Greeks rebel against the Turks; the French against their king.

414

415

The hopes of the Poles were revived by the sight of the Tricolour floating over their capital. This was in July 1830. In November the Polish troops refused, to a man, to march against the French and Belgian revolutionaries. This news was received in Paris with enthusiasm, but by September 1831 the Russians were once more masters of the situation. A French minister conveyed this news to the Chamber in these deplorable words: 'Order reigns at Warsaw'. Meantime the secret lodges of the Carbonari endeavoured to rouse Northern Italy against the Pope and the Princes, but the Austrian army immediately intervened to preserve the old régimes. Nevertheless the breath of the liberal revolution, which in Italy and Poland served to fan the spirit of national liberation, was never to leave the thrones of Europe in peace. Without realizing that their passion for the sovereignty of their own peoples was hardly compatible with their desire for universal brotherhood, the liberal intellectuals called earnestly for the moral unification of Europe on a republican basis. Mazzini, an exile in Marseilles, initiated there in 1831 the Young Italy movement, the forerunner of Young Europe which he was to inaugurate at Berne three years later.

The attempts of the German students of the Jena confraternity to introduce liberal measures met with no success. In 1833 their turbulent revolt

414

415

416

The national flags are unfurled while men dream of brotherhood.

Electricity and steam promise a new pattern of life.

417

416 against the Diet of Frankfurt was sternly suppressed. Prussia, in point of fact, though hardly deserving to be called a liberal state, was nevertheless designated by no less a person than Hegel as a rational state which, by the superiority of its educational system, the quality of its universities and the competence of its administrators enabled its subjects to enjoy a sufficiency of liberty, provided they fulfilled their collective obligations.

Maassen, one of the Prussian ministers, supposing that national power would in future be more safely based on sound economic founda-

418

tions than on intellectual or political considerations, initiated on 1st January 1834, the *Zollverein* or Customs Union of Prussia, Württemberg and Bavaria, which other German states joined before long. By this means Germany, a name but not yet a reality, whose component parts had been crippled by increasing customs duties and other internal taxes inherited from the Middle Ages, was restored to life at the very opening of the industrial era.

The birth of the century had been marked by an invention which was one day to revolutionise human life. In a letter addressed on 20th April 1800 to the Royal Society in London, and later at a successful public demonstration staged in Paris, at which Bonaparte assisted, the Italian, 417 Volta, showed how by means of his battery electricity could be generated in a continuous current.

In 1801 Richard Trevithick, a mechanical engineer, constructed a steam-propelled vehicle which reached a speed of ten miles an hour and was one of the highlights of London life. 418

In the year 1807, Fulton, the son of Irish emigrants to Pennsylvania, made the first successful trials of his steam-boat, and in 1819, the American steamship *Savannah*, braving the ocean, 419 completed the voyage from New York to Liverpool, using sail and steam, in 25 days.

419

Nineteenth century maps unfold black riches, mines and industries.

420

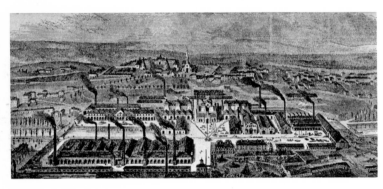

421

422

As the nineteenth century advanced, the map of Europe changed. Attention of students was focused less and less on administrative and political frontiers and geographical divisions and more and more on the coloured patches signifying industrial regions and the great cities. The English textile industry, the first to employ machinery, was supreme in Europe and made the future of Lancashire.

In 1784 England used four million pounds of cotton. By 1833 this figure had risen to three hundred millions. The future of the textile industry depended largely on the producing countries overseas, on the ports of transit, the ships which carried the precious raw material and the insurance companies which covered the risks. Once started, an endless chain of capitalistic endeavour came into being, comprising, link after link, the whole economy of commerce and industry. The substitution of mined coal for charcoal in metallurgy caused the transfer of the great English metal works from the wooded regions of the south to the valley of the Clyde, to Northumberland and Yorkshire, the country of rich mines, the 'Black Country' of the north. France was transformed by similar industrial changes. The new English techniques of spinning, weaving and printing were introduced into Normandy and Flanders and Alsace with revolutionary results. The northern and central coal mines were developed and with them the metal industry. In 1836 the brothers Schneider bought at Creusot a collection of glassworks, foundries and mines from bankrupt owners. There they established the first French ironworks. In Germany the coal-mining industry was founded in the Ruhr and the Sarre. The firms of Krupp at Essen and Borsig in Berlin grew in power and importance.

420

421

422

The stock exchange is the seat of power; the top-hat replaces the crown.

423

The birth of industrial Europe was accompanied and even overshadowed by enormous financial developments. Joint-stock companies appeared everywhere. Stock-brokers became important members of society. The London
423 Stock Exchange opened its new premises in 1802, and the Paris Bourse established its headquarters in 1826.

The factories and machines, which modified the forms of production so radically, also transformed society. Economic power passed into the hands of the industrial and commercial middle classes. In Great Britain the Reform Bill of 1832 secured for these classes a predominant position in politics, while in France and the whole of Eastern Europe the great land-owners still retained a large part of their old influence.

But all these transformations were not effected without cries of distress and appeals for betterment from the common people. The introduction of machines had either driven the workers from their homes to the factories or simply thrown them out of work and in no case had relieved their distress. Between 1825 and 1848 Europe could only count eight years of prosperity as against fifteen of crisis. The findings of private investigators or commissions of enquiry boldly denounced social injustices. Prominent among these were
424 the Sadler Committee in England, which reported on the employment of children, and in France Villermé's *Tableau* describing the lot of textile workers. And side by side with the rising tide of mechanisation we see the ancient work-
425 men's Guilds striving to preserve the old bonds of brotherhood and to maintain the old standards of skilled labour.

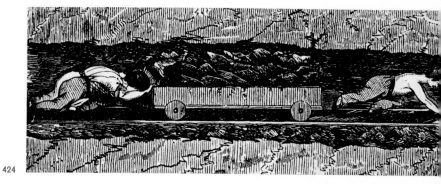

424

425

had studied Hedley's locomotive, introduced the connecting rod, an improved steam blast and the tubular boiler. In 1825 he turned out three engines for the Stockton-Darlington railway, where a passenger train travelled at a speed of 23 miles an hour — a sensational event.

In 1829 the French engineer Seguin purchased two of Stephenson's locomotives and fitted each with a tubular boiler developing much greater power. But Seguin was anticipated by Stephenson himself, who produced his *Rocket* in the same year. The inauguration of the Manchester-Liverpool railway on 15th September 1831 with a locomotive that covered nearly thirty miles in the hour provided one of the great moments in the history of European genius.

Other technical problems of prime importance were solved by Robert Stephenson, the son of George, in connection with rails, points, signals, level-crossings, cuttings and embankments. By

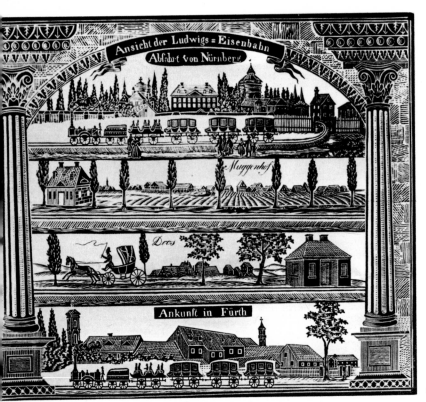

The development of railways, which proceeded amid great popular enthusiasm, concealed for a while the distress to which the industrial revolution had given rise in the economic and social life of Europe. The owners of great mining concerns in England had, since 1750, been using waggons drawn by horses along rails. In 1813 Hedley was able to prove by experiment that the skidding of a steam-propelled machine pulling trucks along these same rails could be eliminated if the engine were heavy enough. George Stephenson, who

1834 the line between London and Birmingham was in working order.

In France the first railways appeared in the central region in 1823. They were built to carry coal from the mines to the rivers. The Belgian minister Rogier proposed a railway connection between Antwerp and Cologne, which would provide the great port on the Scheldt with a Rhenish hinterland. Thus we see the railway becoming the main instrument of vast economic development. For financial reasons as well

The whistle of Stephenson's locomotive announces the railway age.

430

as for those of technical convenience the first great lines terminated in important urban centres guaranteeing a sufficiency of passengers. There was no lack of new ideas and plans. The construction of the Brussels-Mechelen line in 1835 was followed in the same year by that of Nuremberg-Fürth in Germany, built by van Denis, a former graduate of the Paris Polytechnic. There followed the Berlin-Potsdam railway (1838) and the Leipzig-Dresden line (1839). In Spain a line was constructed in 1836 from Reus to Tarragona, and in France a line linking Paris with Le Pecq (1837), soon to be followed by the Paris-Orleans, Paris-Lille, and Paris-Lyon-Méditerranée lines. In Russia Petersburg was connected by rail with Tsarskoe-Selo (1838) and in Holland we have the Amsterdam-Leyden-Utrecht line in 1843.

The steam-propelled vehicle was undoubtedly a national asset. In France Guizot was the moving spirit in the creation of the network of railways radiating from Paris, which was an important factor in establishing a centre of French life. In Germany the economist List saw in the railway system an instrument of political unification.

By now the expression 'railway time' had a real significance for a substantial number of Europeans —for the holiday-making middle classes on their way to the seaside, for peasants going to town, for soldiers rejoining their units and for noble ladies lolling in their first-class carriages. Monumental stations sprang up and strove to compete with the fine buildings of the past—for example Charing Cross in London and the Gare de Lyon in Paris, which was inaugurated with the pomp of a solemn ceremony. Dealings in railway shares were pursued with feverish activity in the stock exchanges. In order to get their scrip printed the British railway companies, swamped by orders, had to send for 400 lithographers from Belgium.

426

427

428

429

430

431

429

431

The noble monuments of this new age will be the railway stations.

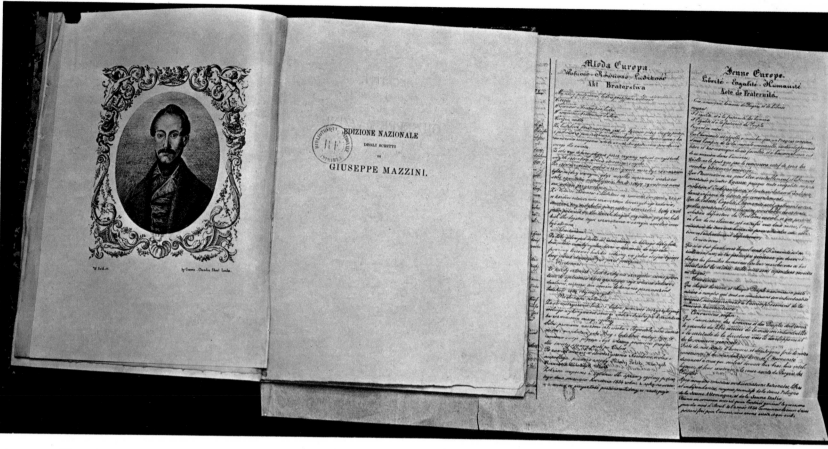

433

The railway was the symbol of an era of unlimited progress towards which a restless or pleasure-loving generation hurried in jolting, gay-coloured coaches. But this newly acquired mobility was to stoke the fires of social and political discord which smouldered since the liberal risings of 1830. Throughout Europe the craze for building railways had taken a heavy toll from public and private funds at a time when a succession of bad harvests had necessitated the importation of large quantities of foodstuffs.

Europe had refused to listen to Malthus when, in 1798, that economist predicted that the natural growth of population would outstrip the possibilities of supporting it. Europeans had not yet learnt to face the consequences of demographic expansion. Achard, a Berliner, and Delessert, a Swiss, had discovered the possibilities of sugar-beet, while Appert, a Frenchman, had introduced great improvements in the canning industry. But these ameliorations seemed insignificant in comparison with the great bread riots which occurred in 1847 at Brussels, in Württemberg, Vienna and northern Italy. The intellectuals of Europe, in their whole-hearted sympathy with the oppressed workers, tirelessly campaigned in their favour. Some of them, particularly if they were Italians, Hungarians, Germans or Poles, made national liberation their slogan, while others proclaimed

their determination to obtain social justice. Mazzini, who appealed unceasingly for a United Europe, became the apostle of the Italian *risorgimento*, while in 1847 Karl Marx issued his Communist Manifesto. The bread of revolution was always baked in the same oven, and Paris, which had given the signal in 1789 and in 1830, rebelled once more in February 1848, when the crowds stormed the Tuileries.

432

433
433

434

434

The revolutionary movement receives its impetus once more from Paris.

435 The throne of the King of France was set on fire on 24th February 1848 and the Republic was proclaimed. The flames of revolution spread to all the countries still adhering to the system established in 1815 and, first of all, to the country which, since the fall of Napoleon, had constituted itself the champion of reaction in Europe : Vienna revolted and, unable to resist the pressure of the insurgents, the Austrian Emperor had to sacrifice Metternich, who fled from the country. When this news was announced, Italy, a country divided among many Italian and foreign rulers, also caught fire.

The question was, whether to re-create a Roman Republic in which these other states should be

435

436

federated as Mazzini proposed? And if so, was this confederation to be placed under the aegis of a liberal Pope or under that of the ruler of Piedmont, a progressive and modern sovereign? At the news of the Austrian rebellion and the flight

436 of Metternich Milan revolted, and during the insurrection, which lasted for five days, forced the Austrian general Radetsky to withdraw. King Charles Albert of Piedmont then declared war against Austria. Beaten at Custozza in July and later at Novara in March 1849, he was forced to abdicate. The insurrection was repressed in Lombardy-Venetia and the constitutions, granted under pressure from the insurgents, were abolished.

At Rome Pius IX was very popular owing to the liberal reforms he had introduced, but he looked with disfavour on the project for the liberation of Piedmont. In February 1849 Mazzini led a revolt in the ungarrisoned capital. The Sovereign Pontiff retired to Gaeta as the Republic was proclaimed, but the French army soon replaced Pius IX on his throne. The newborn republics of Florence and Venice were destroyed by the Austrians, while the police of Naples purged the kingdom of its liberals. This attempt to establish Italian unity was a complete failure. Nevertheless the new king of Piedmont, Victor Emmanuel II, and his minister Cavour, firmly upheld the liberal constitution, for they perceived that it might be possible to unify Italy to their own advantage and without proclaiming a republic. Their method would be to employ the armies of a foreign ally to defeat the Austrian forces, when the time was ripe.

Germany, in which the treaties of 1815 had permitted the survival of thirty-nine sovereign

The wind of liberty blows across the frontiers, fanning national fires.

437

states forming the German Confederation, suffered more from lack of unity than from lack of liberty. Her peoples inclined now towards Austria, conservative and unenterprising, and now towards dynamic Prussia, who was then in possession of the coalfields of the Ruhr and had initiated the Customs Union. Liberal ideals seemed singularly bloodless compared with economic and national ambitions. However, the insurrection in Vienna provoked a revolution in Prussia and throughout Central Germany. On 18th March 1848 the people of Berlin took up arms against Frederick William IV and gained possession of the town. The king accepted the liberal measures imposed on him, but in order to give the restoration of the Empire precedence over any programme of democratic reform, he solemnly declared : ' From now onwards Prussia becomes Germany '.

437

About the same time, in March 1848, a group of intellectuals, assembled in romantic Heidelberg, demanded that a preparatory assembly should be convened to negotiate with the Diet. The idea of a parliament appealed strongly to the Austrians also. After Metternich's flight a constitution had, it is true, been granted, but the slowness with which it was introduced provoked fresh outbursts. The new Viennese Parliament abolished the feudal rights of landowners, while the German Parliament, convened at Frankfurt, concentrated solely on studying the most practical means of achieving German unity. The members hesitated between the idea of a Germany without Austria and a pan-Germanic state. Choosing the first solution, they offered in 1849 the imperial crown to Frederick William IV, but he had already felt the weight of Austrian arms and declined the offer. The example of Austria had shown the magnitude of the difficulties which beset the imperial idea.

438

439

438

439

The flames spread, but Piedmont and Prussia await their opportunity.

440

In the heart of Europe, where the national idea gave life to so many hopes, the Austrian Empire was a true mosaic of peoples distinct from one another in everything—race, religion and language. Under the administration of Vienna these were grouped, after a fashion, into hereditary states for the Germans, the Crown of St Stephen for Hungary, the Crown of St Wenceslas for Bohemia, to which must be added Galicia for southern Poland and the provinces of Lombardy and Venetia. Hungary, influenced by the genius of Kossuth, voted for liberal institutions and claimed autonomy. The Emperor, whose hands were full in Piedmont, needed time to collect his troops,

some of whom had in any case to be sent to Prague, where the crown of Bohemia was seriously threatened. The Czech publicist Palacky had convened a pan-Slav congress at Prague. The Austrian army, with orders to suppress the revolution, occupied the city in June under General Windischgraetz and dispersed the congress. In October the general was at work in Vienna, where the demands, for reforms were rejected and a 'strong' government under Schwarzenberg was formed. However, in Hungary, Windischgraetz had to fight hard in the open country before he captured Budapest. The bravery of the Hungarian insurgents won them a victory over the Aus-

443

The Springtime of the Peoples is a short one; many die in vain.

196

A 13 vértanú közül

Ernő, Lázár Vilmos, Desseffi Aristid és Schweidel Jósef 1849 október hó 6 án reggel fél 6 órakor az aradi vársánczban golyó által történt kivégzése.

441

Historians have long sought to fathom the reasons for the failure of the Revolution of 1848, 'the Springtime of the Peoples', a truly European movement if ever there was one. The lack of interest shown by the peasantry of France and Austria and their indifference towards a purely urban rising, as well as the divergent objectives, here political and there social, had contributed in no small degree to this failure. Nor must we forget how delusive was Mazzini's claim that it would be easy to reconcile the aspirations of different national groups. To these explanations for the defeat of the movement we must add the inactivity of the French Government and the intervention of Russia. But in spite of everything the theorists of 1848 sowed a seed which was not destined to die. In central and eastern Germany the feudal régime definitely ceased to exist and an individualistic society came into being. In France a new social problem presented itself and in no uncertain terms. This was the problem of labour which continued to interest and disturb the public conscience.

Finally, the idea of social emancipation was no longer confined to the great cities. It had spread to the colonies, where slavery, in addition to enriching successive generations of Arab, Indian and European slave-traders, had been for three centuries the mainstay of the local economy. In 1834 the abolition of slavery in the British possessions was proclaimed and the king's ships made war on the slave-traders. In 1848 France followed 443 the example of England, while in the United States the question was the theme of endless and passionate debate, the flames of which were fanned by the publication in 1852 of *Uncle Tom's Cabin*.

trians at Godöllo, and the Emperor had to call in Russian troops to help him. The Magyars, beaten at Temesvar, held out until August 1849, when they capitulated at Vilagos. In Hungary, as elsewhere, the rebel elements were cruelly 441 punished.

Everywhere in Europe reaction set in. The 442 Frankfurt Parliament disappeared at the end of May 1849. The King of Prussia endeavoured to create a limited union by grouping a number of small states round Prussia. But Austria was no more ready to countenance this effort to achieve German national unity than she been to accept liberal reforms. In November 1850 she forced Prussia into an inglorious agreement at Olmütz. In France, where a wave of republicanism had at first swept the country, the Republic did not long survive. Louis Napoleon, appointed President, assumed autocratic power on 2nd December 1851 and stifled the opposition.

442

Reaction sets in everywhere, but the day will come...

197

444

Napoleon III was justified in saying in 1855, 'The Holy Alliance is dead'. This pronouncement was made on the day on which Queen Victoria and Prince Albert landed at Boulogne to make friends with France. But compared with Victoria, who was to reign for more than sixty-three years (1837-1901), Napoleon III filled but a short span of history. The queen, completely British in appearance and spirit, became the grandmother of all the courts of Europe and, as each fresh political wind began to blow, had the gift of choosing ministers able to guide her along the right path. One of the most formidable products of her workshop of statesmen was that champion of compromise, William Ewart Gladstone, whose countenance combined strength, generosity and idealism. The living antithesis of imperialism, this grave and high minded prophet of peaceful solutions would withdraw

444

445

from his office of Chancellor of the Exchequer rather than swim with the current of opinion which favoured the Crimean enterprise.

Turkey, the 'Sick Man of Europe', seemed to be on the point of death. The Tsar proposed to share the estate with Great Britain, but it was against Russia that middle-class English opinion called for war.

Sebastopol is the key to the Crimea and the Crimea the sentinel of the Black Sea. The campaign to capture Sebastopol which opened in the spring of 1854 provided a foretaste of modern war. During the siege the Anglo-French troops nibbled at the enemy positions. Heavy losses, out of all proportion to the importance of the objectives, were sustained on both sides.

This war anticipated those of the twentieth century : though a local conflict, it was, in fact, based on a conflict of ideologies. It was indeed

446

445

446

ВЫЛАЗКА ИЗЪ СЕВАСТОПОЛЯ ПРОИЗВЕДЕННАЯ 18й НА 19й АПРЕЛЯ 1855 ГОДА.

Henri Dunant's symbol, the Red Cross, has a place of honour in Europe.

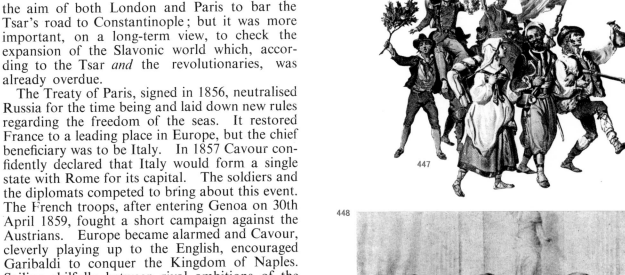

447

the aim of both London and Paris to bar the Tsar's road to Constantinople; but it was more important, on a long-term view, to check the expansion of the Slavonic world which, according to the Tsar *and* the revolutionaries, was already overdue.

The Treaty of Paris, signed in 1856, neutralised Russia for the time being and laid down new rules regarding the freedom of the seas. It restored France to a leading place in Europe, but the chief beneficiary was to be Italy. In 1857 Cavour confidently declared that Italy would form a single state with Rome for its capital. The soldiers and the diplomats competed to bring about this event.

447 The French troops, after entering Genoa on 30th April 1859, fought a short campaign against the Austrians. Europe became alarmed and Cavour, cleverly playing up to the English, encouraged Garibaldi to conquer the Kingdom of Naples. Sailing skilfully between rival ambitions of the Great Powers, the statesman and the *condottiere* succeeded, in 1861, in offering the crown of Italy

448 to their sovereign, Victor Emmanuel.

On this occasion the horrors of war inspired a pacific movement of truly international scope.

449 To quote the words of Henri Dunant, the Genevan: 'At Solferino the sun of 25th June 1859 cast its rays on one of the most fearful spectacles the imagination can conceive. The battlefield was strewn with the bodies of men and horses.' Dunant had already thought out plans for the establishment of a World Court of Arbitration. He now succeeded in persuading the Governments to adopt his idea of 'Societies to help the wounded'. The Red Cross on a white background (the Swiss colours inverted) would in future be the

450 distinguishing flag of ambulances and medical personnel and would proclaim to the world the right of war-victims to protection.

448

449

450

451

Meantime the Paris Bourse was humming with the activities of dealers and stockbrokers. It was 451 difficult to decide whether the wave of bullish speculation which had swept from London to the Continent was a symptom of a dangerous fever or rather the vital impulse of capitalism.

Ton after ton of newly mined gold began to flow into Europe—from California in 1847, from Australia in 1851 and from New Zealand in 1853. There was an increase of three hundred million francs' worth of gold every year. France, the chief beneficiary, absorbed in twenty years 44% of all the gold coinage of the world. The cost of living would have risen indefinitely if a large part of this gold had not been used to finance industrial development as well as going, in smaller quantities, into salaries and savings. To hasten this movement France achieved the triumph of the banknote. Napoleon III, who was thoroughly alive to economic necessities, created various great credit establishments to serve as intermediaries between the possessors of unemployed capital and the owners of concerns needing finance. Wealth attracted wealth when it was invested in industry. It was the railways that created by their arterial system the prosperity of the new factories. The exploitation of mines was facilitated by improvements in the techniques of boring and blasting. In 1855 an Englishman named Bessemer invented his converter, which was to contribute largely to 452 the substitution of steel for cast-iron. Soon the brothers Siemens, Germans, and Martin, a Frenchman, introduced further improvements.

Between 1850 and 1860 there was a lively competition in speed between sail and steam; but the picture of the giant *Téméraire* being towed to her last resting-place, in the sheen of a gold and blood-red sunset, by a small paddle-boat shows 453 how unequal the struggle really was. The clippers carrying up to 4000 square yards of canvas, were able to cover the distance from Havre to New York in eighteen or twenty days and raced each other madly along the tea or wool routes, but the steamers were already winning the day if only through the greater capacity of their holds. When in 1860 they adopter the propeller to replace the paddle-wheel, their supremacy was assured.

452

Gold and steel come into their own; the clippers are on the way out. 453

Through the Alpine tunnels Europeans can now link hands.

454

456

Europe had ceased to exist except in the imagination of theorists or the will of princes. Suddenly she awoke to conscious life. The telegraph and the railway, heedless of frontiers, revealed her to herself. The road which was to lead Europe towards her unknown destiny was to be blazed with international exhibitions. London had led the way in 1851 with brilliant success at the Crystal Palace. Paris followed in 1855 and London again in 1862, adding greatly to the range of these international festivities. In 1867 Napoleon III welcomed all the sovereigns of Europe to the banks of the Seine, among them the Sultan of Turkey, the first of his dynasty to travel outside his own empire. 454

The railways served as a permanent lure for those wishing to attend these tremendous functions. The European mileage had risen from 32,000 in 1860 to 87,000 in 1878. The Alps, at first sight an insurmountable obstacle, were negotiated by gradients and tunnels. Along the old imperial route leading from Innsbruck to Verona by the Brenner Pass a railway line was built which necessitated twenty-two tunnels and sixty bridges and viaducts. When, in 1867, the last blows of their picks brought face to face the two gangs who had attacked the huge massif from opposite ends, the event was celebrated with well deserved acclaim. 455

In 1871 after seven years of work the Mont Cenis tunnel was opened to traffic and a direct 456

455

The telegraph, rotary press and linotype make communications an industry.

connection between Paris and Turin established. The Saint-Gothard tunnel, completed in 1880 after long delays, linked the valley of the Rhine with that of the Po; Switzerland became a bridge between the North Sea and the Mediterranean.

The adventures in scientific progress through which Europe lived in this epoch can well be compared with those of Christopher Columbus

flourish without constraint. Between 1860 and 1878 five million Europeans, with their families and their baggage, crowded on to the decks of vessels, using both sail and steam, in search of fresh horizons. Only the French were reluctant to quit the old continent. It may be that the expansion of urban life satisfied their taste for comfort and the pleasures of existence.

459

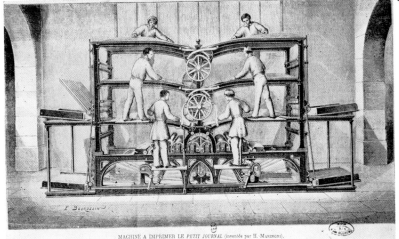

458

MACHINE À IMPRIMER LE *PETIT JOURNAL* (inventée par H. MARINONI).

457

and the conquistadors. The total length of telegraph lines was 43,000 miles in 1858 and 315,000 in 1880. The Russian land-line connected Moscow with San Francisco via Alaska. In 1866 and 1869 respectively England and France were first able to communicate with America by submarine cable. A congress at Berne created the International Postal Union, which laid down the first code of rules for international postal traffic.

Nowhere was the rapid march of progress more welcome than in the printing industry and 457 particularly the newspapers, which owed a great debt and the possibility of high circulation to 458 Hippolyte Marinoni's rotary press.

News transmitted by telegraph was first received and put into shape by the Press Agencies. In 1856 Reuter, Wolff and Havas, all of whom had originally formed part of the telegraph agency of Charles Havas, signed their first agreement regarding the exchange of information.

In 1866 the German electrical engineer Otto Mergenthaler supplied the *New York Tribune* with the first linotype, casting types in lines.

As the frontiers of the world receded, the inventive genius of Europe received a welcome beyond the Atlantic, where new ideas could

459

460

Towards 1850 the rural populations, attracted by the development of technical inventions and the progress of science, everywhere began to flock to the towns, which lived in a permanent fever of activity and entertainment.

Photography, one of the fabulous discoveries of this era, was to leave a living witness of this contemporary movement. Niepce and Daguerre in France, Fox Talbot and Archer in England, perfected this durable means of recording reality. Thus, with the possibility of preserving indefinitely the visual record of men, manners and events and of reproducing it at will, the spirit of Europe acquired a new dimension. The early photographers took as their theme balls, receptions, picnics, middle-class interiors, military reviews, supper-parties—in fact all the cheerful and brilliant aspects of urban life. And so photography became a rival of art and people began to ask themselves whether the nameless photographer or the illustrious painter, Manet, gave a more faithful representation of the pleasures of social life.

460
461

The photographer takes his place beside the painter to portray life.

Advances in medical research result in a rapid increase of populations.

Less obviously, perhaps, than industry or technical invention, because slower to show results, medicine and hygiene contributed powerfully to the transformation of the face of Europe. Infantile mortality declined and men lived longer. Since Jenner's conquest of small-pox in 1796, the doctors had gained many other victories. Englishmen like Parkinson, Bell, Hodgkin and Addison, Frenchmen like Bichat, Laënnec, Broussais and Dupuytren, the Germans Virchow, Traube and Wunderlich, and the Hungarian Semmelweis, who

463

found a remedy for puerperal fever—all these were authors of some of the greatest changes in the life story of the human race. The increase of births over deaths largely explains the emigration of Europeans to all parts of the world which characterised the next half century. This movement was accompanied by a constant influx of country-dwellers into the towns. In England the urban population was 55 % of the total in 1860 and 75 % in 1880. The London of Dickens contained less than two million inhabitants in

1840; by 1880 the figure was practically doubled. Moreover the area of the capital had expanded prodigiously and now embraced many large suburbs. Simultaneously the City began to lose its residents, most of whose homes were converted into offices by the business world. In the time of Oliver Twist, the centre of London had 200,000 permanent residents. This number soon fell to 50,000, but not less than 700,000 persons flooded the offices by day. Urban transport became a capital problem. A great daily migration took place between the suburbs and the centre, forming a unique feature of London life. The fatigue entailed by this daily effort justified the custom of the week-end holiday, which was gradually to create a universal fashion. 462 463

In France, a country of small country-towns, the movement towards urbanisation was much less pronounced. In 1860 the urban population was 29 % of the whole and in 1880 35%. Nevertheless the decline in the rural population was general. Under the joint inspiration of Napoleon III and the prefect Haussmann, Paris intended to take the lead in European city development. Whole quarters of the city, surviving unchanged since the Middle Ages, were thrown down in order to make way for a network of broad avenues. The population rose from one million to more than two. Three of the cities of Eastern Europe were likewise on the up-grade. St Petersburg, Moscow and Vienna could boast respectively of 800,000, 600,000 and 700,000 inhabitants.

A century before, Joseph II had admitted the public to the famous *Prater* in Vienna which became as celebrated as the *Champs-Elysées* in Paris, as splendid a scene of elegance and pleasure. Under the fourfold lines of tall chestnuts, the belles would pass by in their carriages and drive past the Three Cafés, never tired of admiring the scene and of being admired. Like Paris, Vienna had treated herself in 1857 to a circuit of boulevards, the Ring, which followed the line of the fortifications against which the waves of Turkish invaders had dashed in vain. 464 465

Berlin developed on other lines and soon became

462

The capitals are continually embellished.

466 one of the great cities of the world. In 1800 there were 150,000 Berliners : in 1880, over a million. Many fine buildings sprang up and the city became the industrial and commercial capital of Germany, unrivalled for its grain and textile markets, its metallurgic output and ... its university. Though, politically speaking, Berlin was the heart of Prussia, in fact the population contained such a great admixture of descendants of French and Slav immigrants that the citizens of genuine German stock were outnumbered by two to one.

466

464

465

In the economic life of this urban Europe, which presented to the world an unfailing spectacle of elegance and charm and imposed its tastes and fashions on mankind, the ports were focal points. Docks were constructed at the mouths of the Seine, the Scheldt, the Thames and the Elbe to receive sailing-ships and steamers which came from all over the world to discharge their cargoes into the newly built warehouses. Hamburg was the leading port of the Continent, the maritime outlet for the commerce and industry of Central Europe. Liverpool, on the Mersey estuary, was the first of the great European centres where the raw materials from abroad were transformed on the spot and where machinery and other objects of exportation were manufactured locally. Its first dock was opened in 1709; eventually its wharves and warehouses would extend for nearly seven miles. Liverpool was also the port of the great cotton industry of Lancashire, the most populous region of the globe, dominated by industrious Manchester.

Marseilles, the future starting point of the eastern routes, was preparing for its new rôle. In 1860, Napoleon III went there to inaugurate a great programme of public works. Marseilles was to serve as the terminal port for the liners traversing the Indian and Pacific Oceans and was busily constructing basins, quays and docks. The dock space available rose from 112 acres to 317. Thus the Mediterranean recovered the importance which three centuries before she had lost owing to the discovery of the Cape route to the East.

Venice slumbered on among her lagoons, but Trieste was soon able to compete with Genoa and Brindisi on the Indian route in spite of the advantage these enjoyed when in 1871 the Mont Cenis tunnel was opened. Trieste became the 'lung' of Austria. Between 1867 and 1876 the four break-waters, protecting the first of the Continent's great maritime railway stations, were constructed. The Triestine shipowners were soon masters of a fleet superior in tonnage to the ships of all their competitors.

469

470

Keeping pace with the development of world trade, the ports expand.

The lightning of '70 strikes the oak dedicated by Hugo to European union.

However, the Austro-Hungarian Empire was not to remain in control of all the great economic regions for which Trieste provided a natural outlet. From 1862 Otto, Count of Bismarck-Schoenhausen, applied himself with all the force of his powerful will to a task worthy of his genius : the unification of all the German states, which had been Prussia's dream for more than a century. Before he could achieve this he had to humble Austria, which in 1850 had forced Prussia into a humiliating surrender. Thanks to the neutrality of France, England and Russia he broke the Austrian forces at Sadowa in 1866. But as if to show that the future of Germany must be based on coal and iron, no less than on blood and fire, the creation next year of a customs union provided the German states with their first unitary institution.

The Prussian victory gave a rude shock to Napoleon III, who was seeking for a policy likely to enhance his prestige with the French people. In fact he worsened his position by a series of clumsy moves which eventually culminated in an open conflict between France and Germany. On his side, Bismarck thought it necessary, in order to cement the unification of Germany, to break the power of France. He was to succeed in this object in the first days of the year 1871.

471

471

On 14th July 1870 Victor Hugo had planted at Hauteville House 'the Oak of the United States of Europe'. When elected a deputy he made glowing overtures to Germany : 'No more frontiers! Let the Rhine belong to all. Let us form one republic, the United States of Europe ... let us devote ourselves to universal peace! ' In actual fact on 18th January 1871, the 170th anniversary of the coronation of the first King of Prussia, William I of Hohenzollern was invested with the dignity of German Emperor in Louis XIV's Gallery of Mirrors at Versailles.

472

472

473

The consequences of the events of 1866-1871 were fateful for Europe. The ten million Austrians, who remained outside the 'Germanic Community ', had to abandon all hope of influencing Italian or German politics. Italy completed her unification when on 20th September 1870 she re-established her traditional capital in Rome, while the Pope, to mark his estrangement, proclaimed himself a prisoner in the Vatican. Meantime Alsace-Lorraine, which France was forced to cede to Germany, became an ever-

had evolved a system based on a state-controlled technocracy, while Fourier had conceived the notion of harmonious communities of workers. Some of these theorists managed to put into practice their intellectual speculations. The followers of Saint-Simon, for example, prepared plans for important public works. In England, Robert Owen, the son of peasants, who became an employer and was a leader of socialist thought, founded in 1833 a trade union with a membership of 50,000. His successors invented chartism, a

474

475

476

widening rift in the fabric of the New Europe.

Behind the screen of economic and political changes and the dust of war, the awakening of the working classes, restless and at last class-conscious, had for some years been casting menacing shadows on the future of Europe. In countries where industry was highly organised, and particularly in England and France, the workers were henceforth to make their power felt and to call attention to their just claims through their unions 473 and even by means of strikes, thus opening a new chapter in European history. The working class only came into political prominence after a long period of thoughtful preparation. There had been no lack of doctrinaires who had sought to build on the ruins of the society, which had been overturned by the revolution of 1789, a new society with new moral standards. Saint-Simon

labour movement designed to prepare society for socialism by introducing democratic principles into politics. Meanwhile everywhere in Europe the established order was severely criticised. Auguste Comte held that the Middle Ages were 474 the era of theology, the intervening centuries the era of metaphysics, while the future of mankind was to be governed by positivism — the religion of humanity, based on reason and morality, the twin goddesses of the universe.

John Stuart Mill, for his part, formulated an 475 ethic designed to create general happiness. It would need the support of universal altruism and would entail the abolition of all private landed property. Herbert Spencer insisted that the biological evolution of man would lead him to the progressive betterment of his lot in a future in which industry and liberalism would co-operate. 476

The philosophers give the leading role to an obscure actor — the worker.

Scientists and philosophers equally discount the supernatural.

The British empirical school claimed to be able to prove that man, *homo sapiens*, was progressing indefinitely towards perfection. In 1859 Charles 477 Darwin published his ' Origin of Species ' and in 1871 his ' Descent of Man '. In his view, the fittest survive by adapting themselves to their environment and transmit to their descendants the characteristics they have acquired.

' Is it true ,then, that men all descended from monkeys? ' This question, while it excited heated polemics, gave a fresh impetus to progress in biological study. The laws of existence were

477

henceforth to be based on material and measurable data. Huxley and Haeckel are the leading champions of this school. There is no room for God if the evolutionary sequence from the primary cell to man remains unbroken. At any rate that is how the heirs of the philosophers of the ' Age of Reason ' interpreted Darwin.

478 Renan concluded from the findings of the Germans that the supernatural did not exist. In 1863 he published his ' Life of Jesus ', an imaginative novel in which he also discusses some of the vexed questions of theology. Three centuries in the course of which the origin and destiny of life had been constantly called into question seemed now to have come to a conclusion. The scientists and the philosophers united to prove that man alone can master the secrets of life and alone is responsible for his own destiny.

478

Was there not something utopian in this affirmation? By what means could man at once fulfil his destiny and achieve the ideal harmony? Many solutions were offered. Proudhon, for 479 example, said that ' if you do not transform the system of ownership, you will achieve nothing '. Man can only find himself in the familiar realities of the workshop and the community, in which he has to face the problems of daily life. These social cells will acquire vitality and unite in groups to form a flexible society with innumerable components and living by mutual service. As a final stage, federalism will endow war and nationalism with nobler aspirations and will become the political régime of the human race. ' The twentieth century will either usher in the era of federations or humanity will be doomed to a second purgatory for a thousand years '.

Socialism not only found expression in books and pamphlets. Its supporters formed themselves into parties and associations. The ebullient Ferdinand Lassalle, represented by the popular 480 cartoonists as brandishing the sword of universal suffrage to cut down the golden calf and demolish the altar of capitalism, laid the foundations of the

479

212

The International baptised by Marx makes its first attack on Capitalism.

480

481

tional held its first congress at Geneva in 1866, embodying the slogan which Marx had launched in 1847, ' Workers of the world, unite '. The Marxist doctrine, expounded in *das Kapital*, affirmed the principle of determinism in economic and social evolution.

The war of 1870, which had diverted French socialists into patriotic channels, and the violent suppression of the Commune in Paris, had powerful repercussions on the Marxist International which declared itself dissolved in 1876. But it had given a sharp impetus to militant socialism. In 1874 British trade unions had more than a million members. French syndicalism, more unpopular with the youthful Third Republic than it had been with the Second Empire, showed less initiative but, in 1874, the workers succeeded in convening at Paris the first national congress.

481

482

Das Kapital.

Kritik der politischen Oekonomie.

Von

Karl Marx.

Erster Band.

Buch I: Der Produktionsprocess des Kapitals.

Zweite verbesserte Auflage.

Das Recht der Uebersetzung wird vorbehalten.

Hamburg
Verlag von Otto Meissner.
1872.

German socialist party, which was officially recognised in 1875, eleven years after his death.

In 1864 a meeting held in St Martin's Hall decided to found the Workers' International. The inaugural address, drafted by Karl Marx, proclaimed : ' At last the people have returned to play their part, conscious of their power, standing up boldly to face political tyranny and to fight monopoly and economic privilege '. The Interna-

482

Conflicts across the Atlantic have their repercussions in Europe.

483

One may well wonder how the stern, shrewd face of Abraham Lincoln came to take its place among 483 Europe's family portraits. The leader of the American nation 'conceived in liberty and dedicated to the proposition that all men are created equal ' was one of the links in the long chain of European political thinkers who have worked untiringly to ensure that ' the government of the people, by the people, for the people, shall not perish from the earth '

In the southern states, the owners of sugar estates and cotton fields were determined to force the Union to recognise the enslavement of negroes as a federal institution. The northerners, industrialists and traders, replied that freedom was the birthright of mankind. The war lasted for four years, from 1861 to 1865, and ended in a victory for the North and American unity. The conflict engaged the serious attention of European politicians and revealed the importance of the United States in the affairs of the world. It deprived the European textile industry of its cotton and reduced hundreds of thousands of English and French workers to total or partial unemployment, while causing a notable increase in India's share of the world's cotton production. One came to feel more than ever that the safety of Europe lay outside Europe. Napoleon III believed this so strongly that, profiting by the civil war in the United States and in defiance of the Monroe Doctrine, he intervened in the affairs of the American continent. ' In order to shed the rays of his beneficent influence from north to south ', the Emperor sought to organise an expedition in which Britain, France and Spain should act together ' in the interests of civilisation '. His real objective was to obtain possession of the zone through which the canal linking the Atlantic with the Pacific would pass, thus blocking the possibilities of United States expansion in Central America. Archduke Maximilian of Austria, whose vanity and weakness had allowed him to be drawn into the contrivance, paid with his life for his rashness in accepting the 484 crown of Mexico.

But it mattered little to Europe if America closed its doors to European penetration. The cutting of the Isthmus of Suez had brought India as well as the Far East and the fertile archipelagoes of South-Eastern Asia much nearer to her ports. Sailing up the Suez Canal on board her yacht *l'Aigle*, Eugénie, Empress of the French, led the procession of sovereigns. All the national flags of 485

484

The Empress of the French opens the Suez canal, short cut to Asia.

Europe fluttered in the breeze—from Spain to Norway, from England to Russia, all were present. It was already nine months since the waters of the Mediterranean had flowed into those of the Red Sea. This great exploit had been the work of one man, achieved in spite of all the obstacles placed in his way by the Great Powers:
486 that man was Ferdinand de Lesseps. The distance from Europe to the Far East had now

zone, it is true, became wealthy and westernised and the Chinese living there quickly acquired, thanks to their qualities as men of business, a privileged position, but the interior remained impervious to western ideas. The techniques of agriculture and medicine had, centuries ago, reached their peak. Mistrust of European exploitation and a conservative inertia combined to hinder the progress of westernisation.

485

486

been reduced by two thirds and Egypt had, by the same token, recovered her personality as a nation.

It is true that Europeans had not waited for the miracle of Suez before taking an interest in the Asiatic continent. From 1840 they had dreamed of transforming China. England first and then France and the United States had obtained the free entry of their ships into five great Chinese ports. The English and French, not yet satisfied, had landed an expeditionary force which, in 1860,
487 succeeded in capturing Pekin and dictating terms to the Chinese. After a veritable political revolution Japan for her part agreed, in 1868, to do business on a large scale with Europe, hoping, by rapidly modernising her methods, to recover her former power. But what of China? The coastal

487

Impecunious travellers like Livingstone and Brazza mapped out Eurafrica.

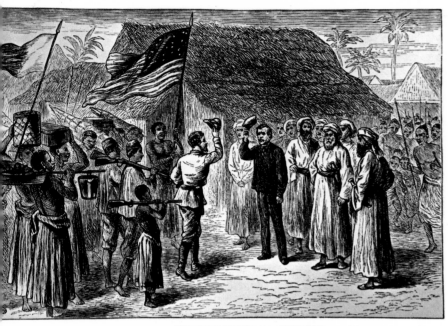

A footing had already been obtained by the English in Egypt, the French in Algeria (since 1830), the Germans in East Africa with the connivance of the Arab Sultan of Zanzibar and the Dutch in South Africa. The French marched eastward from Senegal and southward from North Africa. The English were trying to link the Cape with Cairo and to discover the source of the Nile, down which Burton had sailed in 1860, starting from the Great Lakes. The German Nachtigall trekked from Tripoli to the country of the Nyam-Nyam. But the most remarkable figure which illumined the early days of Europe in Africa was that of the Anglican missionary David Livingstone, a philanthropist, a sworn enemy of slavery, a scientist and a trader. After leading several expeditions, he remained for three years in the heart of South-East Africa. His friends had given him up for dead. Then an Anglo-American journalist, Stanley, set out to find him. At last he encountered him in a village in the bush, a ragged and weary old man, and greeted him with the classic words, ' Dr. Livingstone, I presume? '

While Africa was to remain for several years longer the hunting-ground of the pioneers, India, a continent in her own right, had become an integral part of the British Crown possessions. On 1st January 1877, at a Durbar in Delhi, Queen Victoria was proclaimed Empress. The words ' colonialism ' and ' imperialism ' originated in England, where they were to acquire high-sounding variations. Prime Minister Disraeli, the offspring of Venetian Jews, set to work to make an Empire out of a miscellaneous collection of colonies. By the end of the century the Empire had an area of nearly sixteen million square miles and a population of 396,000,000 — roughly a quarter of the population of the world. There seemed to be some justification for the opening words of the song Rule Britannia '.

Savorgnan de Brazza, with his keen but kindly glance, exercised an immense influence over countless Africans. This Italian, an officer in the French navy, was first and foremost a lover of peace. In 1875 he sailed up the Ogowe and the Congo and placed the riverside tribes under the protection of France, in token of which he gave

But there was a better mission-field than China with its ancient, unchanging civilisation. Africa could offer Europe not only countless economic outlets, but also the opportunity to make a whole series of valuable discoveries, geographical, ethnographical and linguistic, calculated to stimulate religious and humanitarian zeal. Africa was nearer, more primitive and more malleable. Slavery and the slave trade flourished there together with animistic superstitions and fetishism.

them tricolour flags. With a capital of 300,000 francs and no one to help him he created the French Congo, a colony larger than France.

We are still in the era of the lone wolves, the indomitable adventurers who compelled their governments to give them a free hand in Africa. Stanley was the first great reporter in the modern style. Behind his humanitarian proclamations the aims of a shrewd man of business are not hard to detect. He certainly succeeded in implanting in public opinion in more than one country the view that the chief mission of Europe in Africa—the abolition of the slave trade—can easily be reconciled with good business. In October 1877 it was learnt that Stanley had traversed the whole of Central Africa and sailed down the Congo river, whose lower reaches alone were known to explorers. The enthusiasm aroused by his adventur-

ous journeys attracted the interest of the covetous.

Meanwhile, far from Africa, a few officers and traders succeeded in placing the Indo-Chinese Peninsula under the influence of France. After occupying Cochin-China, the French captured the principal towns of the Tonkin delta, among them Hanoi and Haiphong. Disavowed by their government, these Frenchmen concluded a treaty of friendship with the Emperor of Annam.

The frontiers of the rising colonial empires had already been clearly traced and it was now essential to secure the sea-routes by establishing strong-points in various places. Great Britain made of Singapore a sort of commercial turntable between Europe and the Far East. Its situation opposite Batavia, for two centuries the capital of the Dutch East Indies, was very appropriate for this purpose.

This taste for discovery grows in business and with colonial empires.

Foreign adventure encourages a renewed interest in education.

494

Only the Japanese who, nevertheless, remained firmly attached to their deep-rooted traditions and faithful to their own particular genius, found themselves able to adopt certain long-established features of European civilisation such as the Gregorian calendar, vaccination and conventional male attire. Thus the European businessman on a visit to Japan was hardly distinguishable from
493 his hosts. But Europe, for her part, was preparing to take a new step forward. It may be that her recent contact with countries yesterday unknown had made her realise her own inadequacies. In any case the enthusiastic ovation
494 which greeted Edgar Quinet and Michelet at the *Collège de France* was symbolic of the interest which all nations were henceforward to take in education. History, doubtless because it is the prop and stay of nationalism, was the subject first in favour. Men like Mommsen, Sorel and Stubbs invested the realities of the past with the warmth of the present, while bringing to their work a meticulous accuracy. The struggle against illiteracy took a decisive turn. Compulsory schooling became general and free from England to Hungary. It seemed as if a new epoch was unfolding itself, in which science and knowledge would contribute to man's happiness and help him to enjoy greater freedom. Jules Verne was the romantic herald of this dawning age. His novels acclaim
495 the knights of the future, aeronauts and submarine captains, skimming over continents and flying to the moon. Their theme is that to the man of good will nothing is impossible.

493

495

the evil and the remedy at the same time? In 1877 Pasteur conceived the idea of vaccinating fowls against cholera. He had the courage, a little later, to apply the same remedy to a human, when little Joseph Meister was faced with the alternatives of death from rabies or safety by inoculation. Men of science could make no more splendid gift to mankind than the conquest of the great epidemics. And in a few years Europe was to offer this gift to the whole world thanks to the labours of the German bacteriologists Loeffer, Hansen, Eberth and von Behring, the Frenchmen Yersin and Roux, and Metchnikoff the Russian.

On every front there were victories for progress and feats of audacity crowned with success. Since the day when the Belgian engineer Neuville introduced the open-web girders, no building device seemed too fanciful. In 1879 an Englishman named Thomas found out how to dephosphorise cast iron, making it possible to produce

496 Justus Liebig was, in the eyes of his contemporaries, the leader of the band of illustrious chemists striving to hasten the tempo of progress. By *concentrating* the meat which South America provided in enormous quantities, he supplied food to Europe and at the same time provided a new source of wealth to the Latin-Americans. He also explained the precise rôle of phosphates in the growth of plants and invented chemical manures. Was famine now a thing of the past?

By the time Liebig died, in 1875, most of the great discoveries of modern chemistry had come from his laboratory. Since the simultaneous discovery by Murdock and Lebon of lighting by gas, no one had taken further interest in this stinking residue of the factories, until the German, August von Hofmann, a professor at London University, managed to extract benzene from the residual coal tar and from benzene, in turn, extracted aniline. His English pupil Perkin went still further, for it was he who compounded the first synthetic colouring matter thus initiating the endless chain of organic chemistry. Marcelin Bertelot laid the foundations of a new science: the fabrication in the laboratory of natural products, a technique in which Germany was soon unrivalled.

It was also Germany who led the way in the search for the infinitely small—the science of bacteriology. The development of the microscope accomplished by a German physicist, Abbe, and the improvement in the new processes of colouration helped the campaign against the bacilli which ravage humanity. A cluster of brilliant scientists combined to identify these subtle enemies. The best known of these was
497 Robert Koch, who in 1882 discovered the bacillus of tuberculosis and later isolated that of cholera.

But where would all these research-workers
498 have been without Louis Pasteur, who discovered

Chemistry and physics enlist the genius of Koch, Pasteur and many others.

The development of sinister war-weapons is not, however, neglected.

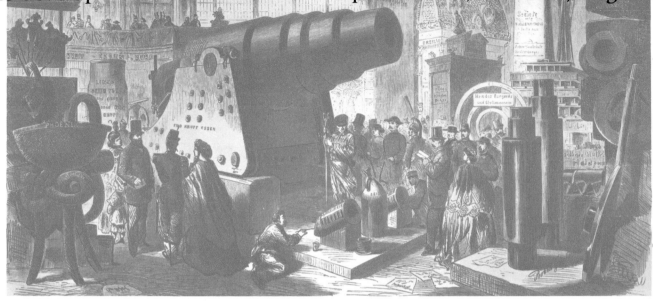

499

steel at will by utilising the very abundant deposits of iron ore of which no use had hitherto been made. The great iron works had not waited for the supremacy of steel to be finally established before launching out into ever-increasing production. Essen could already compete with Sheffield, and Birmingham with Creusot. In 1844 Krupp manufactured the first weapons cast from molten steel at the very time when Schneider was putting his great steam hammer into operation. The fifty-ton cannon which Krupp exhibited in the Paris exhibition of 1867 revealed to the clear sighted how easily the armaments race could bring the world to ruin. But one could not deny that there was a positive side to all these inventions. The exact calibration of machine parts and the technique of special steels, worked out in England, was of as much value to agricultural machinery, to steam navigation and to household plumbing as to the artillery. Moreover the triumphant accla-

mations that welcomed the birth of a new form of energy gave man ground for hope in the permanent collaboration of science and peace. Gramme, an unassuming Belgian joiner, manufactured the first dynamo in 1869, thus creating a source of power, heat and light. This invention was soon to be followed by the most wonderful adaptations. It was Edison who perfected in the United States the electric light bulb, but only after drawing lessons from the ideas of Goebel, a German watchmaker, and Swan, an English inventor, and not until the Russian engineer Joblochkoff had produced the electric candle.

The application to industry of electric power dates from 2nd October 1882, when ,at the Munich exhibition, the French engineer, Marcel Deprez worked a dynamo on a quarter h.p. current transmitted along a telegraph wire from the town of Miesbach, 35 miles away.

500

500

Europe acquires a new land-mark : the Eiffel Tower.

Europe with distant oilfields. In 1865, an American trader named Rockefeller combined the existing petrol refineries into the Standard Oil Company which by 1878 controlled 90 % of the market. On the Caspian the Russians were the first to fuel their steamers with 'mazout'. But Europe, herself scantily supplied with oilfields, had no inkling of the part which petroleum would play in her future. Men's minds were far more occupied with the great French Exhibition of 1889 organised to commemorate the centenary of the Revolution. It was then that the Eiffel Tower rose proudly into the skies of Paris, at 503 once a trophy, a witness and a herald of the greatness of Europe.

Feeling, or perhaps imagining, that her future lay overseas, Europe hastened, in 1878, to settle 504 the conflict which had broken out in the Balkans, where the Bulgarian population aided by Russia, the protector of the Slavs, had revolted against

501

501 It is a question whether Alfred Nobel, the Swedish inventor with 129 patents of his own, would have endowed the Peace Prize in 1895 had he not, thirty years before, played an important part in the armaments industry. Nobel was the father of dynamite, the first explosive that could be at all safely handled, and he founded plants for its manufacture all over the world. He left his great fortune to the Swedish Academy with instructions to use it for the honour of Europeans.

In proportion with her growing needs, the dependence of Europe on the other continents increased. As the working-class populations adopted cotton as their staple material for under-linen, sheets and table-cloths, the amount of the raw material needed by European industry multiplied. Import agents crossed the seas to 502 visit New Orleans or Bombay and activate their buying offices.

Another bond was formed which one day was to link the political and economic destinies of

502

503

222

their Turkish masters. Bismarck, now reconciled with Austria, presided at the Congress, which decided on the independence of Roumania, Serbia and Montenegro and the autonomy of Bulgaria, while leaving unsolved many problems capable of giving rise to future conflicts. But the statesmen believed that large-scale modern industry would be unable to accelerate or even to maintain the tempo of its production if it could not rely on new countries with a rich consumers' market and a wealth of raw materials. At a moment when nationalism was everywhere gaining ground, it was easy to argue that colonial expansion was a sign of physical, intellectual and military vitality. Men of better understanding felt that the destiny of Europe was to awaken the peoples of other continents not only to more rational forms of material existence, but also to new conceptions of social and political life.

Three men arose as the champions of these

505

506

504

505 different principles. Joseph Chamberlain, son of
      a London shoe manufacturer, created in England a
506 regular creed of Imperialism; Jules Ferry persua-
      ded the French people to undertake the conquest
      of Indo-china and to occupy Tunisia. Meanwhile
507 Leopold II of Belgium directed his own colonial
      policy. His claim to international recognition of
      the 'Congo Free-State' caused the second
      Congress of Berlin to be convened in 1885, when
      the division of the Dark Continent into spheres
      of influence was worked out on the principle that
      the hinterland belonged to the nation occupying
      the coastal zone.

507

The Nobel prize is founded on profits from the manufacture of dynamite.

508

509

510

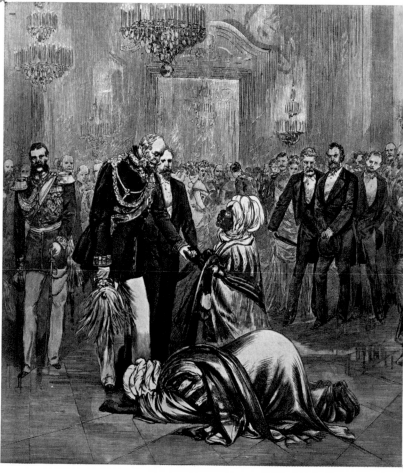

508 In September 1882 the British had landed troops at Ismailia. As principal shareholders in the Suez Canal Company they had sent a naval squadron to assure the safety of the Canal, a vital link in imperial communications. With time, Britain would come to occupy the whole of Egypt.

509 A dozen years later Kitchener, a figure typical of the Victorian empire-builders, succeeded in re-establishing British suzerainty over the Sudan. By a singular reverse of fortune Egypt was to become, more than half a century later, the leading Arab independent nation, organised on modern lines. Mohammed Abdu, a disciple of Spencer, led a movement to rejuvenate Islam and restore its dynamism. Thus for the first time the contributions of European thought were to become the seed of future hostility to the presence of Europeans.

510 Our illustration shows the Cameroon chiefs in their sober white robes prostrating themselves before the Emperor of Germany. Bismarck himself was loth to compete in the race for colonial aggrandisement, but his hand was forced by German explorers and traders. Lüderitz, Rohlfs and Nachtigall brought East-Africa, Togoland and the Cameroons under German rule. The navy occupied certain islands in the Pacific. The whole was big enough to call itself an empire.

In Madagascar the French protectorate, im-

In the Middle East, Europe sows the wind, later to reap the whirlwind.

511

posed in 1885, was breached by the feudal chiefs of the Hovas and the royal princesses called on the people to revolt. An expeditionary force had to be despatched in 1895 to restore protectorate, which was subsequently transformed into a colony and pacified by Galliéni.

South Africa, which was thought to have become less important since the opening of the Suez Canal, suddenly came into prominence again. The English, who owned the Cape Colony, had recognised the right of the Boers, farmers of Dutch stock, to the Orange Free State and the Transvaal. Suddenly diamonds in abundance were discovered in the south of the Orange Free State and immensely rich goldfields in the Transvaal. Immigrants flowed into the country. Cecil Rhodes, the son of an Anglican clergyman, became a diamond king and dreamed of establishing a peaceful British dominion throughout the whole of South Africa. His grand aspirations clashed with the patriotism of the Boers and of their leader Paul Kruger, President of the Transvaal. A filibustering expedition led by Dr Jameson was defeated by the Boers. It needed a long and cruel war (1899-1902) before the Boers consented to form part of a Union of South Africa under the British Crown.

511

512

512

Cecil Rhodes and Paul Kruger shape the history of South Africa.

513

514

The year 1897, the sixtieth of Victoria's reign, was a year of apotheosis for the British. For her diamond jubilee Victoria Regina, 'the grandmother of the Courts of Europe', received the homage of the whole world.

Her grandson William II, the young Emperor of Germany, entertained ambitions no less vast than those of England. By his entry into Jerusalem in 1898 he assured for his country commercial outlets in the Arab world, henceforth susceptible to German influence. He opened the Near East to German businessmen and his friendship for the Sultan of Turkey enabled him to compete with the Tsar as a protector of the Christian population of the Ottoman Empire. He also aimed to obtain access to the Persian Gulf by building a railway which would link Berlin with Baghdad and Basra, creating a rival route to India, and curtailing the ambitions of the English.

513

Europe, as an entity, no longer existed. There was only a patchwork of nations competing with one another for expansion in the outside world.

Major Marchand had left Brazzaville at the head of 120 soldiers and a gang of bearers, who crossed Africa with the individual parts of the S.S. *Faidherbe*. He hoped to reach the upper waters of the Nile before the Cape to Cairo route could be mapped out. This would place in French hands, not Egyptian, the sources of the Nile to which the latter country owed her prosperity.

514

In September 1898 Kitchener sailed up the Nile in command of Anglo-Egyptian forces. His gunboats reached Fashoda to find Marchand in occupation. He had just arrived after an exhausting march of over 4,000 miles. Diplomatic instructions prevented a clash between the two forces; on 3rd November Marchand found himself compelled to evacuate Fashoda and the Egyptian flag was hoisted over the outpost.

515

As a compensation for this setback, the territory from Algeria to the Congo was recognised by the British as a French sphere of influence.

515

spike the cannons of the West.

National rivalries, so rife in Africa, had no place in the Far East, where the European in quest of zones of influence had become the public enemy. The Boxer uprising of May 1900 was inspired by the Empress of China herself, a foe to all forms of modernisation. The fanatical Chinese concentrated their fury on the symbols of western civilisation, demolishing railways, telegraph lines and steamships as well as slaughtering foreigners and Chinese Christians. In June the European Legations in Pekin were besieged by the Boxers, but two months later an amphibious expeditionary force numbering 18,000 men, led by Field Marshal Count Waldersee and containing German, French, Russian and British units, captured Pekin. This victory marked the end of all attempts to partition China among European nations. In the same year a group of reformers headed by Sun Yat Sen set to work to borrow from Europe the instruments of European power.

516

Japan won the first real victory over the Whites. The Japanese had no intention of watching with folded hands the attempts of Russia to extend her influence over Northern China. The Russian Far Eastern Fleet, reinforced by warships that had passed through the Suez Canal, was powerless against the attacks of Admiral Togo who, on 8th February 1904, sank three Russian ships in the harbour of Port Arthur.

517

In April, Admiral Makharov's flag-ship struck a mine and went down with the admiral on board. Sustained by the moral support of England, Japanese forces routed the Russian armies in Manchuria. Meanwhile, St. Petersburg despatched a fresh fleet from the Baltic to the Korean Sea, but disaster awaited it at Tsushima. There, on 27th May 1905, Admiral Togo, a brilliant pupil of the British Navy, proved that Europe could be forcibly deprived of those instruments of war which she herself had forged. The consequences were incalculable. Tsushima sounded the tocsin of nationalism in India and Indo-China.

518

516

517

518

227

There followed a short spell of peace. Europe, more disunited than ever, could not ward off for long the perils that threatened her. Attempts had indeed been made to further the cause of peace. In 1899 the delegates of twenty-eight States had met at the Hague, but beyond laying down the rules of war, they accomplished nothing.

The alliances concluded or renewed during this period reveal the aggressive nature of European diplomacy. To counter the Triple Alliance of Germany, Austria and Italy, initiated by Bismarck in 1882, France and Russia signed a defensive pact in 1893. England at length issued from her 'splendid isolation' and the *Entente Cordiale* with France was born. While the Egyptian question was settled in favour of England, Morocco, the last independent country in Africa, was declared a French sphere of influence.

The Moroccan delegates who attended the Conference of Algeciras in January 1906, were in fact no more than lay figures in the discussions which were to settle the fate of their country. Germany, the last great nation to become conscious of a colonial vocation, had something to say, both to promote her prestige and to protect her material interests. The Act of Algeciras did not prevent the occurence of serious incidents and a further compromise had to be found. After agreement with Germany, a French protectorate was established over Morocco in March 1912 and the danger of war was temporarily exorcised.

But Europe continued to be divided into two camps. Public opinion naturally regarded the Triple Entente, concluded between England, France and Russia in 1907, as designed to encircle Germany.

Moreover, new threats to peace began to appear. The weakness of the Turkish Empire became a source of complications. The Italians intervened in Tripolitania; the Austrians annexed the Turkish provinces of Bosnia and Herzogovina; Bulgaria declared herself independent; Serbia sought to create a federation of Southern Slavs. Montenegro declared war against Turkey.

In this illustration we see Montenegrin women gallantly carrying supplies to their husbands in the firing line; but the issues at stake could not be measured in terms of local heroism. Austria was perturbed by the successes of the Serbs; and the Bulgars, though backed by the Austrians, were reduced to impotence by their former allies. Turkey lost almost all of her European possessions, and four times between 1905 and 1913 Europe was on the brink of war.

We should not assume that the history of Europe in this epoch could be epitomised in the ambitions of her rulers and the intrigues of her governments. Democracy, which was everywhere gaining ground, often succeeded in identifying the people with their government. Universal suffrage was introduced on the creation of the German Empire and the Third French Republic. It found

Algeciras, Montenegro : Europe poses on the «brink of war».

The century is closing, and Socialism is coming of age.

521

523

522

its way into the Swiss Confederation in 1874 and was practised in Belgium in 1883. It was adopted in Spain in 1890, in Norway in 1898 and in Italy in 1912. The vote was extended in Great Britain, Austria and Hungary, while in Scandinavia and the United Kingdom women could vote in municipal elections.

However, the views of the public were often relegated to the background. Everywhere men were moved by a common desire: to provide the people with their daily bread and to sustain their dignity in the face of the technical and financial 'progress' which threatened to crush them. Conscious at last of the real power which, as voters, they had acquired, the workers joined the socialist parties in the different countries— in Germany in spite of Bismarck's discriminatory laws, in France thanks to Jaurès, in England, where it took the name of Labour Party, in Sweden and Belgium. The governments could not remain indifferent to this movement and Bismarck, to canalise it, created a massive system of compulsory insurance which was subsequently imitated in other lands.

Pope Leo XIII's encyclical *Rerum Novarum* called upon all governments to protect the working classes. Evolution along these lines was not effected without collisions. The prolonged economic depression that lasted from 1875 to 521 1895 caused strikes and movements sometimes accompanied by violence with after-effects which disturbed the political atmosphere. Even Lon-522 don had its troubles, but the constitutional reform party was too strong for the champions of direct action. Encouraged by the methods of the Russian Nihilists, who after five attempts succeeded 523 in murdering Tsar Alexander II, the Anarchists waved the banners of revolt across the Continent and in Lyons, Madrid, Paris, Barcelona and Rome, their agents made illustrious victims.

On the operatic stage Wagner and Mussorgsky steal the thunder.

524

526

525

As the twentieth century approached, the world of thought, and especially the world of music, was lit up by bright flashes of new genius. Wagner claimed not only to have demolished the obsolete technique of Italian opera. He aimed to combine music, poetry, drama and scenery in works better fitted than any before them to depict the destiny of man. After giving to the world *The Flying Dutchman*, *Tannhauser* and *Lohengrin*, he set out to illustrate his aesthetic theories by composing *The Ring of the Niebelungs*, a monumental cycle of four operas. To these he added *Tristan and Isolde*, *The Mastersingers* and *Parsifal*. In order to find a fitting theatre for his immense tetralogy, which took him a quarter of a century to compose, he established at Bayreuth, in Bavaria, 'the Jerusalem of a new artistic tradition'. The opening of his theatre on 13th August 1876 was a truly European occasion. On that day Siegfried, the unblemished warrior, full of hatred for

the meannesses of conventional humanity and for gold, the corrupter of mankind, took his place in the Pantheon among the heroes of all time.

The Wagnerian style, grandiose and allegorical, produced as many imitators as critics. The latest reaction came from Russia, where the Five—Moussorgsky, Balakirev, Cui, Rimsky-Korsakov and Borodin—embarked on the task of freeing Russian music from the romanticism of the West. Moussorgsky, by giving the Russian people the principal rôle in *Boris Godunov* and by mingling with the folksongs of his country echoes of the orthodox liturgy, created an effective counterpoise to the attractions of Wagner.

In Germany, Brahms made himself the champion of the classical instrumental tradition, in opposition to the Wagnerian music-drama. The latter, in spite of its triumphs, did not succeed in eclipsing Italian opera. Far from it. Verdi, born in 1813, the same year as Wagner, was a

Verdi instills new life into the aria; Brahms prolongs a great tradition.

527

529

528

530

new scion of this ancient tree. Recognition came to him early and his career was full of achievement. *Rigoletto*, *Il Trovatore*, *La Traviata* and *Aida* (written by order of the Khedive for the opening of the Suez Canal) display, in spite of the poverty of their librettos, a wealth of lyrical beauty.

There was a falling off in the music of Verdi's followers, who, in their reaction against the preponderance of the orchestra in Wagner's operas, assigned undue importance to the human voice. Puccini, breaking loose from the complacency and effusiveness of this school, composed *La Bohême*, *Tosca* and *Madame Butterfly* which appealed to a new and wide public.

The creative storm did not soon die down. Everywhere on the Continent appeared composers eager to exploit the folk-music of their countries. Frederick Smetana and Anton Dvorak emphasised the originality of the Czechs at a

time when, in the Austrian Empire, the diversity of races which composed it was progressively undermining the position of Vienna.

In the North, Edward Grieg gave distinction 530 to the charming folk-melodies of Norway and Jean Sibelius, later to be a torchbearer of the Scandinavian musical genius, was born in Finland.

The Romantic School of writers dating from the previous century hardly survived the glories of Manzoni, Tennyson and Victor Hugo. In 1857 Baudelaire opened up forbidden regions which he was henceforth to call his own, when he issued his collection of poems 'Les Fleurs du Mal', a book which caused delight and consternation. The poems of Novalis and Hoffmann in Germany and the visionary works of Blake in England had already driven a breach into the poetry of ethereal sentiment which had been hitherto in vogue, and had introduced the 'new thrill' which Victor Hugo welcomed in Baudelaire.

531

533

532

531 In contrast to Verlaine with his half-tints and
531 chiaroscuro, Rimbaud, a primitive mystic, seeks
in his poetry to rediscover the original truth of
man's being. He raises the flag of revolt against
civilisation and its sacrosanct traditions. He
journeyed to Abyssinia to forget the storms of his
youth, but this negation of the past seems a constant feature of the European genius and the fruit
of its eternal discontent.

It is a far cry from the lonely laments of Rimbaud to the Russian novelists with their vast
audiences. Tolstoi and Dostoievski take us to
the very root of the mood which seems to constitute the essence of the soul of Europe: man's
incessant preoccupation with his own rôle in the
universe and his urge to challenge all the conclu-
532 sions of past generations. Tolstoi's theory of
history, whereby those very people who control
the destiny of nations are themselves but the
illuded puppets of Destiny, is mutely contradicted
by the evident wilfulness and vitality he imparts
to his characters.

533 Dostoievski, for his part, breaks down all the
moral barriers. He leads his heroes to the void,
beyond the regions of sin, to a realm faintly illumined by a gleam of hope of regeneration.
Though he never says so in so many words his
work is inspired by a sense of the absurd. His
novels would become the breeding ground of
Kafka's myths and of much of the true literature
of the twentieth century.

The poets and the novelists spoke out against
the soulless universe constructed by the clerics,
technicians and politicians of the day. Nor did
the playwrights lag behind. The Norwegian

Rimbaud rebels against the absurdities of life which later provoke the

534

535

534 dramatist Ibsen displayed in all the great theatres of Europe his thirst for absolute truth. An ardent champion of the individual, he pleaded the cause of individualism and self-determination in various plays, among which *The Doll's House*, *The Enemy of the People*, *Brand* and *Peer Gynt* are outstanding. Another Norwegian, Bjoernson, was likewise an apostle of the solitary life and the Swede, Strindberg, was no less critical of a played-out world. It was, moreover, the power of the individual which formed the central

535 theme in the writings of the Prussian Nietzsche. This man, who was regarded as a preacher of pure violence and the herald of a coarse and aggressive pan-Germanism, the prophet of the reawakening of a barbaric age, spent much of his life dreaming of the Mediterranean; he envisaged a return to the spirit of classic Greece which alone could free mankind, stifled and overcrowded. An enemy to Europe's Christian tradition, Nietzsche represented, in a sense, the spirit of courage, resistance and stoicism. But all that his contemporaries borrowed from him were slogans, ready-made precepts, and a form of social snobbery.

536 Rudyard Kipling sought a remedy for European restlessness in India, where the British Raj gave him material for stories synthesising the Western philosophy of action with the marvels of the East. H.G. Wells refused to be depressed by the evergrowing burden of modern techniques. Quite the reverse ! He pushed them to their extreme

537 limits and preached a form of international socialism in which increased production and its attendant comforts would secure for everyone a better life. So, in spite of pessimism and uncertainty, Europeans always found new grounds for hope and incentives to advance.

536

537

Wellsian nightmare.

233

French men of letters, also, had set out to depict the revolt of man against an oppressive society, but their descriptions of manners and customs were better documented than in the past. Flaubert's 'experimental' and Zola's 'naturalistic' novels are written in a style which in sculpture becomes realism. Thus began an aesthetic revolution which was to spread throughout Europe, though in very varying forms. The English Pre-Raphaelites, unable to detect beauty in the age in which they lived, reconstituted with loving care the biblical past and the Middle Ages in order to give, by means of an exact picture of a bygone age, a soul to the world of today. Dante Gabriel Rossetti and Burne-Jones were the foremost representatives of an art full of harmony and gentle melancholy.

538 Realism in painting led to violently conflicting tendencies. The academic painters strove to copy nature in her most flattering, splendid or anecdotal aspects. A rival school grew up alongside them, led by Courbet, determined to paint 'nature in the raw'. Writing of the great picture he painted in 1854, Courbet says: 'It is the moral and physical portrait of my studio. The figures all represent my followers and collaborators'. Baudelaire (on the extreme right) is among them, but the foreground is occupied by common mortals and women careless of conventional beauty. This school insisted that painting should help man to see himself as he is, miserable and undone, but never vulgar. That ideal was to influence Wilhelm Leibl of Munich and the Spaniard, Sorella. With it, too, we must associate Rodin, the richness and variety of whose work entitle him to a place among the great sculptors of all time.

The influence of Edouard Manet caused a speedy transformation in the values of realism. Addicted, like Courbet, to the portrayal of daily life, he became, in 1863, the champion of the young independents in revolt against the academics. His technique suppressed modelling and half-tones and employed bright colours, the better to depict the finesse and the vigour of landscapes and human figures. He was the father of impressionism based upon the correctness and spontaneity of observation of the play of light. No one was a more devoted slave of sunlight—devoted to the point of madness—than the Dutchman Vincent Van Gogh. When he painted the church of Auvers, Van Gogh used brilliant colours reminiscent of the sunbathed skies of Provence. His manner of laying on paint in serpentine strokes, along the forms, gives a flamelike twist to the humble Gothic lines of the church. Outstripping the impressionists, Van 539 Gogh hastened madly in quest of colour, anticipating *fauvisme*.

Impressionism was the strongest aesthetic movement that European painting had known for several centuries.

Courbet paints nature in the raw; Van Gogh bathes it in sunlight.

541

In 1870, we see in *L'Atelier des Batignolles*, grouped round Manet seated at his easel, the most ardent apostles of the newest aesthetic: Astruc, Renoir, Schelderev, Zola (conversing with Bazille), Edmond Maitre and Monet. We can easily understand that the essence of impressionism, a movement rather than a school, could not be compressed into a formula. The movement gave inspiration to a world of painters extraordinarily rich in talent. Pissaro, who came from the Danish West Indies, Monet and Sisley display impressionistic technique in the purest form. But the impressionists seemed to have the power of diffusing a sort of enduring gaiety, a radiance of light and joy; who better than Renoir, the painter of flowers and fruits and buxom beauties, could convey this message? Degas, more of a realist, sought by a skilful use of light and exceptional draughtmanship to catch the nuances of his models' attitudes.

Gauguin, following an opposite course, conceived of a new aesthetic, employing a linear technique and areas of flat colour. Cézanne, who started as an impressionist, sought in the vibrations of light permanent and enduring volumes, planes and forms and thus served as a link between impressionism and cubism.

540
541
467
527
542

540

Manet plays truant from the academies, but Gauguin goes further afield.

The internal-combustion engine adds a third dimension to travel: the air.

543

of the new firms of motor-builders came into prominence. In France there was the Panhard-Levassor, founded in 1890, followed by Peugeot and then by Renault in 1899. The German Mercedes dates from 1901; the English Daimler from 1898, the Rolls from 1904 and the Austin from 1906. The Italian firms of Fiat and Lancia date from 1899 and 1905 respectively.

The credit for having first fitted a steam-engine to a heavier-than-air machine, which actually left the ground, goes to the Frenchman, Clément Ader, who made his first flight in 1890. The Franco-Brazilian flyer, Santos-Dumont, re-enacted this

545

Science and mechanics were also evolving. Since that day in 1863 when Étienne Lenoir had started a kerosene engine running on the road from Paris to Joinville, men had been eagerly searching for the best way of substituting petrol for steam. Beau de Rochas had developed the theory of the four-stroke cycle, the first example of which had been shown by the German engineer Nicolas Otto at the great exhibition of 1878. Then in 1886 Daimler, Otto's mechanic, constructed the first oil-driven motor, which Karl Benz mounted on a vehicle capable of covering 12 miles in an hour. Finally Rudolf Diesel, with his internal combustion engine, clinched the victory of petroleum over steam.

543

544 The London-Brighton race of 1896 made history, putting an end to the official ostracism to which the infant automobile industry had hitherto been subjected. The invention by John Dunlop of the pneumatic tyre in 1888 had revealed the immense possibilities of these machines which many people thought frightful. Soon the makes began to increase in number and the names

544

exploit for the benefit of a public audience in 1906
545 at Bagatelle; in this instance, the steam-engine
was replaced by an internal-combustion engine.
But the foremost student of the problems of flight
was the German Otto Lilienthal, who spent years
observing the behaviour of his aircraft before
being killed in a crash. Further experiments by
the pioneers of flight, among whom the best
known are the American Wright brothers, soon
made the aircraft practicable for commercial and
military use.

Following the discoveries of the Englishman
Crookes, a German physician, Wilhelm Konrad
546 Roentgen, discovered in 1895 the X-rays and
thereby opened the path to the knowledge of
radioactivity. In 1896 Henry Becquerel observed
547 the properties of uranium from which Pierre and
Marie Curie succeeded in isolating the radioactive
element. Rutherford and Kelvin took radioactivity as the basis of their research into the atomic
constitution of matter. In 1900 Max Planck
formulated his quantum theory, a few years
before the young Einstein came onto the scene.
Already in 1888 Hertz had demonstrated the
existence of electro-magnetic waves and on
24th March 1895 the Russian Alexander Popov
transmitted in morse two words, 'Heinrich
Hertz', on the waves proceeding from his oscil-
548 lator. However, it was Guglielmo Marconi
who foresaw that in future distance would be
eliminated and, making use of all the previous
discoveries in this field, succeeded in extending
the range of wireless to trans-continental distances.
His first successful attempt in sending sound
waves across the Thames was followed five years
later, in 1901, by the despatch of wireless messages
over the Atlantic.

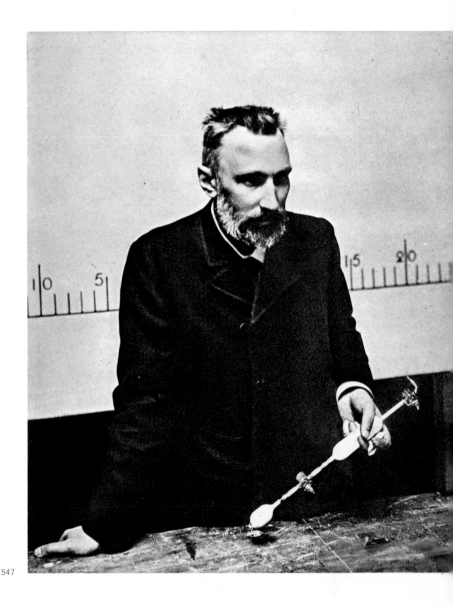

547

546

548

X-rays, radium, the wireless: the possibilities of science seem endless.

At a time when the great art-movements of the recent past—Wagnerism, Impressionism, Naturalism—seemed to be worked out and to be turning into profit-making concerns, it was hard to conceive of new fashions of seeing, hearing and thinking. Art, however, never pauses to rest.

549   Claude Debussy sought, implicitly, to contribute to music what impressionism had contributed to painting or symbolism to letters. At its first performance, *Pelléas and Mélisande*, an opera based on Maeterlinck's play of that name, was hailed as a revolutionary innovation. Debussy introduced into his music an irrational note but while affecting an exaggerated lack of constraint, he constructed his compositions with the utmost sobriety. There was soon a reaction

581   to his methods, led by Igor Stravinsky, whom Diaghilev attached to the famous Russian ballet,

550   with Nijinsky as its brightest star, in its tour of Europe. Stravinsky made his *Sacre du Printemps* the spear-head of his attack on musical impressionism. His shattering orchestral effects, his novel rhythms and sounds unknown to music shocked but conquered his hearers.

In literature, Marcel Proust was at work on a 551 masterpiece which was to put all previous forms of novel-writing out of joint. *A la Recherche du Temps Perdu* began to appear in 1913. The essential, unformulated, self-chosen content of a man's consciousness is the subject of the story. The meticulous naturalistic analysis designed to display a man in his proper setting seemed out of date after Proust, no less than the exaltations and enthusiasms of the Romantics.

The first cinema performance was given by the brothers Lumière in 1895, but it was Georges Meliès, a Parisian, who created the cinematogra- 552 phic entertainment. With the help of all sorts of devices, often complicated ones, he led his public into a magic world. It was not long before the detective story and the historical film could compete on the screen with the comic picture. After France, Italy, Germany and England produced their directors, their star-actors and their theorists of the art of the cinema. Sweden showed its first film in 1909.

Since the eighteenth century there had not been so many readers of the new books. Gabriele

With Proust, art becomes an instrument to probe man's consciousness.

architectural conception of related shapes. The subject, whether a human face or a man smoking a pipe, has to be presented in all its aspects at once. This 'cubism', which claimed among its devotees Juan Gris and Léger, shocked many but created a school, while the 'futurism' of Marinetti revolted against the tyranny of harmony and good taste. Paris, the capital of the modernists, also encouraged isolated efforts, backed by no school. Thus Modigliani revived the cult of the human face which, from Byzantium to Siena, from Lorenzetti to Botticelli, had been one of the finest themes of European genius.

556

557

552

553

554

555

557

d'Annunzio, Fogazzaro, Paul Bourget, Barrès, Anatole France and many other writers were famous throughout Europe. The Russian and Norwegian novelists were translated into all languages. Germany furnished a brilliant recruit to the naturalistic school in the person of Gerhart
553 Hauptmann, while Stefan Georg, strongly influenced by Mallarmé, became one of the great poets of his country.

All England echoed with the mocking, unsen-
554 timental tones of Bernard Shaw, a useful counter-irritant to the effusions of the patriotic school. But it was Vienna that won the laurels in the first year of the new century when, in his work
555 on the interpretation of dreams, Sigmund Freud laid down the principles of psychoanalysis, the art of coaxing into the light man's hidden forces and preoccupations, often unsuspected by himself. Freud's life work was akin to that of Proust in a different setting.

The painters also sought to create a new vision. Braque and Picasso, reacting against the tyranny of optical sensation and the extreme chromatics of the Fauves, sought to limit themselves to an

556

Freud penetrates the subconscious mind, which the Cubists illustrate.

241

558   559

This group shows the two reigning families of England and Russia with King Edward VII and Tsar Nicolas, close kinsmen, and their children

558 and grandchildren. The old-fashioned Europe of the monarchies was nearing its end, soon to pass away in a tragic display of deadly fireworks. At Sarajevo on 28th June 1914, a Bosnian student

559 murdered the heir to the throne of Austria. Thereafter for five long years, Europe was to battle in blood, hearing no voice but that of the cannon. Since the troubles of 1912 and 1913 Austria had not ceased to fear the menace of a Serbian hegemony in the Balkans. Using the Archduke's assassination as a pretext, she presented an ultimatum to Serbia on July 23rd. The Serbs were ready to come to terms, but on the 28th Austria declared war. In a few days the conflict began to spread, for it seemed that all Europe considered it unavoidable. Though the direct causes of the war were accidental, it was the fatalistic assumption that war was inevitable that caused the outbreak of hostilities, and no government was free from blame.

On 29th July Russia began to mobilise in support of Serbia. On the 30th, the German government sent an ultimatum to St. Petersburg and to Paris. On August lst Germany was at war with Russia and on the 2nd her armies invaded Luxemburg. On the 3rd she declared war against France and by the 4th her troops were already in Belgium. Great Britain went to the defence of the Belgians whose neutrality she had guaranteed. Only Italy and Roumania remained neutral.

Three million men, in approximately equal numbers on both sides, faced one another on French soil. The French army, outflanked in the north-west, yielded before the attacks of the

560 better equipped German forces who had brought

561

An incident at Sarajevo pushes Europe into the so-called inevitable war.

242

up their reserves and were following a bolder plan of campaign, and began a general movement of retreat. The German General Staff thought they could crush the French armies in a few weeks, and instead of entering Paris, they advanced rapidly on the other side of the River Marne, where a tremendous battle was fought in September. After a flank attack the French, who had thrown in their reserves and were supported by their British allies, began to drive the Germans back, foot by foot, towards the north-east. In October and November the French, Belgians and British succeeded in stabilising their front line which extended from the North Sea to Alsace, a distance of more than 400 miles. The static trench warfare which ensued was to last for more than three years. The trenches, built in curving lines to avoid being raked by flanking fire, and protected by barbed-wire entanglements, were destined to shelter during endless days and nights the hopes, the heroism and the misery of the fighting men.

561 562 563

562

560

The divisions between nations become a terrible reality: the trenches.

At Verdun, the war is revealed in all its heroism and its horror.

563

In the liquid mud of the trenches the soldiers led
564 a bestial life animated by desperate heroism.
During their protracted martyrdom the best of
the younger generation perished. The war
became 'total'. The engines of war became more
efficient and destructive. The Germans started
using poison gases in the spring of 1915, a practice
which became general. In the autumn of 1916
565 the English put their first tanks into action; this
arm, of which the allies made massive use, contributed largely to their final victory. Aircraft
were employed for observation and bombing.
Artillery, light or heavy, became more and more
important as it was adapted to trench warfare.
Lighter machine guns were introduced. Their
control of the sea enabled the British and French
fleets to establish an economic blockade of Germany and the Germans replied with the submarine
weapon. The civilian populations, often short
of food, shared in the struggle both by their moral
support and by their work in the munitions factories. Moreover the importance of women
both in economic and social life was enhanced
by the exigencies of war. In 1915 Italy declared
war on Austria and subsequently on Germany.

564

565

By the autumn of 1918 the war has swallowed up over eight million men.

Nevertheless the struggle seemed endless. The Russians, defeated by Hindenburg at Tannenberg in August 1914, were forced to withdraw from Eastern Europe in May 1915. The defeat of a small Turkish force on the Suez Canal was more than set off by the failure of the French and British at the Dardanelles. Meantime the Germans had entrusted their High Command to the hands of Hindenburg and, even more, Ludendorff, but were unable to break into Verdun. In 1916 all the combatants suffered reverses and the Austro-Hungarian Empire could no longer conceal its exhaustion. But the accumulated passion and hatred, and the sacrifices already made, were too heavy to allow any prospect of success to the peace proposals suggested by the United States, advanced by Germany, and supported by the neutral states and the Papacy.

In 1917, the aspect of the war was altered by the entry on 2nd April of the American forces on the side of Britain and France. Among the reasons for America's overcoming her isolationism were the need to re-establish her European market, her desire to impose a just and durable peace, and the constant threat to her sea-communications provided by the U-Boats. The intervention of America, greatly underestimated at first, was to have an enormous influence on the course of the war, for Russia, undermined internally, began to show clear signs of collapse. At the same time a crisis occurred in the morale of the French army, while on both sides the resistance of the civilian

567

568

566

population was wearing thin. Then in Britain and France Lloyd George and Clémenceau, both men of action, came into power, and with the arrival of the Americans, the morale of the allies was restored.

Ludendorff decided in the spring of 1918 to attempt a decisive blow. Uniting before the German avalanche, the Allies decided to entrust the supreme command to Marshal Foch. Between April and June they had to endure three fresh German attacks and Paris was once more threatened. But on 18th July two French armies drove the Germans back over the Marne, while in August, from Dunkirk to Nancy, the Allies launched a great concerted offensive. Simultaneously the allied forces based on Salonica attacked in the Balkans and the Italians captured Trent and Trieste. At last, in November, the central powers asked for an armistice. The soil of Europe was strewn with the bodies of eight and a half million men, killed in the prime of life. Europe herself had been thrown hopelessly out of gear.

568

The requirement in its constitution that any decisions must receive unanimous assent condemned the League of Nations to a régime of compromise ; but this was man's first attempt in modern times to organise the relations between states on a basis of mutual understanding.

On the other hand the war of 1914-1918 seriously constrained Europe's traditional love of liberty. In all countries freedom of thought and criticism had, during the war years, been subject to severe constraint. Obedience to commands was obligatory, and in order to bolster up the morale of the people the governments learnt how to wield the weapon of propaganda. Thought became state-controlled.

Was this the 'Decline of the West' announced by Oswald Spengler? The foundations of free capitalism had been undermined by a flood of paper money and by the interference of the State in the organization of business. Revolutionary doctrines, in sympathy with the Russian revolution, made headway in many countries and regained their lost vitality. Bolshevism was all but victorious in Germany and Hungary. Democracy was threatened by social and economic movements which the people could not control. The dictators were on their way in.

The accession to power of Mussolini after his march on Rome, October 1922, confirmed 571 the trend away from democracy. Meantime the Poles, though now, once more, they had a country of their own, found little satisfaction in their condition. The campaign against Russia dragged on until Pilsudski assumed power, brought the war to a successful end and fixed the frontiers of the country. He was openly proclaimed dictator in 1926 after a *coup d'état*.

The first state to be completely overturned was Russia. Victorious after three years of pitiless civil war, in which Europe intervened half-heartedly,
569 Lenin found himself able to establish the power of the Soviets on a solid basis. Adapting the principles of Marxism to the Russian situation, he replaced democratic parliamentarianism and the capitalist economy by a new type of state based upon the *Soviets*, consisting of a hierarchy of workers' and peasants' councils constituted in the framework of the factory, the canton, the town or the province.

At the Congress of Versailles convened in January 1919, to which twenty-seven nations sent their delegates to settle the problems of the peace, the 'Big Three', Wilson, Lloyd George and Clémenceau, found themselves obliged to revise
570 the whole map of Europe. Competing ambitions and ideals were reflected in their policy. Wilson considered that fourteen articles would be sufficient to settle all the questions, provided the frontiers were rectified in accordance with the principles of nationality, and believed that a League of Nations could provide great and small countries alike with guarantees of political independence and territorial integrity. Lloyd George's principal aim was to prevent the French from dominating the Continent, while Clémenceau felt that Germany should be rendered incapable of any future offensive. Six new states were erected on the ruins of the Austro-Hungarian Empire: Czechoslovakia, Poland, Roumania, Jugoslavia, Austria and Hungary. Germany was cut off from East Prussia by the Polish corridor. These arrangements were, after all, accepted by President Wilson and M. Clémenceau.

Does the advent of Bolschevism and Fascism mark the decline of the West?

Lloyd George and Briand welcomed with satisfaction the entry of Germany into the League of Nations in 1926, which seemed to forecast a reconciliation, in the spirit of Geneva, of yesterday's enemies. On the banks of Lake Léman the delegates of the great nations of Europe believed, during these years 1925-1930, that they were going to be able to realise in practice the theories of President Wilson. The League, which had dealt only with minor conflicts and the work of technical reconstruction, now came alive.

During the lull which accompanied the return of economic and financial stability, the most ambitious dreams were formulated by men whose proudest boast was to be 'European'. The agreements signed at Locarno on 16th October 1925 mark the zenith of political illusions. While negotiations for a perpetual peace were proceeding freely and good-humouredly, the partition of Eastern Europe was being debated as keenly as ever. Great Britain was coming to occupy the position of arbiter in this field, while Germany regained political independence as well as material prosperity. She owed this independence to Stresemann and his keen sense of compromise. His interview at Thoiry with Briand, in September 1926, could have established the basis of a final settlement of Franco-German differences if on both sides public opinion had supported the statesmen. But the exhausted public were more easily allured by spectacular programmes which left the real problems unsolved. That is what happened in the case of the Briand-Kellogg pact, born of the pipe-dreams of Briand and the U.S. State Department. In August 1928, all the members of the League of Nations signed this pact 'to outlaw war'. The pact explicitly freed the United States from any obligation to intervene in European affairs.

This was the moment for Europe to show wisdom and vitality. When Briand proposed the adoption of Coudenhove-Kalergi's plan for a United Europe, based at first on economic ties, the idea received some support from the parliamentarians of different countries, but was finally wrecked by the rising tide of totalitarianism.

The League of Nations speaks too softly to make itself clearly heard.

Dadaism, a movement born in Switzerland in 1917, raised the standard of revolt against rational thought, now declared bankrupt. The surrealists, successors to the dadaists, also repudiated rational man and the world he had constructed.

The Italian dramatist Pirandello sought to show that art was no more than a melancholy abstraction in comparison with the fleeting reality of human existence. *Six Characters in Search of an Author* caused a riot at its première in Rome in 1921. The success of *Tonight We Improvise*, written in 1930, was confirmed in 1949 when it was played in Paris and Milan by the *Piccolo Teatro* Company. The Czech writer Kafka died in 1924. His work was marked by unrelieved pessimism. The Irishman James Joyce loosened up both time and language.

In philosophy, too, the spirit of revolt was at work. Nicolas Berdiaeff desired the return of a new version of the Middle Ages to stem the invasion of the technicians. Edmond Husserl, in Germany, laid the foundations of a philosophic method in which thought, completely independent of facts, opens the door to the only true knowledge, that of pure consciousness. Martin Heidegger, more of an innovator, suggested that authentic values could be perceived only in isolation from practical contexts.

But in her distress, no less than in her revolt, Europe was passionately seeking for new reasons to believe, to hope and to create. Could not the appeasement men dreamed of be brought about by a better mutual comprehension, transcending frontiers, and by a simpler, clearer understanding of national literatures and the concepts expressed by them? While Paris was becoming the centre

574

575

576

Painters and writers look for an escape outside reality.

of a restless cosmopolitanism, which, it is true, gave fresh life to American letters, Valéry Larbaud in France, Ernst Robert Curtius in Germany and Romain Rolland in Switzerland stood out as the standard-bearers of an art and a literature which were truly European.

Other writers with messages of comfort and inspiration appealed to a public no less numerous. Norway could be grateful to Knud Hamsun for having treated with a dazzling virtuosity themes of high adventure, proud individualism and nostalgic romance which, since the days of the Vikings, had counterbalanced the prosaic realism of peasants and traders. The German philosopher-novelist Thomas Mann lent his support to the movement to improve the human condition. His political attitudes coincided with his spiritual convictions. The philosopher Bergson had, since 1897, been asserting the supremacy of intelligence over matter, clothing his creed with a vital, creative impulse and a generous ethic. Ramuz discovered in the natural beauties of the Swiss landscape the image of a way of life of a pure, almost supernatural, innocence, while Ladislas Reymont gave expression to his Polish motherland's song of hope. The German poet Rilke found in poetry the gateway to the life of the spirit. Claudel sought in his poems to recover the virile faith of the Middle Ages, overcoming the assaults of the flesh and the despair of the spirit. The *Satin Slipper*, his masterpiece, composed between 1919 and 1924 but not staged until 1943, tells how a man in sacrificing an impossible love achieves divine happiness.

To sum up, European thought in the years 1920-1930 was rebellious, exacting and hopeful.

580

577

578

579

But hope still survives in Rilke and inspires Claudel.

581

582

583

584

581 There were no less novel manifestations in the progress of music. Stravinsky abandoned the violence of his youthful method in favour of clarity and simplicity inherited from the classics, while other composers introduced into music the cult of the abstract which painters were making fashionable. In 1912 Arnold Schoenberg, a Viennese, had revolutionised music by his *Pierrot Lunaire*, composed in the twelve-tone scale, a work in which the abstract in music is pushed to its extreme limits. He was greeted as 582 a scandalous innovator. Paul Hindemith, Schoenberg's junior, still retained a measure of romanticism and abstained from the purely abstract with its contempt for sensuousness. He did not demolish, but renewed the fabric of the past and his work paved the way for a new classicism.

583 Maurice Ravel (whom the illustration shows playing a piano duet with Nijinsky) possessed a Mediterranean conception of music. His repu-

tation and influence are justified by his technical artistry, his humour, an extreme modesty in the expression of his feelings, a deep restlessness and a delicacy masked by a spirit of adventure.

Bela Bartok derived from the folk music of his 584 native Hungary the inspiration for his compositions, whose diversified rhythms and audacious harmonies entitle him to rank among the great musicians of the century.

The orchestral conductors of international reputation, such as Furtwaengler and Toscanini, 645 added lustre to the world of music.

The fauvisme of Matisse, Vlaminck, Derain and the cubism of Picasso, Gris, Braque and Léger, which were at their zenith in 1906 and 1910, did not survive as schools or movements after the first world war, but they left a rich posterity.

Fauvisme had a swarm of devotees in Dresden and Munich—art-centres which also gave birth to expressionism. This art-form seeks to strip

The twelve-tone scale lends itself to abstraction in music.

Painters favour the abstract, but Matisse and Rouault go their own way.

objects of their accidental aspects in order to express their essence. It made the reputation of the Russian Kandinsky, who pushed *fauvisme* to its extreme limit. Since 1910 he produced numerous works of an abstract, non-representative nature. The Dutchmen Van Doesburg and Mondrian followed the same path. Between 1920 and 1930 first at Dessau and then at Weimar the architect Walter Gropius, Klee, a Swiss artist, and Kandinsky trained a whole generation of painters and decorators in the principles of abstract art. At the same time the movement made progress in Paris encouraged by the influence of cubism and surrealism.

But abstract art was far from monopolising the painting of the 'thirties. Matisse, from having been a leading light of *fauvisme* and succumbing briefly to the temptations of cubism, pursued his solitary way. He employed with great skill brilliant and daring colours without relaxing the rigour and severity of his line.

Rouault makes no attempt to dazzle us with his colours. He portrays the tragedy of mankind. Chastising with the rigour of a Daumier the failings, vices and falsehoods of society, he proposes the challenging figure of Christ—the arch-victim of cruelty and violence—to point the moral. The horrors of the prolonged war inspired him to make a series of engravings—the *Miserere* series—full of dramatic intensity. One of these, the *Bella matribus detestata* is reproduced here.

Painting, with its continually revised technique, its intellectual adventures, its spiritual pilgrimage, is unquestionably the expression of the genius of Europe in this troubled age.

586

587

585

251

At this period the popularity of the cinema and its artistic merit were mainly due to the actors. Outstanding among them was Charlie Chaplin, a little English comedian who had made a success in the United States from about 1914. A succession of films like *The Kid* in 1921, *The Pilgrim* in 1923 and *The Gold Rush* in 1925 (the latter a genuine masterpiece), made Chaplin a unique figure in the film world. This little man, undaunted by all his humiliating experiences, was the

588

589

588

sole popular and universal hero thrown up by the age. Behind a façade of raillery he gave the world lessons in courage and hope.

In spite of the competition of the American screen, Europe nevertheless found competent directors. The film drama became an art—an art still voiceless, but one in which images, faces and objects were given great powers of suggestion. Between 1920 and 1927 the European nations did themselves full justice. In France, Abel Gance

invested the Napoleonic era with a romantic light. René Clair, whimsical and imaginative, recreated the atmosphere of the comedy-ballet. In Germany, G.W. Pabst, producer of *Street without joy*, in describing the miseries of post-war Vienna threw on to the screen a blend of romance and realism which won him a European reputation. Fritz Lang made a film of the *Niebelungs* full of static beauty, before producing *Metropolis*, an apocalyptic vision of the city of the future entirely dominated by its machines. Dreyer, a Dane, a leading European director, produced in France, entirely in close-ups, *The Passion of Joan of Arc* with Falconetti as the star. Among the Scandinavians, Stiller in *Gôsta Berling's Saga* revived the poetic atmosphere of Selma Lagerlöf's novel. In Soviet Russia, Eisenstein borrowed the scenario of *The Battleship Potemkin* from a well-known episode of the 1905 revolution. This film, at once violent and sober, includes the classic scene showing the massacre of the people of Odessa, when successive lines of soldiers march down the steps slowly and inexorably shooting down all before them.

589

590

By the time the film sound-track had become practicable in the United States, and had crossed the Atlantic, with revolutionary consequences to the art of the cinema, the European screen had already won notable triumphs.

590

Chaplin, René Clair, Eisenstein raise the cinema to a high level of art.

The nightmare Caesars soon turn the post-war period into pre-war years.

591 August 1933. Here we see Hitler and Goering beside Marshal Von Hindenburg, presiding over a celebration of Tannenberg Day. Hitler had carried out a revolution which was to weigh heavily on the destiny of Europe and of Germany. In the thirteen years of his ascent to power, he had reached his goal by the constitutional method of election, supported by the parties of the right and called to office by the Head of the State. He was not yet in possession of full dictatorial powers, but after a year in office he was strong enough to grasp them. Between February 27th, when the Reichstag was burnt down, and the plebiscite of December 12th, he assumed full powers, suppressed the political parties, abolished what remained of provincial autonomy, excluded the Jews from the German community and opened a concentration camp at Buchenwald to house his rebellious compatriots.

The wave which had carried him to power revealed in Germany a totalitarian tendency latent throughout Europe. The Treaty of Versailles had left all the belligerent nations unsatisfied, the winners because their victory had proved barren, and the losers, because the penalties of their defeat seemed unduly prolonged. An unprecedented financial crisis had declared itself in the United States in 1929 and quickly spread to Europe, whose liberal system of economy was based on fragile foundations.

592 The crowds who cheered Hitler at his well-drilled rallies could rely on the indifference of Europe. But no nation can make itself felt otherwise than by opposing other nations. Many people began to foresee that war would be the consequence of Versailles, the only point in doubt being how long the next pre-war period would last.

591

592

With the triumph of the dictatorships the peace is in grave jeopardy.

593

in Germany, the opposition was gagged. The intellectuals who could not or would not bow the knee to the Nazi ideology had to go into exile. Among these were Einstein, Thomas Mann and Jaspers, who were made welcome in the United States and in Switzerland. Bertold Brecht, who clung to Marxism, took refuge in many countries. The scene of his *Mother Courage* was laid in the 594 Thirty Years' War to express his horror of the tragedies which accompany all wars.

Meanwhile, France was traversing one of the gravest political and social crises of her history. The fear of Fascism, the failure to resist the successive encroachments of Hitler's Germany, the consequences of the economic crisis—all these resulted in the victory of the parties of the left in the elections of 1936 and the formation of the *Front Populaire*. The socialist leader Blum 595 became Prime Minister and found his government faced with a far-reaching series of strikes accompanied by the occupation of factories. A new social charter resulted from the conflict. It could have restored internal peace, but the people of France were more divided than ever, while no flaws were visible in the armour of the dictators.

A movement of rebellion against the Popular Front, which had also come to power in Madrid, started in Spanish Morocco on 17th July 1936 and quickly spread to Spain. Led by General Franco, it divided the country into two camps. The siege of the Alcazar at Toledo and the bom- 596

The Europe of the liberal democracies was on her way out. Since 1924 Stalin had been ruling the U.S.S.R. with a rod of iron. Dictators were enthroned, under different guises, not only in Germany and Italy, but also in Turkey, Hungary, Poland, Portugal, Yugoslavia, Austria, Bulgaria, the Baltic States and even in Greece. The unco-ordinated and clumsy attempts to prevent the different fascist régimes from uniting, the ever-closer *rapprochement* between the two dictators 593 Hitler and Mussolini, and the exaggerated claims of Hitler to rule Europe, illuminated the last years of peace with a murky, tragic glow. On 14th June 1934 Hitler met Mussolini at Venice, in preparation for the Vienna *putsch* in the course of which Chancellor Dollfuss was murdered.

It was the Ethiopian question which caused the landslide. The campaign starting in October 1935 ended in a victory for the Italians in May 1936. It brought about the downfall of the Negus of Abyssinia but no less that of the League of Nations. French policy, directed by Laval, favoured a compromise settlement acceptable to the totalitarian powers, causing a rift with the British who frowned on the imperial ambitions of Rome.

By this time Europe had become a stage for the display of passions where loyalty to a party or a political creed was of more account than patriotism. In the Fascist régimes, especially

594

254

The holocaust of the Spanish Civil War foreshadows a greater slaughter.

596

595

bing of Guernica provided scenes of heroism and
of horror. Though various European states
had asserted the principle of non-intervention,
both Nazi Germany and Fascist Italy took an
active part in the civil war. An international
brigade of volunteers brought help and encoura-
gement to the Spanish Constitutionalists, and a
few Russian detachments took part in the fighting.
When on 1st April 1939 General Franco proclaimed his victory, this ideological war had accounted for 1,200,000 victims: 450,000 soldiers and
750,000 civilians. This tragedy foreshadowed,
even in its details, the great world drama which
was drawing ever closer.

On 25th October the Rome-Berlin axis announced the indissoluble union of the Fascist and Nazi
dictatorships, while in France the efforts of the
government to stabilise the financial and economic
situation brought about its downfall.

Was Marxism the last word in political theory?
André Malraux, deeply influenced by the spectacle
of the Chinese communist revolution of 1923,
597 seemed to think not. He visited Gorki in Russia
and later joined the International Brigade in
Spain, but his philosophy, consisting of a mystical
search for intensity and aventure, lays no foundations for a political system.

597

599

It was at this critical moment in the drama of European history that the International Exhibition of 1937 made its strange, paradoxical entry on to the scene. Its promoters sought to give an account of the achievements of thought and to show that transcending national frontiers, the world republic of intellectuals had not forfeited the esteem of mankind. In honour of electricity Dufy covered an enormous canvas with figures of scientists of every race, with Europeans—Russians, English, French, Germans and Italians —in the foreground.

598

A lonely voice was heard through the grumbling of the approaching storm, that of Saint Exupéry, an airman and a writer, who became the spokesman of the great community of brothers in misfortune.

599

The great encounter was near at hand. On 12th March 1938 Hitler annexed Austria, who, had she been loyally supported by the great powers, could have continued to enjoy her well-deserved freedom. But the powers did not move. They preferred to attribute to historical necessity the suppression, pure and simple, of one of the oldest states of Europe. Pursuing his rearrangement of the map of Europe according to linguistic frontiers, Hitler came to the second item on his programme: the absorption of Czechoslovakia. The excessive centralisation practised by the Government of Prague encouraged the Sudeten Germans to revolt. No one denied that there were three and a half million Germans living in Western Czechoslovakia, but Hitler, filled with a pathological hatred for the Czechs, wanted to blot their country out. He took the chance of war in full knowledge of what he was doing, deliberately wrecked all the British attempts to find a settlement and finally won his case at the Munich conference, when Edouard Daladier and Neville Chamberlain ratified, in presence of Mussolini, the results of his blackmail, and saw Czechoslovakia deprived of her right to exist. Poland and Hungary competed for the spoils until on 15th March 1939 Hitler annexed the country to satisfy his need for vital space.

600

Then, casting his eyes eastwards, he claimed the right of access to Dantzig and East Prussia across the Polish corridor. At last the eyes of the men who had signed the Munich Agreement were opened. Paris and London counted on the support of the U.S.S.R., the fanatical enemy of Nazism, in their resolve to protect Poland, but at the climax of the crisis the world learned with stupefaction that a pact of non-aggression was to be signed between Germany and the U.S.S.R. At 5 a.m. on the morning of September 1st, German armies crossed into Poland. England and France called for their immediate withdrawal and, receiving no answer declared war on Germany on 3rd September.

598

600

Not all the goodwill of the International Exhibition could prevent war.

601

603

602

Warsaw capitulated on 27th September 1939 and the Soviet armies, who had also invaded Poland, lost no time in effecting a junction with the German forces. While the U.S.S.R., concerned 601 about the future of the 'Baltic Lake', invaded Finland in November, encountering a tough resistance, Hitler was able to operate freely in the West. After his successful invasion of Norway in April 1940, he contemptuously violated the neutrality of Belgium and Holland. Between May 10th and 15th the *Wehrmacht* smashed the Dutch army, drove the Belgians before them and breached the French front from Sedan to Namur. On 28th May the British troops, hemmed in to landward, were forced to evacuate Dunkirk by 602 sea, while endless columns of refugees choked the roads of France. On 14th June the *Wehrmacht* reached Paris. France capitulated, and 603 Hitler was now able to maintain an unbroken cordon of troops from the Bay of Biscay to the North Cape. Fascist Italy now entered the war. Hitler aimed to reorganise the Continent but in spite of appearances, the spirit of freedom was very much alive: and nowhere more so than in London during the intense bombardments of September and October, when St. Paul's cathedral was ringed with a garland of flame and smoke. 604

Winston Churchill, called to power on May 10th, took charge of the defence of Europe. His inspection of the coastal defences in company with the Mayor of Dover, seen here wearing a bowler hat, was symbolic of his heroic activities. 605

England, unprepared for the outbreak of war and still unprovided in 1939 with a conscript army, had to expect an invasion by air or sea. Churchill placed the civilian population on a war footing by creating the Home Guard, whose duty was to report enemy attacks and prevent

Refugees, armies, nations are swept away by the flood-tide.

604

infiltration. Thus Europe became familiar with
a 'Total War' far more intense than that of
1914-1918. It was no longer simply a war
involving armies confronted in battle: the civilian
populations were exposed to danger, and suffered
hunger on account of the blockade. The whole
world had once more to participate in the conflict
in order that Europe might be saved. It was the
Far East that gave the first sign that the war was
going to spread like a forest fire. On 27th September 1940 Japan signed a pact with Germany
and Italy of an aggressive character in which the
United States could read the future fulfilment of
a threat. The re-election of President Roosevelt
was pregnant with consequences. It could mean
that in the future Great Britain would no longer
be alone. In the early months of 1941 the English
counter-attacked vigorously in the Mediterranean,
in Libya and Cyrenaica where Rommel's *Afrika
Korps* was bolstering up the Italian army, and
in Ethiopia, where Haile Sellassie was fighting to
recover his throne.

The second stage of the gigantic conflict began
in the summer of 1941, when Hitler invaded
Russia and forced open a door he was never able
to close. For six months the German troops
drove ever deeper into Russia till in December
they were within a dozen miles of Moscow, where
the Soviet armies under Zhukov held them up.
Hitler tried to push on to the Caucasus in an
attempt to reach British territories in the Middle
East and thus simultaneously to defeat both of his
adversaries. He was not alone in attempting a
coup of such dimensions. In December 1941 the
Japanese in a treacherous attack destroyed many
units of the American Fleet at Pearl Harbor,
after which they induced their allies Germany and
Italy to declare war on the United States.

605

John Bull keeps a watch in England, and freedom harries murder.

606

The war now extended from the Pacific to the Caspian. By the autumn of 1942 German troops had reached the Volga and penetrated into Egypt, threatening the Suez Canal. But this same autumn of 1942 was destined to see the collapse of Hitler's strategy. On 3rd November, Montgomery's army, breaking through at El-Alamein, transformed Rommel's brilliant advance into a rout. On the 8th, American troops landed in Morocco and Algeria. On the 12th, the *Wehrmacht* launched a new offensive against Stalingrad. It was to be the last. Overwhelmed by the Soviet armies, Marshal Von Paulus surrendered on 2nd February 1943.

Meantime, Occupied Europe suffered ever greater hardships from famine and violence. Agricultural and industrial production, already seriously diminished by labour shortage, was further reduced by the massive demands of the occupying power. Opponents of the régime were liquidated by imprisonment, torture, deportation or execution. Everywhere perquisitions and reprisals were carried out and curfews imposed. Forbidden zones were created, foreigners were set to forced labour in German factories, while the German penal legislation against the Jews was ferociously enforced. Systematic deportation and subsequent annihilation accounted for the death of more than six million Jews. Poland was hardest hit by this terrible persecution. In all the occupied countries, from Norway to France and Italy, resistance groups were formed from rebels and young people who refused to work for the Germans. The network of secret channels of communication organised by the *maquis* was of great value to the armies fighting the Germans. The partisans kept in touch with their governments in exile, whose headquarters were in London. There could be found the representative of France, General de Gaulle, who crossed to Algeria after the Anglo-American landings, General Sikorski representing Poland, Dr. Benes of Czechoslovakia, the governments of King Haakon VII of Norway, of Queen Wilhelmina of the Netherlands, of Pierlot and Spaak of Belgium, and of King George II of Greece. Sometimes dissensions broke out among the partisans, foreshadowing future conflicts. Thus in Yugoslavia Tito's secret movement, supported by the U.S.S.R., gained an armed victory over the Serbian patriots owing allegiance

606

609

Terror reigns on the Continent, but its subjects are rebellious.

610

to King Peter II in London.

But nowhere was the torch of liberty extinguished. One example among millions of others is the story of Anne Frank, a Jewish girl of 13, who started to write her diary on June 12th 1942 in the upper story of an office building in Amsterdam which she shared as a hiding place with her parents and other Jewish friends. Two years later she was arrested by the Gestapo and died in a concentration camp in the last year of the war.

607

On July 10th 1943, French, English, American and North African troops, supported by units from the British Commonwealth, landed in Sicily. Their advance up the Italian peninsula was marked by numerous battles, including the many months of savage fighting for the possession of the great abbey of Monte Cassino founded in the 6th century by St. Benedict. By now the *Wehrmacht* had been brought to a standstill in Russia, defeated in North Africa and put on the defensive in Italy, while the Anglo-American Air Forces dropped hundreds of thousands of tons of bombs on the industrial cities of Germany. The bombers hit not only Berlin, Cologne, Munich, and Hamburg, but also Hitler's nerve centres in the occupied countries of Europe, which suffered seriously from the bombardments.

608

609

On 6th June 1944, an immense Anglo-American armada landed a great host of soldiers on the Channel Coast of France. This operation had been organised with unprecedented care and

610

skill. Two months later Paris, Brussels and Amsterdam had been liberated. Their numbers swelled by the French and American divisions who had marched northwards up the Rhône Valley, the allied armies under General Eisenhower reached the Rhine in December 1944.

608

From the steppes, from the sea the armed hordes press forward to Germany.

The giants sit on the ruins of Europe and divide the spoils of victory.

611

613

611 The difficult problems of the peace had already been preoccupying the allies some time before the war was over. It was the task of the Big Three—Churchill, Roosevelt and Stalin—to work out solutions. They met at Teheran in November 1943 and later at Yalta to establish a common policy effective during the transient period of instability. Did they foresee that this instability

would last for a very long time? In any case, on 26th April 1945 at 4 p.m. a new chapter of the history of Europe opened at Torgau on the Elbe, when the Russian and American soldiers made contact. They did not then meet as rivals but 612 greeted one another warmly as brothers in arms.

That at least was the mood of Eisenhower and Zhukov, the commanders of the victorious armies. 613

614

Germany lies in pieces while Russia reorganises its eastern frontier.

The unconditional surrender of Germany was signed at Rheims and in Berlin on 8th May. Roosevelt died at the moment when his policies were triumphing. Stalin had not waited till then to establish his suzerainty over the whole of Eastern Europe and in particular over Poland, whose independence had been the issue which had brought the western allies into the war.

The last bludgeon-stroke of the Second World War was delivered in the Far East. On the 6th and 9th August 1945, American atom bombs raised their monstrous mushroom clouds over Hiroshima and Nagasaki. Without them, and by the sole use of conventional arms, the world had, in six years, lost 55 million inhabitants of whom 45 million were European. Berlin had become an enormous heap of rubble.

The Soviet Union and Germany had been the hardest hit. They had each lost 10 % of their populations—25 million Russians and 8 million Germans. Civilian losses had been substantially as high as military, for extermination had been an instrument of war among all the belligerents. The technique of saturation bombing complemented the movement of the populations.

And now the essential problem was what to do with Germany. On 5th June 1945, the American, British, French and Soviet Governments published a common declaration that they were taking over the supreme authority in Germany, which was to be divided into four zones of occupation. However, the rapidity with which Russia dealt with the territories occupied by

612

Soviet armies soon gave rise to fresh tension.

In five months there was no German population left to the east of the Oder, where an area equal to one fifth of that of Germany was handed over to Poland in compensation for the territory occupied by the U.S.S.R. in the east. Between nine and twelve million Germans emigrated to the west. Austria, a meeting-point of the allied armies, was also divided into four zones of occupation with Vienna as the federal capital.

615

615

While the U.N. strives for union, the Iron Curtain enforces division.

616

Lines of barbed wire, observation posts and police patrols were to separate Eastern from Western Europe with an iron curtain. The severance was emphasised by an economy dictated by Moscow and by the refusal of the communist régimes to tolerate any kind of opposition. Agrarian reforms, often justified by the archaic conditions of land tenure, the persecution of the Catholic and Protestant Churches, and the priority accorded to industry over agriculture were among the leading characteristics of the people's republics. Only in Yugoslavia did a discord break the harmony of this concert. There, without dropping the principle of state ownership and control, the Government favoured a neutralist attitude in regard to the rival American and Soviet blocs. Though condemned to give up hope of political peace, Europe continued to furnish proof of her vitality. 618

616 Between the 17th July and the 1st August 1945 the Big Three met in conference at Potsdam to determine their policy in regard to the German problem. They declared the following points to be essential: the disarmament and demilitarisation of Germany, the liquidation of the Nazi Party and its influence, and the payment of reparations. The future political status of Germany was not defined in precise terms. The British and Americans took note (without doing more) of the revolutionary changes introduced in Eastern Europe while reserving their legal rights in respect of the ultimate delimitation of the Polish frontiers. The final status of Berlin was left undetermined. In the meantime this island in the Soviet zone was divided into four occupation zones, to which free access by air, road and rail was guaranteed. The Potsdam agreement was not long to remain a valid instrument.

Grave ideological differences soon separated the U.S.S.R. from the Western Powers. England, France, Belgium, Italy and Holland declared their solidarity with the views of the United States. But Marshal Tito had imposed communism on Yugoslavia in the winter of 1944-5, thus creating the first of the people's republics. Similarly in the different countries occupied by Russian forces Europe could observe the progressive elimination of the traditional political parties by the Communists. Poland, Roumania, Bulgaria and Hungary became in their turn people's republics. By creating the *Cominform*, the Soviet Communist Party was able to dictate a single common policy to Eastern Europe.

Greece, in spite of a rebel pro-communist government, and Finland, though still occupied, remained outside the sphere of Soviet encroachment. But Czechoslovakia did not escape.

617 Edward Benes was obliged to surrender to the communist leader Gottwald, who assumed power.

617

618

622

620

621

The United Nations Organisation (U.N.O.) preferred New York to Europe as a headquarters but it is significant that UNESCO, the international association for the preservation of the five freedoms—of movement, of residence, of religion, freedom to criticize and the free right to work—chose Paris in which to erect the striking edifice which the Spaniard Miro has enriched with a wall in many-coloured ceramic.

619

A new era had opened, that of space travel, atomic science and electronics. The U.S.S.R., who launched the first successful satellite, and the U.S.A. engaged in a keen contest in the scientific and technical fields. What was the rôle of Europe among these Titans? First, that of an initiator. In 1937, Whittle, an Englishman, had conceived the first jet-engine. The German scientists at the Peenemunde base had produced the first war-rockets; these self-propelled projectiles were used in 1944, under the name of V2's, to bombard London and Antwerp. These scientists, later prisoners of war in America or Soviet Russia, made important contributions to the staggering development in interplanetary navigation. As far back as 1924, the school of Copenhagen, led by Bohr and Heisenberg, had played an important part in atomic physics and before 1939 the European physicists Fermi, Otto Hahn, Sziland, Wigner and Joliot had discovered the theoretical principles on which the subsequent utilisation of atomic energy was based. In June 1940, by a feat worthy of these heroic times, French physicists managed to transport from Norway to England via France 185 litres of 'heavy' water—virtually the entire world stock—which was indispensable to nuclear research. In December 1942, the Italian Fermi constructed at Chicago the first atomic pile in graphite. Largely outstripped during the war, and because

620

In the field of nuclear physics and electronics many dreams are realised.

of the war, Europe subsequently developed various methods of using atomic science for peaceful ends. In 1958, at the Brussels Exhibition, an Atomium worthy of the aspirations of Europe was displayed. 621

The English biologist Fleming, who discovered in 1928 the healing properties of penicillin, opened the road for the science of antibiotics, which Oxford scientists in 1940 brought into industrial production. 622

The share of European science in the development of electronics was no less considerable. The Englishman Crookes, the German Lénard, the Frenchman Jean Perrin were the gifted precursors in this field. In 1904 J.A. Fleming patented the diode which, as the result of constant improvement, not only resulted in the radio valve but also in a host of specialised electronic tubes.

Radar, invented by the British physicist Robert Watson-Watt, protected Great Britain against invasion in 1940 and later became an essential auxiliary in all aerial navigation.

On 27th June 1926, Baird gave his first display of television. On 6th June 1954, six European television stations, from Glasgow to Naples, from Paris to Copenhagen, relayed the Feast of the Narcissi celebrated at Montreux. This was the official birthday of Eurovision. 623

In the domain of the arts Europe retained her position. The cinema, influenced by Italian neorealism of which *Bicycle Thieves* was among 624 the masterpieces, was shedding its sentimental conventionality in favour of the authentic. The tragic years, 1939-1945, had accentuated the success of existentialist philosophy. Sartre, Jaspers and Camus, each in his own way, pays tribute 625 626 to its value or preaches its extension. The necessity to rebuild did much to develop architecture. Le Corbusier born a Swiss but naturalised French, created a style and a school, of which examples are everywhere to be found and particularly in Brazil. Even industrial buildings, formerly predestined to ugliness, were now given elegant outlines, like the Olivetti works, overleaf. 627

623 624

625 626

Neo-realism is built up on the debris of illusions destroyed in the war.

Risings in Eastern Europe prove the quality of the People's democracy.

The genius of Europe continued to assert itself in all fields, although European equilibrium was still not wholly achieved. Before the progress of Soviet influence in the countries of eastern Europe, the western powers adopted, in 1948, a policy enabling Germany to recover her national sovereignty. The reply of the Soviets was to suppress all railway traffic between West Berlin and its sources of supply. This manœuvre proved fruitless owing to the air-lift maintained during eleven months by Britain and the U.S.A., 628 in memory of which this monument was erected.

On 8th May 1949, a parliamentary council adopted a constitution for the Federal Republic of Germany, granting to each of the eleven *Lander* a large measure of economy, while safeguarding the power of the central institutions.

Similarly the Soviet-occupied zone transformed itself into the German Democratic Republic, thus entering the system of people's republics sponsored by the U.S.S.R.

The announcement of Stalin's death on 5th March 1953 and the adoption by his successors of a more liberal policy caused two risings, indicating the political and economic difficulties of the communist system in eastern Europe. On 17th June 1953, Russian tanks fired on demonstrators in East Berlin, while on 24th October 1956 the population of Budapest staged an insurrec-629 tion. The intervention of Russian tanks and the ruthless suppression of the rising accentuated the rift in the European continent.

Only Austria, gradually evacuated by the four occupying powers, achieved, on 15th May 1955, liberty and independence.

628

629

627

631

The Second World War did much more than transform the map of Europe and upset the balance of political power in Europe. It also hastened a large-scale rearrangement of nationalities throughout the world. The colonial empires founded late in the nineteenth century disappeared one by one.

This disintegration started in Asia. In 1945, the French and English abandoned their concessions in China. In 1947, England granted independence to India and Ceylon. India was partitioned into two states—India for the peoples of Hindu faith and Pakistan for the Moslems. In 1948 Malaya was proclaimed independent. The elastic formula of the British Commonwealth, which became a political reality in 1926, survived as the link which united the former metropolis with the liberated nations. Burma, however, stayed outside the Commonwealth. Supported by the U.S.S.R., the Chinese communists defeated Chiang Kai-Shek's nationalists in 1949 and under the leadership of Mao Tse Tung created a new China with a population of six hundred millions. The China of Mao would soon be able to speak as an equal with the Russia of Khrushchev. 630 Indonesia, ten times more populous and fifty times larger than its former suzerain, acquired its independence in 1950.

The combined efforts of the Chinese, the English, the Japanese and the Americans brought about a trial of strength between France and a combination of communists and nationalists in Indo-China. From 1946 to 1954 France spent her strength waging a war which ended in the grim disaster of Dien Bien Phu. The treaty signed at Geneva in July 1954 recognised the full independence of all the states of the Indo-Chinese peninsula.

In the light of the emancipation of Asia, from Pekin to Saigon, from Karachi to Jakarta, the conference which was convened at Bandoeng in Java was an event of historic significance, one of the most important of the post-war period. Mr. Soekarno, President of the Indonesian Republic, presided over a conference containing delegates from twenty-nine Asian and African nations, representing populations totalling 1,250,000,000. These were sharply divided between the partisans of neutrality, the friends of the West and the pro-communists, and their discussions led to no concrete results, except to a unanimous vote expressing their determination to preserve their independence. The conference made it plain that the nations of Asia and Africa had come to realise what a counterweight their union would provide against the ambitions of the Western Powers. To act in unison was, of course, another matter.

For historical, strategic and economic reasons

630

Europe intervenes on the Suez canal but is reminded of Bandoeng.

632

England and France had maintained a hold over certain states of the Middle East. But from 1946 onward all these countries had broken away from European guardianship. Iraq, Jordan, Saudi Arabia, Syria and the Lebanon were completely independent. Nevertheless, they were subjected to the powerful and contradictory influences of the U.S.S.R., the U.S.A. and Egypt. The Egyptian monarchy had been overthrown by that same storm of feeling which in the past had so often united Islam against Europe. Colonel Nasser, the head of the new regime, aimed to create an Egyptian hegemony over all the Arab states. In 1956 he nationalised the Suez Canal. The armed intervention of England, France and Israel, the youngest of the independent nations, failed on account of the concerted opposition of the U.S.S.R., the U.S.A. and the United Nations.

631

While two North African states, Tunisia and Morocco, achieved independence in 1955, Britain and France were endeavouring to set up new political systems in black Africa. Thus in 1957 Britain granted sovereign status to the Gold Coast which became the State of Ghana. Two theories found their advocates. The first recommended a regrouping of the African states and their total liberation from European influence. The partisans of the second believed that Africa could never enjoy real independence except by close collaboration with Europe. It was in this spirit that in 1958 the men and women of the former French colonies voted for the creation of the *Communauté Française*, a free association of autonomous states grouped round France. Vast economic developments, holding promise of social progress and material benefits both to Africans and Europeans, would link Europe and Africa. The exploitation, after years of obstinate prospecting, of petroleum and gas in the Sahara, was one out of many such possibilities.

632

633

633

The African states awake to a sense of national identity.

636

634

635

At a reception held in his honour in September 1946 by the University of Zurich, Winston Churchill said: 'We have to create a kind of United 634 States of Europe. Our first step towards this end must be to set up a Council of Europe.' And so the idea put forward in Aristide Briand's memorandum of 1st May 1930 was reborn after tragic vicissitudes.

Several organisations supporting this idea came into being almost simultaneously : the European Federal Union, the Socialist Movement in favour of the United States of Europe, and Winston Churchill's United Europe Movement. Meanwhile Count Coudenhove-Kalergi's scheme for a United Parliament of Europe was resuscitated. In May 1948, the Congress of Europe was held at the Hague, giving rise to the Movement for a United Europe, with Winston Churchill, Léon Blum, P.H. Spaak and De Gasperi as its first 635 636 presidents. Simultaneously efforts throughout the West induced in governments a consciousness of the necessity to 'raise themselves above the passions that had caused the ruin of Europe'.

The nations of Europe, victors and vanquished alike, found themselves facing the gigantic task of restoring an economy bankrupted by six years of warfare. On 5th June 1947, General Marshall, the U.S. Secretary of State, had invited the nations of Europe to work out a common scheme of relief to be supported by American contributions. The U.S.S.R. and the satellite countries declined the invitation, but sixteen nations accepted and in April 1948 the Organisation for European Economic Co-operation (O.E.E.C.) was founded.

The division of the world into two blocs and the accompanying 'cold war' was soon to encourage the consolidation of Western Europe by the creation of a more comprehensive pact. On March 17th 1948, England, France, Belgium, Holland and Luxemburg (the Five) signed in Brussels a treaty of collaboration, based on the principle of collective legitimate defence, the application of which was to extend to the economic, social and cultural fields.

In 1948, when the Berlin crisis seemed likely to cause another conflict, the Five presented Washington with the scheme for an Atlantic Alliance, which Norway, Denmark, Iceland, Italy and Portugal were prepared to join. On 4th April, twelve nations, including Canada, signed the North Atlantic Treaty. The addition of Greece and Turkey in 1952 and then of the German Federal Republic brought the numbers of N.A.T.O. to fifteen. Basing their action upon the European Movement, the Five then prepared the statute of the Council of Europe, which they signed in London in May 1949. Ten other countries later subscribed to this instrument.

But over and above the diplomatic and military alliances, often of short duration, and the discussion of principles, it was necessary to pull Europe together by means of her material assets, those

637

Wedged between opposing blocs Europe is compelled to unite.

272

639

which influenced the daily life and welfare of
637 nations and individuals. Robert Schuman, the
French Minister of Foreign Affairs, proposed
placing the whole Western European coal and
steel production under a supreme authority.
The European Coal and Steel Community,
which was set up in Luxemburg on 25th July
1952, comprised six nations: Germany, Italy,
France, Belgium, Holland and Luxemburg. In
1957 these six nations signed an agreement in
Rome instituting the European Economic Community, which established a common market, and
another treaty creating the European Community
of Atomic Energy (Euratom).

Strasburg, over which fly the national flags of
638 the members of the Council of Europe, became
a meeting place and a clearing-house. Meetings
between Heads of States and government leaders
became frequent. A meeting between General
639 de Gaulle and Chancellor Adenauer was regarded
as the symbol of a time when age-old quarrels
would be forgotten.

It is not surprising that the birth of a European Community was attended by so many difficulties and hesitations. Our history, certainly
shows the existence of many common denomi-
nators. But it also shows that each nation of
this westward-looking promontory has succeeded
in creating its own culture, its own language, and
its own political, economic and social structure,
often providing an example to its neighbours and
by no means averse from spreading its own
doctrines. The ideal of today is an equilibrium
—and a very delicate one. The European Community does not rule out, on the contrary, it
presupposes, a Europe divided into nations.

638

Strasburg, former site of discord, is now the capital of hope.

644

645

640

641

Our panorama is coming to a close. Three thousand years of history compressed into one volume! But in this review of the past we can foresee the history of the future. And what our conspectus of history has recorded for us first and foremost is the diversity of Europe and her constantly creative spirit. Is it possible to affirm that some impulses in the current of European history have been stronger than others? Is it possible to pin-point certain events, certain men, certain dates, and declare that the fate of Europe depended on them? 753 BC, when Rome was founded, or 52 AD, when St Paul landed on the shores of Greece? Or 1454, when Gutenberg opened his printing works? Or 1789, which saw the proclamation of the rights of man and of the citizen? Or 1917, when the Revolution broke out in Russia, or 1945, when Russian and American soldiers shook hands on the banks of the Elbe? Dates, often a temptation for the historian, are here of only limited use. Moreover,

every nation has contributed to the light which Europe has shed upon the world since the earliest times. The philosophy and science of Greece, the Pax Romana, the France of St Louis, the golden age of Spain and of Holland, the Italy of the Renaissance, Elizabethan England, and the Germany of the romantic era, (to say nothing of more modern examples)—these have all left deep imprints on our civilisation.

Europe has never rejected anything that came to her from outside. Graeco-Buddhist art, Etruscan civilisation, the Judaic message, the skills of Tartar horsemen or of Egyptian monks, the refinements of the Arabs, the inventions of the Chinese and more recently the art of the South Seas and of Black Africa—Europe has absorbed all these gifts of Africa and Asia and enriched her new acquisitions in the use to which she has put them.

No less valuable than the creative movements within a nation and the vitalising currents from out-

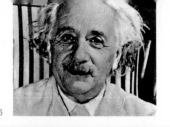

642

643

side has been the cosmopolitan cultural tradition of Europe, a tradition embodied alike in poets and painters, musicians and architects, philosophers and scientists.

As Europe has received, so has she given. She has been the heart of the world, and its countenance. From the first she has revealed the world to itself. She has brought forth a new civilisation, that of industry, which has changed from top to bottom the conditions of human life. But will Europe remain the most precious quarter of the globe, will she maintain the initiative in world history?

Today, when greatness is too often measured by material power, by population, area, wealth of raw materials, has Europe cause for envy? No, indeed, for her people do not form a homogeneous bloc: they are split up into a multitude of nations, each with its own physiognomy, its own spirit, each providing incentive for constant emulation.

640   These illustrations show a procession of pilgrims

testifying to their faith, a crowd of students, gay or   641
earnest, crowds of spectators at an air display   642
watching as new speed records are broken, throngs
of onlookers at the Olympic Games where the   643
time-honoured tradition of athletic contests is
renewed every four years. Whether it is hope which
assembles these gatherings, or duty, they are united
by a common destiny.

Standing out above the masses of men by virtue
of intelligence and genius, there are numerous individual personalities of exceptional brilliance, men to
whom Europe will continue to give birth, as she
always has. There is Schweitzer, a man of exem-   644
plary life; Toscanini, who has brought to his task   645
the power and vitality of an original mind. There
is Einstein, who showed how the courage of the   646
lonely research-worker can open all doors, even,
may be, that which leads to the absolute. And
then there is Hunt, an example of what endurance   647
and resolution can achieve.

648

The peculiar quality of Europe is well expressed in her landscapes. Like the different quarters of an immense city, her countries border on each other, from Gibraltar to the North Cape, from the Emerald Isle to the Black Sea, separate but interpenetrated.

Europe has many faces. Here, for instance, is one—that of Portugal, with its barefooted women **648** wearing their shawls, and its little white houses squatting beside the huge blocks in Lisbon's new quarters. The new has not dispossessed the old — by subsisting side by side they enrich the store of national tradition. Venice, once the dazzling metro- **649** polis of a maritime empire, continues to attract visitors to its festivals and exhibitions. Ever since the first great bankers and traders built their sump- tuous palaces along the Grand Canal and became foremost patrons of the arts, Venice has enjoyed a place in the mainstream of Europe's cultural life. Here is Zermatt, mantled with pines, in its sleeping **650** valley high in the Swiss Alps. And here, a donkey stands before one of the windmills of Greece — **651**

650   651

652

655

653

windmills turning at the breath of the same wind
as that which filled the sails of Odysseus' ship,
and those of the Argo, bound for Colchis.

652   Grenada, meantime, climbs gently up the hillside
towards the sun—Grenada, where Ahmed, the
young Moorish prince, used to caress the flowers
653   and talk with the animals. And here is London
at Christmas-time, its crowds of shoppers preparing
for the festivities with the same expectancy as that
which marked the Dickensian Christmas scene.
      The diversity of Europe and of her children can
654   never be overstressed. Here, a town in Holland
records the patient, ceaseless efforts of man against
655   the encroaching waters, while the Rhine, a river
which enshrines numberless legends, such as that
of the Lorelei, flows broad and free towards the
656   ocean. In Paris, the lighted shop-windows of the
Champs-Elysées reflect man's need for luxury and
657   beauty. Stockholm is to be ranked among the
great capitals of commerce, cities where the prosperity of a nation is forged.

657

654

656

The essential harmony of Europe is incomparable. Tradition, ceaselessly rejuvenated, vies with a future jealously seeking to outdo the achievements 658 *of the past. The amphitheatre of Mediterranean* *stone, and the powerhouse of industry, both bear* 659 *testimony to her greatness.*

And what testament of greatness is not first of all a testament of union? It is clear that the task

of the Europe of tomorrow, indeed of today, is to unite, to help, to reconcile, to save. Her different peoples, eastern and western alike—who have conquered the ocean, fertilised deserts and pushed back the boundaries of the known world—these people, who have lived through the most intense spiritual experiences, are faced now with the greatest adventure of all, the adventure of brotherhood.

TOO MANY WARS, TOO MANY EXPEDITIONS HAVE TORN THE CONTINENT. TOO MUCH EGOISM, TOO MUCH VIOLENCE HAS DISFIGURED IT. BUT IS THE SPIRIT OF THE CATHEDRAL-BUILDERS QUITE DEAD? THE WORK OF RECONCILIATION, OF REVIVING MEN'S HOPES, OF PROVIDING FOR THEIR WELFARE AND ALLEVIATING THEIR DISTRESS—THESE ARE TASKS THAT MAY WELL BE COMPARED, THOUGH ON A VASTER SCALE, WITH THAT OF BUILDING THE GREAT, MAJESTIC CATHEDRALS OF OLD.

WE LIVE IN AN AGE OF IMMENSE POSSIBILITIES: HOW WE SHALL USE THEM WE CANNOT YET KNOW. IN THE MEANTIME, A NEW EUROPE IS FORMING, SHARPLY CONSCIOUS OF THE NEED FOR COHESION.

AS ALWAYS, THE WRITERS, ARTISTS AND THINKERS OF EUROPE ARE IN THE VANGUARD OF HISTORICAL CHANGE. HER CREATIVE SPIRIT, AS LIVELY AS EVER, YET TEMPERED BY AGE-OLD TRADITION, IS ALREADY SOWING THE SEEDS OF THE WORLD'S FUTURE.

'WE WISH TO EXPLORE THE GOOD, A GREAT, SILENT COUNTRY,' SAID THE POET GUILLAUME APOLLINAIRE. LET US KEEP OUR FAITH IN EUROPE, CONFIDENT IN OUR HOPE THAT AN ERA OF JUSTICE AND BROTHERHOOD WILL SHORTLY BE REALIZED, AND THAT HER CIVILISING INFLUENCE WILL CONTINUE AS HER HISTORY UNFOLDS.

chronology

DATE	POLITICAL AND MILITARY EVENTS	ARTISTIC AND LITERARY EVENTS	ECONOMIC, SOCIAL AND RELIGIOUS EVENTS	PERSONS
BC				
5000				
			First organised states in the valleys of the Indus, Tigris, Euphrates and Nile. 11.	
4000				
3000		3rd millenium: Birth of Sumerian art in Mesopotamia. 11.	3000: Foundation of Mohendjodaro on the banks Indus. 11.	
		2600-2300: Egyptian civilisation, the Pyramids. 11.		
2500		2500: Invention of writing in China. 11.		
		2400: Cretan civilisation. Palace of Cnossos built. 13.		
2000			c. 2000: Beginning of Bronze Age in Europe. 13.	
1500	1400: The Achaeans destroy Cnossos and settle in Greece. 15.	c.1500: Spread of Mycenean civilisation in the Aegean. 14.		
	1180: The Trojan War. 15.			
1000				
900				
	850: The Etruscans settle in Italy. 26.			
800		9th century: Homer's Iliad and Odyssey. 15.		
			753: Foundation of Rome. 27.	
700			c.700-550: Greek commerce expands along the Mediterranean shores. Magna Graecia colonised. 21.	
600				
	509: The Roman Republic founded. 28.			
500		495-405: Sophocles. 19.	500-300: Beginning of Celtic civilisation. 24-25.	Pericles (499-429 BC).18
	490: Battle of Marathon between the Greeks and the Persians. 22.	480-406: Euripides. 19.		Socrates (468-400 BC). 20
	480: Battle of Salamis between the Greeks and the Persians. 22.			
450				
				Plato (429-347 BC.). 20.
		447-438: The Parthenon built. Phidias sculpts the Panathenaeae. 18.		
400			381: Foundation of Alexandria. 22.	
				Demosthenes (384-322 B.C.). 19.
				Aristotle (384-322 B.C.). 20.
				Alexander (356-323 B.C.). 22.
350				
	334-331: Alexander's conquests. 22.			
300				
		270-200: Hellenic civilisations (Alexandria-Pergamum). 23.	270: Roman expansion in Italy. 28.	
	264-241: 1st war between Rome and Carthage. 28.			
250				
	241: The Kingdom of Pergamum founded in Asia Minor. 22.			
200				
150				
	146: The destruction of Carthage. 2nd century,			
100	The Roman legions conquer Macedonia: Greece, Asia Minor, South-West Gaul, and Spain. 28.			

DATE	POLITICAL AND MILITARY EVENTS	ARTISTIC AND LITERARY EVENTS	ECONOMIC, SOCIAL AND RELIGIOUS EVENTS	PERSONS
		78 BC-14 AD: " The Augustan Age ". Summit of Roman classical art. Cicero, Caesar, Virgil, Ovid, Propertius, Tibullus, Horace.		Augustus (63 BC.-14 AD).
50	58-50: Caesar conquers Gaul. 28.			
	31: Octavius' victory at Actium. 29.	48: Library at Alexandria burns down 23.		
A D			14-37 AD: The Pax Romana. 29	The public life of Jesus.
	37-68: The conquest of Britain, under Claudius and Nero. 31.		45-67: Beginnings of Christianity. St Paul's missionary journeys. 33-34	
50			64: First anti-Christian persecutions. 34.	
	88: Construction of the 'limes' in Germany. 33. 96: Advent of the Antonine dynasty. The Roman Empire at its height. 31-32.			The Antonines (98-180). Trajan (98-117).
100		2nd century: Construction of temples, bath, arches, arenas at Arles, Nimes, Verona, etc. 31.	100: Paper invented in China. 2nd century: Roman provincial administration. Roads, bridges, acqueducts built. Roman law, language, currency, institutions spread throughout Europe 31.	
150				Hadrian (117-138). Antoninus (138-161).
200				Marcus Aurelius. (161-180).
250				
300				Constantine (274-337). 35.
	306: The accession of Constantine. 35.		313: Constantine authorizes Christianity. Edict of Milan. 35.	St Martin (316-397). 42.
350			325: Council of Nicaea. 330: Foundation of Constantinople. 35. 360: St Martin founds first French monastery. 42. 380: Theodosius' edict: Christianity the official religion.	Theodosius (346-395).
400	395: Death of Theodosius. End of Roman unity. Germanic invasions. 36. 410: Visigothic invasion. Alari csacks Rome. 36. 441: The Anglo-Saxons complete the conquest of Great Britain. 37.		432: St Patrick starts conversion of Ireland.	
450	450: Attila invades Gaul. 37. 476: The Western Empire disappears. 38. 486: Theodoric, king of the Ostrogoths, occupies Italy. 38		496: Clovis converted to Christianity. 38.	Theodoric (454-526). 38. Clovis (465-511). 38. Justinian (482-565). 39.
500	509: Clovis unites the Franks. 38. 527: The accession of Justinian. 39.	6th century: Gregorian chant. 44.	528: St Benedict found sabbey of Monte Cassino. 43.	
550			563: St Columba starts conversion of the Picts. 43.	Gregory the Great (540-604). 44.
	590-604: Pontificate of Gregory the Great. 44.		596: St Augustine starts conversion of England. 44.	
600	622: The Hegira. The beginnings of Islamic preponderance. 45.	7th and 8th centuries: the Anglo-Saxon Church, hearth of civilisation.		Mahomet (570-632).
650		653: The Koran written down.	653: The Lombards converted to Christianity.	Charles Martel (686-741). 45.
	696-708: The Arab conquest of North Africa. 45.		698: The conversion of Germany. St Willibrord founds abbey of Echternach. 44.	
700	711-713: The Arab conquest of Spain. 45.		722: St Boniface consecrated bishop of Germany. 45.	
	732: Charles Martel halts the Arabs. 45.			Charlemagne (742-814). 46-47.
750	768-814: The reign of Charlemagne. 46-47.	773: Arab numerals introduced. 54.		
	793: First Norse attacks on England. 49.	Revival of learning under Charlemagne. 48.		
800	800: Pope Leo III crowns Charlemagne emperor. 47.	c.800: Arab translation of Ptolemy's geography. 54.	802: Charlemagne administers Christian Europe: provinces organised into counties. Missi dominici. 46.	
850	843: Charlemagne's empire dismembered. Treaty of Verdun.			
	856-861: The Norsemen ravage Normandy and the Ile-de-France. 49. 862: The Hungarians invade Germany. 50.		870: The conversion of the Bulgars. 50. 878: The conversion of the king of Denmark.	
900			910: Cluny Abbey founded. 51. 911: The Norman chief Rollo baptised.	
	919: The Saxon dynasty established in Germany. 52.			Otho 1st (912-973). 52.

DATE	POLITICAL AND MILITARY EVENTS	ARTISTIC AND LITERARY EVENTS	ECONOMIC, SOCIAL AND RELIGIOUS EVENTS	PERSONS
950				Avicenna (980-1057). 55.
	987: Hugues Capet elected king of France. 52.		985: Baptism of St Stephen of Hungary. 50. 988: The Russians converted by Byzantine missionaries. 997-1035: Conversion of Hungary. 50.	
1000	1001: Stephen I receives the crown of Hungary. 50. 1017-1035: Canute, king of Denmark and England. 53. 1042-1066: Reign of Edward the Confessor.		1027: Beginning of the Truce of God. 68.	Edward the Confessor (1004-1066). 53. William the Conqueror (1027-1087). 53.
1050	1054: Final separation of Rome and Constantinople.	1065: The Song of Roland. 56. 1066: Abbey church of Monte Cassino built. 61.		
	1066: William the Conqueror crowned. 53. The Normans conquer England. 53. 1076-1077: Conflict between the Emperor Henry IV and Pope Gregory VII. 63.	1088: University of Bologna founded. 87. 1088-1130: Building of abbey church at Cluny. 57. 1093-1133: Durham cathedral built. 79. 1094: St Mark's Venice, consecrated.		
	1099: The Crusaders capture Jerusalem. 70.		1095: The First Crusade preached. 69. 1098: Robert de Molesme founds Citeaux. 61.	
1100			12th century: the Feudal system. 65 to 68. 1115: St Bernard founds Clairvaux. 61. 1118: The Order of Templars founded. 70.	
		1120: University of Paris founded. 87. 1130: Oxford University founded. 87. 1132: The abbey church of Vezelay, and Autun cathedral completed. 58.		
	1147-1148: Second Crusade (failure at Damascus). 70.			
1150	1152-1190: Reign of Frederick Barbarossa 63-70.	1155-1160: Beginnings of Gothic art. 77-82. 1160: 'Tristan and Iseult' and the 'Niebelungen' written. 67. 1163-1182: Notre-Dame de Paris built. 78. 1175-1192: Choir of Canterbury Cathedral built. 78.		St Bernard (1090-1153). 61. Frederick Barbarossa (1123-1190). 63-70. Philippe-Auguste (1165-1223). 64-65-70. Richard the Lion-heart (1157-1199). 70. St Francis of Assisi (1182-1226). 76. Frederick II (1194-1250). 72.
	1180-1223: Reign of Philippe Auguste. 64-65-70. 1189-1193: Third Crusade (death of Barbarossa). 70.	1194-1260: Chartres cathedral built. 78.		
1200	1204: Fourth Crusade. Capture of Constantinople. 72.		Early 13th century: hinged rudder invented. 99. 1208: St Dominic founds the Order of Preachers. 76. 1215: Magna Carta signed. 64.	St Louis (1214-1270). 72.
	1221: The disastrous Fifth Crusade. 72.	1220-1266: Salisbury Cathedral built. 78. 1225: Cathedral of Toledo started. 82 1232: Alhambra of Grenada started. 93.	1230: Hanseatic League founded. 86. 1232: The Inquisition entrusted to the Dominicans. 76. Consequences of the Crusades: Break-up of Feudal system, civic liberty introduced, charters, expansion of trade in the Mediterranean. 74-75-86.	St Thomas Aquinas (1225-1274). 76.
	1240-1270: Reign of St Louis. 72. 1241: Mongol expedition into Poland and Hungary. 85.	1245: Siena Cathedral started. 82.		
1250		1253: The Sorbonne founded. 87.		Marco Polo (1254-1323). 85. Dante (1265-1321) 90. Giotto (1267-1337). 90.
	1291: Swiss Confederation founded. 89.	1289: University of Montpellier founded. 88. 1290: University of Lisbon founded. 88. 1296-1304: Giotto paints Life of St Francis. 90.	1271: Marco Polo's travels in China. Oriental techniques introduced to Europe. 85.	
1300		1302-1321: Dante's Divine Comedy. 90. 1308: University of Coimbra founded. 88. 1327: Petrach's Canzoniere. 90.		
	1339: Beginning of Hundred Years' War. 92.		1347-1349: The Black Death. 94.	
1350	1365-1409: Empire of Tambulraine. 58.	1364: University of Cracow founded. 88. c.1375: Beginnings of flamboyant art. 95.		
1400		1409: University of Leipzig founded. 88. 1432: Van Eyck's Agneau Mystique. 95.	15th century: the age of the caravel. 99.	Fra Angelico (1387-1455).

DATE	POLITICAL AND MILITARY EVENTS	ARTISTIC AND LITERARY EVENTS	ECONOMIC, SOCIAL AND RELIGIOUS EVENTS	PERSONS
1450	1453: End of the Hundred Years' War. 92. 1453: (May 29th) The Turks take Constantinople. 89. 1461-1483: Reign of Louis XI of France. 47. 1492: The Catholic kings take Grenada: the end of Moorish power in Spain. 93. 1493: The New World divided between Spain and Portugal. 100.	1450: Gutenberg opens his first printing press at Mainz. 106. 1457: Donatello's St John the Baptist. 1497: First editions of ancient mss at Venice (Aldo Manuzio). 106.	1492: Christopher Columbus crosses the Atlantic and discovers America. 100. 1497: Journey of Amerigo Vespucci. 101. 1498: Vasco da Gama at Calicut. 100.	Leonardo da Vinci (1452-1519). 108. Erasmus (1466-1536). 112-113. Machiavelli (1469-1527). 98 Michelangelo (1475-1564). 108. Luther (1483-1546). 111. Charles V
1500	1503-1513: Pontificate of Julius II. 108.	1506: Bramante starts St Peter's, Rome. 108. 1508-1512: Michelangelo paints the Sistine ceiling. 108. 1516: Machiavelli's The Prince. 98.	1503: Albuquerque in the Indies. Beginning of Portuguese Empire. 100. 1507: The name 'America' given to the New World. 101. 1513: Balboa discovers the Pacific. 101. 1517: Luther's 95 theses against indulgences. 111. 1518: Zwingli preaches at Zurich. 111. 1519-1521: Cortez discovers Mexico. 101. 1519-1522: The Straits of Magellan discovered. 101. First circumnavigation of the world.	(1500-1558). 116. Calvin (1509-1564). 113 St Teresa of Avila (1515-1582). 118.
	1525: Gustav Vasa, king of Sweden. 114. 1531: Henry VIII founds Church of England. 114. 1533-1584: Reign of Ivan the Terrible. 130. 1545-1563: The Council of Trent. 115.		1531: The new Antwerp Stock Exchange. 104. 1535: The Reformation at Geneva. 113. 1539: The Society of Jesus organised. 115.	Montaigne (1533-1592). 122. (1542-1591). 118. Francis Bacon Cervantes (1547-1616). 122
1550	1555: Diet of Augsburg (to settle the religious question in Germany). 227. 1556: Charles V abdicates. 117. 1556-1598: Reign of Philip II of Spain. Spanish hegemony. 118. 1558-1603: Reign of Elizabeth of England. 120 1571 (7th October): Battle of Lepanto. 117. 1572: " Beggars " revolt in the Netherlands. 118. 1579: Union of Utrecht: formation of the United Provinces. 119. 1588: Destruction of the Spanish Armada. 119.	1563-1584: Philip II builds the Escorial. 118. 1568-1575: The church of Gesu built in Rome. 133. 1569: Mercator's map of the world. 123. 1580: Montaigne's Essays. 122. 1582: The Gregorian calendar.	1566: Royal Exchange founded in London. 139. 1577-1580: Drake sails round the world. 120. 1587: Raleigh founds a colony in Virginia. 120	St John of the Cross (1561-1626). 123. Shakespeare (1564-1616). 122. Galileo (1564-1642). 123. Rubens (1577-1640). 124 Descartes 1596-1650). 136. Bernini (1598-1680). 133. Cromwell (1599-1658). 129.
1600	1611-1632: Reign of Gustavus Adolphus of Sweden. 127. 1619: Beginning of Thirty Years' War. 127.	1603: Shapespeare's Hamlet. 122. 1605-1615: Cervantes' Don Quixote. 122. 1607: Monteverdi's Orfeo. 123. 1611: Rubens' Descent from the Cross. 124. 1623: St Peter's, Rome, completed. 133. 1631: Rembrandt's Anatomy Lesson. 135. 1632-1675: Vermeer of Delft. 135. 1636: Harvard University founded. 126. 1636: Corneille's Le Cid. 137. 1637: Descartes' Discourse on Method. 136. 1643: Molière starts the Illustre Théâtre. 137. 1647: Velasquez paints The Lances. 134-135.	1609: Amsterdam Bank. 140. 1610: Galileo's telescope. 123. 1620: The Mayflower pilgrims reach America. 126.	Rembrandt (1606-1669). 135. Corneille (1606-1684). 137 Milton (1608-1674). 138. Newton (1642-1727). 136. Leibnitz (1646-1716). 136
	1645-1676: Reign of Alexis Romanov. 130. 1648: Treaty of Westphalia. 129. 1648-1658: The Commonwealth under Cromwell. 139. 1648-1668: John Casimir, king of Poland. 130.		1649: The Quakers are founded.	
1650	1654-1660: Reign of Charles X of Sweden. 130. 1661: Louis XIV starts his reign. 132-141.	1666: Molière's Misanthrope. 137. 1667: Racine's Andromaque. 137. 1667: Milton's Paradise Lost. 138. 1675: St Paul's Cathedral built.	1651: The Society of Foreign Missions founded. 1665: The Great Plague in London.	Swift (1667-1745). 138.
	1682-1725: Reign of Peter the Great in Russia. 142.		1679: The Habeas Corpus Act guarantees individual liberty in England. 138. 1681: Pennsylvania founded. 164. 1682: Newton discovers the law of gravitation. 136.	

DATE	POLITICAL AND MILITARY EVENTS	ARTISTIC AND LITERARY EVENTS	ECONOMIC, SOCIAL AND RELIGIOUS EVENTS	PERSONS
	1683: Turks besiege Vienna. 143.			
	1688-1697: War of the League of Augsburg. 132. All Europe against Louis XIV (treaty of Ryswyck).			Handel (1685-1759). 161 Bach (1685-1750). 161.
		1690: Locke's Essay concerning Human Understanding. 138.	1689: Declaration of Rights in England. 138. 1694: Bank of England founded.	
1700	1701: Frederick I takes title of King of Prussia.		1705: Newcomen's pump. 151.	Voltaire (1694-1778). 149. Tiepolo (1696-1770). 155. Franklin (1706-1790). 165
	1713: Treaty of Utrecht. 132-145. 1715: Death of Louis XIV, accession of Louis XV. 146.			Rousseau (1712-1778). 149-166.
		1719: Defoe's Robinson Crusoe. 168. 1721: Watteau's L'Enseigne de Gersaint. 1724: Bach's St John's Passion. 161. 1726: Swift's Gulliver's Travels. 138.	1719: Beginnings of industrial developments in Lancashire. 168.	Kant (1724-1804). 150.
	1740-1780: Reign of empress Maria-Teresa. 145. 1740-1786: Reign of Frederick II of Prussia. 146.		1735: Abraham Derby uses coal for smelting. 151.	Haydn (1732-1809). 162. Washington (1732-1799). 165.
		1742: Young's Night Thoughts. 166. 1744: Hogarth's Marriage à la Mode. 154.	1748: The ruins of Pompeii discovered (Winckelmann) 150.	Goya (1746-1828). 175. Goethe (1749-1832). 167.
1750		1751: First volume of the French Encyclopédie (d'Alembert, Diderot). 148.	1755: Lisbon destroyed by an earthquake. 140.	
	1756-1763: Seven Years' War. 146.	1760: Macpherson, Poems of Ossian. 166.	1760: The Enclosures in England. 168.	Mozart (1756-1791). 162. Schiller (1759-1805). 167.
		1761: Rousseau's Nouvelle Héloïse. 149.		
	1762-1796: Catherine II, empress of Russia. 147.	1762: Gluck's Orfeo. 162. 1762: Rousseau's Social Contract. 149.		
	1763: Treaty of Paris. 146.	1764: Voltaire's Dictionnaire Philosophique. 149.		
			1767: Watt's steam engine. 168. 1768-1771: Cook's first voyage. 150.	
	1772: First partition of Poland. 147.	1774: Goethe's Werther. 167.		Napoleon (1769-1821). 172-176. Beethoven (1770-1827). 167. Turner (1775-1851). 179.
	1776: 4th July : Independence of the United States. 164. 1783: Treaty of Versailles. 165.	1785: Mozart's Marriage of Figaro. 162.	1776: First use of rail-ways. 190. 1783: Montgolfier's balloon experiments. 151. 1785: Blanchard crosses channel by balloon. 151. 1786: Galvani's experiments. 151.	
	1789 (5th May): The States-General meet in Paris. 170. 1789 (14th July) Capture of the Bastille. 168.		1789: (26th August) Declaration of the rights of man and of the citizen. 170.	Byron (1788-1824). 178. Shelley (1792-1822). 178.
	1793 (21st January): Louis XVI guillotined. 171. The Reign of Terror in France. 171. 1793 (April): The first anti-French coalition. 171.	1794: Goethe and Schiller. The Romantic Movement in Germany. 167.	1793: Metric system adopted in France. 172.	
	1795 (August to November): The second coalition. 172.	1798: Haydn's Creation. 162. 1799: Birth of Pushkin, Balzac, Heine.	1796: Jenner starts his vaccine experiments. 206. 1798: Malthus's Essay on the Principle of Population. 193	Schubert (1797-1828). 181. Leopardi (1798-1837). 179. Mickiewicz (1798-1855). 179. Balzac (1799-1850). 179.
1800			1800: Volta invents the electric battery. 187. 1800: Gas-light introduced.	
	1802 (25th March): Treaty of Amiens between France and England. 173.		Early 19th century: rise of English textile industry. 188.	Victor Hugo (1802-1885). 179.
	1804 (8th May): Napoleon proclaimed Emperor. 173.	1804: Schiller's William Tell. 1804: Beethoven's Eroica symphony. 167.		
	1805: Napoleon, king of Italy. Third coalition. 174. 1805: Battles of Trafalgar and Austerlitz. 174. 1806: Berlin Decrees. Continental blockade. 175.			Mazzini (1805-1872). 193.
	1807: Treaty of Tilsitt. 175. 1809: Fifth Coalition. Battle of Wagram. 175. 1809-1848: Metternich, Chancellor of Austria. 177-194.	1807-1808: Fichte's Speeches to the German Nation. 175.		Garibaldi (1807-1882). 199.
		1810: University of Berlin founded. 1812: Byron's Childe Harold. 178.	1810: Krupp works founded. 188	Cavour (1810-1861). 199. Chopin (1810-1849). 181. Dickens (1812-1870). 206· Wagner (1813-1883). 230.

DATE	POLITICAL AND MILITARY EVENTS	ARTISTIC AND LITERARY EVENTS	ECONOMIC, SOCIAL AND RELIGIOUS EVENTS	PERSONS
			1814: Stephenson's locomotive. 190.	
	1815: The Hundred Days. Waterloo. 176.			Bismarck (1815-1898). 210 Marx (1818-1883). 213.
			1819: Atlantic first crossed by a steamboat. 187.	
	1821: Greek insurrection. 185.			Dostoievsky (1821-1881). 233.
	1822: Brazilian independence proclaimed. 185.			Pasteur (1822-1895). 220.
		1826: Leopardi's Canti. 179.		
		1828: Berlioz's Symphonie Fantastique. 182.		
1825	1830: July revolution in France. Fall of Charles X. 185.	1830: Victor Hugo's Hernani. 179.	1830: Faraday's experiments.	J. Verne (1828-1905). 819. Ibsen (1828-1906). 233.
	1830: Belgian independence. 185.		1830: Manchester-Liverpool railway opened. 190.	
			1832: English Reform Bill.	
	1834: the general Zollverein established. 187.		1834: Slavery abolished in the English possessions. 197.	Brahms (1833-1897). 230
		1835: The Kalevala, collection of Finnish folksongs.	1835-1843: Construction of railway networks throughout Europe. 190-191.	
		1843: Wagner's Flying Dutchman. 230.		Moussorgski (1839-1881). 230. Zola (1840-1902). 234. Grieg (1843-1907). 231. Nietzsche (1844-1900). 233. Gauguin (1848-1903). 236.
	1844: Mazzini founds " Young Europe ". 186.			
	1848: Liberal revolutions in the Italian states. Revolution at Vienna, and in the Germans tates. Revolts against the Austrians in Bohemia and Moravia. 193-196.		1848: Slavery abolished in the French possessions. 197.	
	1849: Liberals quelled in Italy. 195.	1849-1850: Dicken's David Copperfield. 206.		Strindberg (1849-1912).233.
1850			1850: Reuter agency founded in London. 203.	
	1851: Liberals quelled in Germany. 196.	1851: Verdi's Rigoletto. 230.		Van Gogh (1853-1890). 234. Freud (1856-1939). 241. G.B. Shaw (1856-1950). 241. Joseph Conrad (1857-1920). Bergson (1859-1941). 249
	1854-1856: Crimean War. 198.			
		1857: Baudelaire's Les Fleurs du Mal. 231.		
	1859: Battles of Magenta and Solferino. 199.	1859: Darwin's The Origin of Species. 212.		
	1859-1861: Cavour achieves Italian unity. 199.			
	1860: Lincoln President of the U.S.A. 214.			Hamsun (1860-1952). 249.
	1860: Anglo-French expedition in China. 215.			
	1861-1865: American Civil War. 214.			
		1863: Renan's Life of Jesus. 212.		d'Annunzio (1863-1938). 240.
			1864: Foundation of the 1st Internationale. 213.	
			1864: Foundation of the Red Cross. 199.	
	1866: Battle of Sadowa. 210.			Kipling (1865-1936). 233. H.G. Wells (1866-1946). 233. Croce (1866-1952). Pirandello (1867-1936). 248. Gorki (1868-1936). 255. Claudel (1868-1955). 249 Lenin (1870-1924). 246. Proust (1871-1922). 240.
		1867: Karl Marx' Das Kapital. 213.		
			1869: Suez Canal inaugurated. 215.	
	1871: Foundation of the German Empire. 210.			
		1873-1877: Tolstoy's Anna Karenina. 232.		
1875		1874: Impressionism (Monet). 236.	1874-1877: Stanley's African expedition. 216.	Churchill b. 1874. Mann (1875-1955). 249 Rilke (1875-1926). 248. Stalin (1879-1953). 254. Picasso (b. 1881). 241.
		1876: Renoir's Le Moulin de la Galette. 236.		
	1882: Triple Alliance: Germany-Austria-Italy. 228			
			1883: Deprez contrives long-distance transmission of electricity. 221.	Mussolini (1883-1945
		1884: Nietzsche's Thus Spake Zarathustra. 233.		
			1885: Pasteur's vaccine. 220.	
			1886: Hertz discovers electro-magnetic waves. 239.	
			1886: Daimler's motor. 238	
			1891: The Encyclical Rerum Novarum. 229.	Hitler (1889-1945). Eisenhower (b. 1890).
			1895: Nobel Peace prize instituted. 22.	
			1895: The origins of the cinema (Lumière brothers). 240.	
			1896: Modern Olympic Games started.	
	1898: The Fashoda incident. 226.			
	1899-1902: The Boer War. 224.			
1900	1900: British Labour Party founded.	1900: Freud's Interpretation of Dreams. 241.	1900: Planck's Quantum theory. 239	
		1902: Debussy's Pelleas and Melisande. 240.		
	1904-1905: Russo-Japanese War. 227.			
		1905: The Fauves (Matisse, Derain, Dufy). 251.	1905-1915: Einstein's work on relativity. 239.	
	1907: Triple Entente: Britain, France, Russia. 229.			
			1909: Anglo-Iranian Oil Co. founded.	
		1910: Cubism (Picasso, Braque). 241.		
		1910: Futurism in Italy, Expressionism at Munich. 251.		

DATE	POLITICAL AND MILITARY EVENTS	ARTISTIC AND LITERARY EVENTS	ECONOMIC, SOCIAL AND RELIGIOUS EVENTS	PERSONS
	1912-1915- War in the Balkans. 229.			
	1914: World War I breaks out. 242.			
	1914: First battle of the Marne. 243.			
	1915: Italy enters the war. 244.			
	1917: The U.S. enters the war. 245.			
	1917: October revolution in Russia. 246.			
	1918 (November 11th) : Armistice signed. 245.			
	1919: Peace Conference opened in Paris.	1919: Proust's A l'ombre des jeunes filles en fleur.	1919: Rutherford's experiments with the atom.	
	1919: League of Nations established. 246.			
1920	1919: Treaty of Versailles. 246.			
		1921: Pirandello's Six Characters in Search of an Author.		
	1922: Mussolini comes to power. 247.	1922: James Joyce's Ulysses.		
	1922: The U.S.S.R. is formed.			
		1924: Eisenstein's The Battleship Potemkin.		
	1925: The Locarno pact. 247.	1925: Charlie Chaplin's The Gold Rush.		
	1928: The Briand-Kellog pact. 247.		1928: Fleming discovers penicillin.	
	1933: The Nazi party in Germany. 253.	1933: Malraux' La Condition Humaine.		
	1935: Italy attacks Abyssinia. League of Nations sanctions against Italy. 254.			
	1936: German re-occupation of Rhineland.			
	1936: Spanish Civil War begins. 255.			
	1936: Mussolini proclaims Rome-Berlin axis. 255.			
		1937: Paris exhibition.		
	1938: German troops invade Austria.			
	1938: Munich treaty. 257.			
	1938: German annexation of Sudetenland. 257.			
	1939: Britain and France recognise Franco government. End of Spanish Civil War. 255.			
	1939: Hitler invades Czechoslovakia. Italy annexes Albania. 257.			
	1939: Russo-German pact. Germany invades Poland. 257.			
	1939: (3 September): Opening of World War II. 257.			
1940	1940: France overrun. Battle of Britain. 258.			
	1941: Hitler invades Russia. Japan bombs Pearl Harbor. 259.			
	1942: Battle of El-Alamein. Battle of Stalingrad. 260.			
	1943: Allied landings in Sicily and Italy. Conference at Teheran. 262.			
	1944: Yalta Conference. 262.			
	1944: Allied landings in France. 261.			
	1945: Germany surrenders. 262.			
	1945: United Nations Charter. Potsdam agreement. 264.			
	1945: Atom bombs used against Japan. Japanese surrender. 262.			
	1947: Independence of India, Pakistan and Burma. 270.			
			1947: Conference in Paris on Marshall Plan. 272.	
	1948: Communist coup d'état in Czechoslovakia. 264.			
	1948: State of Israel founded. 271.			
	1948-1949: Berlin blockade. 269.			
			1948: W.E.U. and O.E.E.C. inaugurated. 272.	
	1948: Congress at the Hague. 272.			
	1949: Communist victory in China. 270.			
	1949: Atlantic Pact signed. 273.			
	1949: Council of Europe statute signed. 273.			
1950	1950: Indonesian independence. 270.			
	1950: Korean War begins.			
	1952: Nasser comes to power in Egypt. 271.			
			1952: European Coal and Steel Community. 273.	
	1953: Riots in Berlin. 269.			
	1954: Indo-Chinese independence. 270.			
	1955: Independence of Morocco and Tunisia. 271.			
	1955: Occupation troops withdrawn from Austria. 269.			
	1955: Afro-Asian conference at Bandung. 270.			
	1956: Egypt nationalises the Suez canal. 271.			
	1956: Hungarian revolution. 269.			
			1957: Common Market treaty signed at Rome. 273.	
			1957: U.S.S.R. launches first Sputnik. 266.	
	1958: Ghana acquires sovereignty. 271.	1958: Brussels International Exhibition. 266.		
	1958: De Gaulle returns to power in France.			
	1959: Geneva Conference on Germany.			

index of illustrations

Pages 9/20

1. The rape of Europa by Francesco di Giorgio (1439-1502) — Musée du Louvre (**Ektachrome Franceschi**). 2. Map of Europe in relief (**Geographical Projects Ltd, London**). 3. Carved head of bearded man — Mohandjo Daro, India, 2600-2300 BC (**Larkin Bros**). 4. Sumerian bas-relief — Detail: the king of Lagash, Our nina, carries on his head bricks for the foundation of a temple, 2000 BC — Musée du Louvre (**Franceschi**). 5. The three great pyramids of Cheops, Chephren and Mykerinos (2525-2425 BC) at Giza, Egypt. In the foreground, the little pyramids of the queens of Mykerinos (**Aerofilms Ltd**). 6. Female statuette of the aurignacian era — Willendorf, Austria. 7. Head of a bull — Lascaux caves, France. Fresco from ceiling of the great hall (**Pierre Ichac**). 8. Stone circle at Stonehenge, England (**Aerofilms Ltd**). 9. Archer in bronze — Archaeological Museum, Cagliari, Sardinia (**Yan**). 10. Female figure known as 'La Parisienne', fragment of wall painting from the palace of Cnossos, Crete (1600-1500 BC). 11. Prince with a crown of feathers, known as 'of The Fleurs de Lys' — Relief in polychrome stucco (1600-1500 BC), palace of Cnossos, Crete. Discovered by Sir. A. Evans. 12. Wall painting of a bull fight (1550-1450 BC) from palace of Cnossos, Crete — Museum of Candia (**Association Guillaume Budé**). 13. Interior of tomb, known as 'the Treasury of Atreus' — Mycenae, Greece (**Boissonnas, Geneva**). 14. Golden mask (VIth century BC) — Mycenae, Greece (**Marburg**). 15. Warriors — Detail from a vase of the Creto-Mycenean period — National Museum, Athens (**Marburg**). 16. Ulysses and the Sirens — Detail from a vase — British Museum. 17. The Acropolis, Athens (**Boudot-Lamotte**). 18. Ajax and Achilles playing dice — Detail from a vase — Musée du Louvre (**Ektachrome Franceschi**). 19. Temple of Athena Nike, the Acropolis, Athens (**Jean Roubier**). 20. Mounted Ephebes — Procession at the great pan-Athenian festival — Detail from the western frieze of the Parthenon. British Museum. 21. Hermes — Painting on a vase. S.A. (**Hirmer**). 22. Discobolos — Detail from a Greek amphora (circa 490 BC) — Vatican Museum, Rome (**Alinari**). 23. Bust of Aristophanes — National Museum, Rome. 24. Theatre of Dionysus, Athens (VIth century BC) (**Boudot-Lamotte**). 25. Demosthenes — S.A. 26. Athenian voter's pebble, in metal — Petit Palais, Paris. 27. Head of Socrates — British Museum. 28. Plato and Aristotle — Detail from 'The School of Athens' by Raphael — The Vatican (**Anderson**).

Pages 21/30

29. Temple of Segesta, Sicily, seen from the Greek theatre (**Viollet**). 30. Person holding distaff, emblem of the industry of purple cloth at Tarentum. Coin of Tarentum, southern Italy, IVth century BC — Cabinet des Médailles — B.N. 31. Carriage drawn by mules — Coin of Rhegium, southern Italy, IVth century BC — Cabinet des Médailles — B.N. 32. Alexander fighting — Mosaic from Pompeii; detail from the Battle of Darius — Museum of Naples (**Anderson**). 33. Head of Devato — Graeco-Buddhist art — Musée Guimet, Paris (**Giraudon**). 34. The Pharos at Alexandria, Egypt — XVIIth century print. 35. The astronomer Ptolemy as king of Egypt, with his bride Astronomy — Manuscript from the monastery of Alderbach, early XIIIth century — M.St. (**Marburg**). 36. Gaul killing his wife — School of Pergamum — Museo delle Terme, Rome (**Chris Marker**). 37. Hermaphrodite — School of Alexandria — National Museum, Rome (**Anderson**). 38. Stone dwelling in the Celtic tradition — Basses-Alpes, France (**Roubier**). 39. Gallerus oratory, east of Smerwick Harbour, Eire, built in the VIIIth century in the tradition of Celtic dwellings — (**Co. Kerry Department of External Affairs, Dublin**). 40. Celtic head from Mseche Zehrovice, Czechoslovakia (**Giraudon**). 41. Bust of a Celtic warrior — Museum of Nîmes, France (**J. Roubier**). 42. Female statuette in bronze — Ancient Gaul — Musée historique de l'Orléanais, Orléans, France (**J. Roubier**). 43. Huntsman and dog pursuing a boar — Ceremonial chariot found at Merida, Spain, end of 1st millenium (**Giraudon**). 44. Ceremony with human sacrifice — Vase of Gundestrup — Copenhagen Museum, Denmark. 45. Gaulish coin — Solar boat — Cabinet des Médailles — B.N. 46. Etruscan gateway adorned with three heads — Volterra, Italy (**Boudot-Lamotte**). 47. Etruscan dancer in bronze — Cabinet des Médailles, B.N. (**Franceschi**). 48. Bust of a man, in terracotta — Ist century BC — Etrusco-Roman — Villa Giulia, Rome (**G.F.N.**) 49.

The she-wolf suckling Romulus and Remus, known as 'The Wolf of the Capitol' **(Giraudon).** **50.** Map of Imperial Rome — A XVIth century reconstruction. **51.** Gaulish captives — Monument at Carpentras, France **(J. Roubier).** **52.** Cavalry — Detail from a Gallo-Roman sarcophagus at St Trophime d'Arles, France **(J. Roubier).** **53.** Bust in basalt of Julius Caesar — Museum of Berlin **(Alinari).** **54.** Augustus — Vatican Museum **(Alinari).** **55.** Ethiopian slave in bronze — Cabinet des Médailles, B.N. **(Franceschi).** **56.** Boat laden with casks on the Moselle — Landesmuseum, Treves, Germany **(J. Roubier).** **57.** The payment of the tribute — Ibid. **(J. Roubier).** **58.** 'The Great Cameo of France', apotheosis of Augustus and his family. In the centre: Tiberius, Livia, Germanicus, Antonia, Caligula, Agrippina and Drusus. Cabinet des Médailles, B.N. **(Franceschi).**

Pages 31/40

59. Aqueduct at Segovia, Spain **(Sougez).** **60.** Arles, France — Aerial view: the theatre, the arenas, the Rhône **(Yan).** **61.** Winter — Mosaic in the Roman villa at Bignor, England **(H.P.L.)** **62.** Hexagramme decorating the synagogue of Tell Houm (Capharnaum?) beside Lake Galilee, Israel **(Frédérique Duran).** **63.** Adam and Eve after the fall — Bronze gate of Hildesheim cathedral, Germany, 1015 **(Marburg).** **64.** The Christ of Anastasia striking down death in chains — XIth century mosaic — Church of Daphni, Greece **(Alinari).** **65.** St Paul preaching — XIVth century ivory — Musée de Cluny, Paris. **66.** St Peter — Miniature from the Hours of Marguerite d'Orléans, 1426, B.N. **67.** Sacred fish carrying in a basket the eucharistic species — Fresco in catacomb of St Callixtus, Rome. **68.** Constantine — Medal, B.N. **69.** The baptism of Constantine — Detail from the frescoes in the chapel of the ss Quatro Coronati, Rome **(G.F.N.)** **70.** The finding of the Holy Cross — Miniature, B.N. **71.** The roman cavalry attacks the Sarmatian cavalry — Detail from Trajan's Column, Rome **(Alinari).** **72.** Hadrian's wall, built about 124 AD to protect the north of England against the incursions of the Picts from Caledonia. Northumberland, England **(H.P.L.).** **73.** Panther adorning a shield, from a tomb in Kouban, U.S.S.R. — Scythian, VIIth-VIth century BC **(Marburg).** **74.** Horseman, from period of the Barbarian invasions — Bas-relief, Museum at Halle, Germany **(Marburg).** **75.** Map of the invasions by Michel Fontaine. **76.** Attila — Medal in the collection of the emperor Rudolph II (1576-1611) in the Cabinet of Vienna. **77.** "The Triumphal Way", Roman ruins **(Mario Ruspoli).** **78.** Ostrogoth eagle **(Rheinisches Bildarchiv, Cologne, Germany).** **79.** Iron crown of the Lombard kings, in the Treasury, Monza, Italy. **80.** Justinian — Detail of mosaic in San Vitale, Ravenna, Italy, VIth century. **81.** Theodora — Ibid. **82.** The horses of St Mark's, Venice **(J. Roubier).** **83.** Monastery of St Paul, Mount Athos, Greece **(J. Lang).**

Pages 41/50

84. The offering of the empress Theodora — Mosaic in San Vitale, Ravenna, Italy **(Ektachrome Giraudon).** **85.** Christianised dolmen in Brittany, France **(J. Roubier).** **86.** St Martin sharing his cloak — Church of St Martin aux Bois, France **(Fortier).** **87.** Gospel book, from the abbey of St Willibord, Echternach, Luxemburg — Irish art, circa 690. Miniature of St Matthew — B.N. **88.** Chalice from Ardagh, Eire. 750. Dublin, National Museum. **89.** St Benedict (left) and St Maurus — Miniature of St Matthew — B.N. **90.** St Willibord — German late XVth century woodwork. **91.** The mass of St Gregory — Church of St Mary of the Fields, Swert, Germany. **92.** Tombstone at Niederdollendorf, VIIth century. A man surrounded by the symbols of pagan mythology, notably the serpent. Landesmuseum, Bonn, Germany **(Marburg).** **93.** St Boniface baptizing-Sacramentary of Fulda (975) — Library of Göttingen University **(Retzloff).** **94.** Charlemagne — Cabinet des Médailles, B.N. **(J. Roubier).** **95.** Charlemagne presents to the Virgin the cathedral of Aix-La-Chapelle — Cathedral Treasury, Aix-la-Chapelle, Germany — Reliquary of Charlemagne (circa 1200-1215) **(Marburg).** **96.** Charlemagne crowned in St Peter's, Rome — Miniature by Jean Fouquet, Grandes Chroniques de France, circa 1460. Miniature, B.N. **97.** The Ebon gospel-book, opening of the chapter-index for St John's gospel — Carolingian manuscript, IXth century — Epernay library — A.Ph. **98.** St John the Evangelist — Gospel-book of Charlemagne, the work of the painter Godescalc, circa 780 — Miniature, B.N. **99.** St Adalbert celebrates mass before the Prussians — Bronze door, Gnesen cathedral, Poland, early XIIth century **(Marburg).** **100.** Combat between the Russians and the Bulgars — Slav manuscript in the Vatican library. **101.** St Stephen — Detail from the altar to Mary (1470-1480) — Zipser Kapitel, Dom St Martin, Germany **(Marburg).** **102.** Crown of St Stephen of Hungary — XIth century, Budapest treasury **(Marburg).**

Pages 51/60

103. The storm at sea — Gospel-book of Abbess Hilda von Meschede — early XIth century — Cologne **(Retzlaff).** **104.** The symbol of the lamb — Detail of a sculpture, Abbey of Cluny **(J. Roubier).** **105.** Otho III enthroned — Otho III's gospel-book (circa 1000) M. St **(Marburg).** **106.** Homage of four nations: Slavonia, Germania, Gallia and Roma — Otho III's gospel-book (circa 1000) M. St **(Marburg).** **107.** The first Capets — Statues at the north entry of St Denis cathedral, France **(A.P.R.).** **108.** Duke William's horsemen fighting the inhabitants of Dinan — Queen Matilda's tapestry, Bayeux Museum, France **(A.Ph.).** **109.** The debarkation of the horses — Ibid. **110.** Wido brings Harold to Duke William — Ibid. **111.** King Harold is killed at the battle of Hastings; Harold pulls the arrow from his eye, then falls beneath the blows of a Norman horseman — Ibid. **112.** The mosque at Cordoba, Spain **(Boudot-Lamotte).** **113.** Bucket-Wheel near Murcia, southern Spain **(Yan).** **114.** Moorish and Christian minstrels singing together — Miniature from the manuscript of the 'Cantibas de Santa Maria' — Library of the Escorial, Spain. **115.** Chess players in a tent — Manuscript in the Escorial, Spain. **116.** Avicenna's 'Canon Medicinae', translated from the Arab into Hebrew — XIVth century miniature — Museo Marsili, Bologna, Italy. **117.** Siege of Pampeluna — Reliquary of Charlemagne, Cathedral Treasury, Aix-la-Chapelle, Germany, 1200-1215 **(Marburg).** **118.** Pilgrims — Latin bible, 1435 — Landesbibliotek, Karlsruhe, Germany **(Marburg).** **119.** St James — XVIth century, church of Varennes l'Arconce, France **(Franceschi).** **120.** St James — Wood carving, lower Rhine, XVth century — Stadt Gallerie, Frankfurt-on-Main, Germany **(Marburg).** **121.** Charlemagne's window, Chartres Cathedral — Detail. **122.** Cluny Abbey, France **(J. Roubier).** **123.** Church of Halberstadt, Germany, D.K. **124.** Building a church — Miniature from a Catalan bible, Xth or XIth century. B.N. **125** Tympanum of the inner central portico at Vezelay — Detail: Pentecost, or the dispersal of the Apostles. Above, figures of distant and legendary peoples. **126.** Capital of a pillar in Canterbury Cathedral, England, 1070-1180 **(B.T.H.A.).** **127.** The Devil and the Rich Man — Capital of a pillar in Autun Cathedral, France, XIIth century. **128.** Dance of Salome — Detail of the bronze pillar of the bishop Bernward, XIth century, Hildesheim Cathedral, Germany **(Marburg).** **129.** Two old men of the Apocalypse, with zithers and cups, and above them the angel of St Matthew — Fresco in St Martin de Fenollar, French Pyrenees **(Editions du Zodiaque, Yan).** **130.** Tournai Cathedral, Belgium **(Gus Poncin).** **131.** Pisa Cathedral, Italy **(Boudot-Lamotte).**

Pages 61/70

132. Monastic scribe — Miniature, B.N. **(Giraudon).** **133.** Woodcutters, lay and religious — Manuscript from Cîteaux, 1111, Municipal Library, Dijon, France (A.Ph.) **134.** Monk harvesting — Ibid. **135.** St Bernard of Clairvaux teaching his disciples in Paris — Miniature of Jean Fouquet — Musée Condé, Chantilly, France **(Giraudon).** **136.** Abbey of Montecassino — Miniature — Vatican Library, Rome. **137.** The Emperor of Germany, Henri IV (1056-1106), between his sister, Countess Matilda, and St Hugh, Abbot of Cluny, at Canossa, 1077 — XIIth century manuscript — Vatican Library, Rome. **138.** Bust of Frederick Barbarossa — XIIIth century reliquary, church of Kappenberg, Germany **(D.K.).** **139.** Pope Alexander III blesses the Emperor kneeling at his feet — Fresco by Spinello Aretino in the Palazzo della Signoria, Siena, Italy **(Alinari).** **140.** Edward I of England — Seal — Archives de France. **141.** Philippe Auguste — Miniature from the Chroniques de Hainaut — Royal Library, Brussels, Belgium. **142.** Murder of Thomas Becket — Miniature, 1455 — Manuscript from the B.N. **143.** Caerphilly Castle, Wales — XIIth century **(B.T.H.A.)**
144. Château-Gaillard and the Seine, France **(Photothèque française).** **145.** Marksburg, near Branbach on the Rhine, Germany **(D.K.).** **146.** Stag Hunt — Miniature from the Manesse song-book, circa 1300 —Heidelberg, University Library. **147.** Castel San Giorgio — Ducal palace, Mantua, Italy — XIVth century **(Boudot-Lamotte).** **148.** Castle of Guimaraes, birthplace of the first king of Portugal in 1110 **(Yan).** **149.** A noble hunting with a falcon — Miniature from the Manesse song-book, circa 1300 — Heidelberg, University Library. **150.** Entertainment with music and dancing — Miniature from the Manesse song-book. **151.** Scene of courtly love: The offering of a heart which the Lady pierces with an arrow — French ivory, XIVth century **(A.Ph.).** **152.** Scene from a romance of chivalry: The Holy Grail is brought to the table of the Fisher-King — Miniature from the Roman de Perceval le Gallois by Chrétien de Troyes — XIVth century. B.N. **153.** Accoutrement of the Knight — Manuscrit in the British Museum, London. **154.** A knight and his lady — Miniature in the British Museum, London. **155.** A knight receiving communion — Rheims Cathedral, detail from the back of the façade **(J. Roubier).** **156.** Knights in combat — German ivory, late XIIIth century — Germanische Museum, Nuremberg **(Marburg).** **157.** Urban II preaching the Crusade — Manuscript, circa 1490. B.N. **158.** Christ, appearing to Peter the Hermit in his sleep, bids him undertake the Crusade — Miniature, 1337, romance of Godefroy de Bouillon. B.N. **159.** Crusade of Peter the Hermit; the pilgrims, led by Gaultier the Landless, are set upon by the Hungarian army — Manuscript. B.N. **160.** A Palestinian town attacked by the crusaders. Manuscript in the library of the Escurial: La gran conquista de Ultramar. Spain.

Pages 71/80

161. Philippe Auguste embarks for the Crusade — Manuscript of Sébastien Mammerot, circa 1490 — B.N. **162.** Frederick II and his soldiers — Manuscript in the Vatican Library. **163.** St Louis embarks for the Crusade and exhorts his companions — Manuscript circa 1320 — B.N. **164.** The capture of Damietta — Life of St Louis by Joinville, circa 1360 — Miniature — B.N. **165.** Le Krak des Chevaliers, Lebanon **(Aerofilms, London).** **166.** The Count de Vaudémont back from the Crusades — Musée de Nancy, France **(A.Ph.).** **167.** The walls of Avila, Spain **(Yan).** **168.** The granting of a municipal charter — Manuscript in the Royal Library at Brussels. **169.** The Garisenda and Asinelli towers — XIIth century — Bologna, Italy **(Alinari).** **170.** Ypres with its belfry — XIIIth century seal — Archives de France. **171.** Echevins taking the oath — Manuscript from Olmütz, Germany **(Marburg).** **172.** Pope Innocent III approves the order of St Francis — Taddeo Gaddi — Galleria dell' Accademia, Florence **(Alinari).** **173.** The trial by fire — St Dominic demonstrates to the Albigensians that his book against the heretics is indestructible. Painting by Berruguete — The Prado, Madrid **(Andersen).** **174.** Head of St Thomas Aquinas — Detail from the Crucifixion by Fra Angelico — San Marco, Florence **(Alinari).** **175.** Laon Cathedral, France

— Aerial view (Photothèque française), 176. Legend of St Wolfgang — Detail from the altar by Michael Pacher (1471-1481), St Wolfgang, Austria (Marburg). 177. Salisbury Cathedral, England — Aerial view. 178. Christ teaching, known as 'Le Beau Dieu' — Portico of the Saviour, XIIIth century, Amiens Cathedral, France (J. Roubier). 179. Statue of the Abbess Uta — Naumburg Cathedral, Germany (Marburg). 180. The resurrection of the dead — Detail from tympanum of central door, Bourges Cathedral, France (J. Roubier). 181. Part of the window donated by the decorators and stone-masons to the Cathedral at Chartres: Completion of the statue of a king. 182. Chartres Cathedral, France — Central window of the West Front. The Visitation (Ektachrome Abbé Dierick - Laboratoire St Liévin, Ghent). 183. Siena Cathedral, Italy. 184. The Basilica at Padua, Italy (Aerofilms London). 185. Cologne Cathedral, Germany (Hugo Schmölz). 186. Harvesting spices in lands beyond the seas — Miniature from the Book of Wonders (Ektachrome B.N.). 187. The medieval technique of harnessing draught animals, after the 'Hortus deliciarum', a manuscript written by order of Herrade de Lansberg (1167-1195), abbess of Mont St Odile, and destroyed during the bombardment of Strasburg, 1870. 188. A windmill in the Balearic isles (Boudot-Lamotte). 189. A watermill used in iron foundries, for generating a draught — Cosmography of Sébastien Munster. 190. Spinning-frame — Manuscript in the Ambrosian Library, Milan (G.F.N.). 191. Caravan from the East — Catalan atlas, known as 'Charles V's Atlas' (1375). B.N. 192. View of Cologne — Detail from the Martyrdom of St Ursula by the Maître de la Véronique. Wallraf Richartz Museum, Cologne, Germany. 193. The 'Foire du Lendit' at Saint Denis, France — Miniature, B.N. 194. A class at the University of Bologna. 195. Oxford University — Aerial view (Aerofilms Ltd, London). 196. University of Coimbra, Portugal (Yan). 197. Student performing an autopsy before his master — Engraving from 'Mundinus Anatomia', printed at Leipzig. 198. St Sophia, Istambul, Turkey (Yan). 199. St Casimir — Hungarian school, XVth century — Museum für Bildkünste, Budapest, Hungary (Marburg). 200. The Vavel palace, Cracow, Poland (J. Lang). 201. Dante — Detail of a painting by Andrea del Castagno — Cenacle of St Apollonia — Florence (Alinari). 202. Petrarch — Detail from the 'Parnassus' — The Stanze of Raphael, Vatican (Anderson). 203. The funeral of St Francis by Giotto — Detail — Santa Croce, Florence (Alinari).

Pages 91/100

204. Crossbowman — Detail from the Martyrdom of St Sebastian by Holbein the Elder (Pinacothèque, Munich). 205. The battle of Crécy — Froissart's Chronicle — Miniature in the B.N. 206. The Black Prince — Detail of his tomb in Canterbury Cathedral (Boudot-Lamotte). 207. Joan of Arc brought before the Dauphin — Miniature from the Vigils de Charles VII. (B.N.). 208. Court of the Myrtles or of the Alberca and tower of Comares — Alhambra, Granada, Spain. (Yan). 209. Ferdinand of Aragon — Detail of his tomb — Capella Mayor, Cathedral of Granada. (Yan). 210. Isabella the Catholic — Ibid. (Yan). 211. The surrender of the Moors — Detail from the altar-piece of the High Altar, Granada Cathedral. (Yan). 212. The Virgin reading — Painting by Van Eyck — The Prado, Madrid (Anderson). 213. The triumph of death — Detail from the fresco in the Campo Santo at Pisa (XIVth century), destroyed during the 1939-1945 war (G.F.N.). 214. The punishment of the damned — Detail of a painting by D. Bouts (XVth century), Musée du Louvre (G.F.N.). 215. God the Father — Detail from the High Altar in the church of Breisach, Germany, circa 1523 (H. Retzlaff). 216. Church of Caudebec-en-Caux, France (Giraudon). 217. The Maison du Roi, Brussels, Belgium (J. Roubier). 218. The lists and stands erected for a tournament — Miniature from the 'Livre des Tournois' of René d'Anjou, king of Sicily — Circa 1460-1465 (B.N.). 219. Louis XI — Cabinet des Médailles (B.N.). 220. Supposed portrait of Charles the Bold — Detail from the 'Adoration of the Magi' by Roger van der Weyden — Pinacothèque of Munich (Bay. Staat.). 221. Battle of Grandson (1476) — Swiss miniature. 222. Machiavelli — Portrait in Palazzo Vecchio, Florence (Alinari). 223. Frederick of Montefeltro, Duke of Urbino — Detail from the 'Communion of the Apostles' by Justus of Ghent — Ducal Palace, Urbino (Alinari). 224. Laurence the Magnificent — Bust in the Medici-Riccardi Palace, Florence (Alinari). 225. Leonardo Loredano, Doge of Venice (1438-1521) — Portrait by Giovanni Bellini — Pinacothèque of Dresden (Alinari). 226. Ship with steering-oar — Seal of the commune of Nieuport, Belgium (1237) — Archives Nationales, Paris. 227. Ship with hinged rudder — Seal of the town of Ipswich, England (Giraudon). 228. Astronomer with sextant and chronometer — XVth century miniature — B.N. 229. Polyptych of the Adoration of St Vincent by Nuno Gonçalves — Museum of ancient art, Lisbon (circa 1470) — From left to right: monks, fishermen, St Vincent flanked by prince Henry the Navigator and Alphonsus V of Portugal, who kneels with his son, the future John II, the archbishop of Lisbon, the chiefs of the army and of the navy, nobles, representatives of the city's different colonies, a Moor, a Jew. 230. Christopher Columbus — Portrait by Sebastiano del Piombo — Doria Gallery, Rome (Anderson).

Pages 101/110

231. Amerigo Vespucci navigating by means of the astrolabe — Engraving by Stradano. 232. Bronze plaque from Benin (Nigeria), XVth century, showing a Portuguese mariner (Photothèque du Musée de l'Homme). 233. Magellan — Engraving by Stradano. 234. A map of maritime discoveries and explorations by Michel Fontaine. 235. Cortes in Mexico — Detail from the bandelette de Tlaxcala. 236. Buenos Aires shortly after its foundation. 237. The exploration of Berentz — Bear hunt on an ice-floe — Engraving from the 'Grands Voyages' of De Bry. 238. Mine-working in America — ibid. 239. The Bourse at Antwerp, 1531. 240. Jacob Fugger-Amberger — XVIth century portrait (Bay. Staat.). 241. The Ambassadors: Jean de Dinteville, ambassador, and George de Selves, bishop — Painting by Hans Holbein, 1533 — National Gallery, London. 242. A print-shop in the XVth century, in which all the contemporary equipment can be discerned: press, inking device, case, copy-holder — Engraving from 'La Grant danse macabre des hommes hystoriée' — Lyons, France, 1499. 243. Christian Plantin — Engraved portrait. 244. Susannah bathing — Painting by Altdorfer (1526) — Pinacothèque, Munich. 245. Allegory of Spring — Detail of Botticelli's painting (Alinari). 246. Drawing from a manuscript of Leonardo da Vinci — A hydraulic machine — Paris, Bibliothèque de l'Institut (Giraudon). 247. Basilica of St Peter, Rome — Interior of the Dome (E.N.I.T.). 248. Town Hall, Antwerp, Belgium (J. Roubier). 249. Castle of Chambord, France — Aerial view (Photothèque française).

Pages 111/120

250. Galatea — Raphael's fresco in the Farnesina (Ektachrome Alinari). 251. Luther — Allegorical print of the Reformation. 251 bis. Zwingli — Portrait by Holbein the Younger — Uffizi Gallery, Florence (Alinari). 215 ter. Melanchthon — Cabinet des Médailles. B.N. 252. Erasmus — Portrait by Quentin Metzys — Barberini Gallery, Rome (Ektachrome Alinari). 253. Calvin — Portrait, Library of Geneva (Jean Arland). 254. The Calvinists destroy statues and religious objects — Engraving by Hogenberg. 255. The peasants' war — Painting by Brueghel (Bay. Staat.). 256. Gustave Vasa opens the national assembly at Vadstena — Painting by Martin Elias — National Museum of Stockholm. 257. Henry VIII of England — Cabinet des Médailles, B.N. 258. The massacre at Vassy, 1562 — German engraving. 259. Pope Paul III approves the Society of Jesus 1540 — Print. 260. Interview between Clement VII and Charles V — Painting by Vasari — Palazzo Vecchio, Florence (Alinari). 261. Allegory of Europe — Engraving from the Cosmography by Sebastian Münster. 262. Siege of Tunis — Painting by Coburg — Detail (Marburg). 263. The battle of Lepanto — Engraving. 264. Portrait of Philip II by A. Coelle — Gothic House at Wörlitz (Marburg). 265. The Escorial seen from the South (Roger Viollet). 266. The Spaniards pillage Malines, 1572 — Engraving by Hogenberg. 267. The defeat of the Invincible Armada, 1588 — Cabinet des Médailles, B.N. 268. Queen Elizabeth goes to attend a 'Te Deum' for the victory over the Armada, accompanied by Lord Hunsdon, Lord Cobham, Sir Robert Cecil, the earls of Worcester and Bedford, and Lord Herbert — Painting by Marcus Gheeraertz. 269. Raleigh takes prisoner a Spanish governor — Engraving from the 'Grands Voyages' of De Bry. 270. Sir Francis Drake (H.P.L.).

Pages 121/130

271. Frontispiece from one of the first editions of Cervantes' 'Don Quixote' — B.N. 272. William Shakespeare — A portrait in his birth-place. 273. Montaigne — Portrait — Musée Condé, Chantilly, France. 274. Galileo's telescope — Museum of Physics and of Natural History, Florence (Alinari). 275. Title-page of the 'Fiori Poetici', published at Monteverdi's death — Venice, 1644. 276. Mercator — Engraving. 277. Francis Bacon — Portrait by W. Marshall, 1640. 278. Rubens' studio — An imaginative painting by Corneille de Baellieur — Pitti Palace, Florence (Alinari). 279. Central trading-post of the (Dutch) East India company at Hughi, Bengal, 1665 — Amsterdam Historical Museum. 280. The first colonial establishment on Manhattan Island, New Amsterdam, 1621-1664. 281. Dutch ships of the East India company. 282. The Hostlery of the Germans, Venice, 1616. 283. Fishermen and trappers on the Hudson, 1670. 284. Gustave Adolphus of Sweden — Portrait by Van Dyck (Bay. Staat.). 285. Gustave Adolphus crosses the Lech and pushes back the Count de Tilly, April 1632. 286. Wallenstein — Portrait by Van Dyck (Bay. Staat.). 287. Scene from the Thirty Years' War — Engraving from one of the first editions of 'Simplicius Simplicissimus' by Grimelshausen. 288. Celebration of the peace — Allegorical print published for the Congress of Westphalia. 289. Oliver Cromwell — Cabinet des Médailles, B.N. (J. Roubier). 290. The beheading of King Charles I, 1649 — German engraving. 291. Cardinal Richelieu — Portrait by Philippe de Champaigne — Louvre, Paris. 292. Alexis Romanoff, Czar of Russia — An engraving. —293. Moscow in the XVIIIth Century — An engraving. 294. John Casimir of Poland — Portrait by Daniel Schultz. 295. Louis XIV and the representatives of the Swiss cantons renew their alliance at Notre-Dame de Paris — Gobelin tapestry — Swiss Embassy in Paris (Ektachrome Franceschi).

Pages 131/140

296. The stolen garment, a Dutch print satirising Louis XIV's conquest of fortresses. 297. Palace of Versailles. Aerial view (Henrard). 298. Piazza San Pietro, with the Bernini colonnade. Aerial view (ENIT). 299. 'The surrender of Breda', painting by Velasquez (circa 1647). Prado Museum, Madrid (Ektachrome. Editions Tisné). 300. 'The Syndics of the Cloth Hall', painting by Rembrandt (1661). Amsterdam Museum (Bulloz). 301. The Gardener, painting by Le Nain. Wallraf Richartz Museum, Cologne. (Rheinisches Bildarchiv.) 302. René Descartes, portrait by Franz Hals. Louvre, Paris (Giraudon). 302 bis. Figure from Descartes' work 'Of Man' — B.N. 303. Baruch Spinoza, a portrait. 304. Leibnitz and Charles XII, engraving from 'The Philosophy of Nature' (1769). 305. Newton, a portrait. 306. Frontispiece of 'Cinna' by Pierre Corneille (1643). B.N. 307. Chauveau's frontispiece for 'Andromaque' by Jean Racine. B.N. 308. Molière dressed as Sganarelle, engraving by Simonin. B.N. 309. J.B. Lulli, engraving

by Bonnart. **310.** Milton, a portrait. **311.** Purcell, a portrait. **312.** Jonathan Swift, a portrait by Barford (1744). **313.** Panorama of Stockholm in the XVIIth century. **314.** London bridge in 1616. **315.** The tower of Belem at Lisbon **(Yan)**. **316.** Amsterdam, canal and houses **(J. Roubier)**. **316a.** Genoese senator, engraving by Bonnart. **316b.** Wife of a Strasburg doctor, ibid.

Pages 141/150

317. View of Prague: in the foreground the bridge of St Charles, in the background the castle and the cathedral **(Boudot-Lamotte)**. **318.** Panorama of Budapest (1617). **318a.** A woman from Nuremberg, Germany — Engraving by Bonnart. **318b.** A merchant from Ragusa — Engraving by Bonnart. **319.** The siege of Vienna by the Turks. **320.** Jan III Sobieski, King of Poland. **321.** The Austrian imperial family: the empress Maria-Teresa, the future queen of France Marie-Antoinette. Portrait by Martin de Meytens (1695-1770). Swedish school. Kunsthistorisches Museum, Vienna **(Ektachrome Giraudon)**. **322.** The siege of Prague: the Hungarian army (entering in the background on the right) forces the French troops to retreat (seen leaving in the background on the left). In the foreground, the Czech governor ot Prague (no 10) waits to enter the city, in which the Hradschin is visible (7.8). **322a.** A volunteer from Saxony: an uhlan. Engraving, 1747. **322b.** A volunteer from Saxony: a dragoon. **323.** Louis XV giving an audience on 11 January 1742 to the Ambassador Extraordinary of the Ottomans. **324.** Frederick II of Prussia with his generals. **325.** The coronation of Catherine II (1762). **326.** Catherine II, a portrait by Lander **(Bay. Staat)**. 327. The kings' cake, a print satirising the partition of Poland. **328.** The library of the Convent of St Gall, Switzerland. 1758-1767 **(Retzlaff)**. **329.** Bookshops in front of the Amsterdam stock-exchange. **330.** Homage to Voltaire. **331.** The actor Le Kain gives a reading at Madame Geoffrin of Voltaire's 'L'Orphelin de la Chine'. **332.** Homage to J.-J. Rousseau. **333.** Tahitian dance, an engraving from 'The Voyages of Captain Cook'. **334.** Winckelmann, a portrait by A. Mazon. Weimar museum, Germany **(Marburg)**. **335.** Kant, by Schron von Carosfeld. Dresden, Collection of Prints **(Marburg)**.

Pages 151/160

336. Newcomen's steam engine. **337.** Blanchard and Jeffries leave by balloon. Dover, 1785. English engraving. **338.** Engraving from 'De viribus electricitatis in motu musculari' by Galvani, 1798. **339.** View of the entrance to the castle of Schoenbrunn, Austria. **340.** 'The Dance', a painting by Longhi. Doria Palace, Rome **(Alinari)**. **341.** 'The oyster luncheon', a painting by J.F. de Troy. French school. Musée Condé, Chantilly **(Ektachrome Giraudon)**. **342.** The porter, detail from Watteau's painting 'L'enseigne de Gersaint'. Berlin museum **(Marburg)**. **343.** Beer Street, engraving by Hogarth, 1751. **344.** The tailor's workshop. **345.** The charlatan, painting by Tiepolo **(Giraudon)**. **346.** Departure of the Bucentaur for the Ascension day ceremony. Painting by Guardi. Louvre, Paris **(Ektachrome Edition Somogy)**. **347.** Façade of the church of St Charles Borromaeus, Vienna, 1716-1737 **(Boudot-Lamotte)**. **348.** Nave of the church of Birnau (Lake Constance), built by Peter Thumb **(Retzlaff)**. **349.** The old chapel of Ratisbonne, Germany, erected in 1002, interior rococo style from 1751 to 1765 **(Retzlaff)**. **350.** Pygmalion and Galatea, Sèvres porcelain after the work of Falconet 1763 **(Retzlaff)**. **351.** Performance given in Rome of La Contesa de' Numi, in honour of the birth of the French Dauphin. Painting by G. Pannini. Louvre **(Giraudon)**.

Pages 161/170

352. J.S. Bach, portrait at the age of 35. **352 bis.** The opening of Bach's 4th 'Invention'. **353.** Handel, a portrait. **354.** A. Scarlatti, a portrait. **355.** Tea at the Prince de Conti's. At the piano, the child Mozart. Louvre, Paris **(Giraudon)**. **356.** Haydn, a portrait. Schwerin Museum **(Marburg)**. **357.** Glück at the harpsichord, detail from a painting by Duplessis. Museum of Vienna **(Bulloz)**. **358. Frontal view of a ship at anchor,** ready to set sail. **359.** The wool market at Breslau, by J. Wagner. Breslau Museum **(Marburg)**. **360.** The port of London, engraving by Hogarth. **361.** The founding of Pennsylvania by William Penn, 1681. **362.** The Declaration of Independence of the United States of America. **363.** French print paying tribute to American independence. **364.** Benjamin Franklin, a portrait by Greuze **(Bulloz)**. **365.** La Fayette visiting George Washington at Mount Vernon. **366.** Lord Cornwallis surrenders to Washington, Rochambeau and La Fayette. **367.** Moreau Le Jeune's frontispiece for Young's 'Night Thoughts'. **368.** Ossian's Dream. Detail from a painting by Ingres. Museum of Montauban **(Giraudon)**. **369.** Young Gœthe looking at his silhouette. A painting by Georg Melchior Kraus. Weimar **(Marburg)**. **370.** Engraving by Duplessis-Berthaut for 'Werther'. **371.** Beethoven as a young man. Portrait by Neugass **(Giraudon)**. **372.** 'The morning walk', **a painting by Gainsborough.** London. **373.** Watt's steam engine. **374.** The storming of the Bastille, 14 July 1789. A coloured print. **375.** The oath in the jeu de Paume. **376.** Allegorical revolutionary illustration about Equality between Men. B.N.

Pages 171/180

377. The freedom of the press. A print from the Revolution. **378.** The meeting at Pillnitz, 25 August 1791 (the emperor of Germany, the king of Prussia, the prince of Saxony). **379.** The departure of the volunteers in 1792: the Genius of War calling the French to arms. Bas-relief of 'The Marseillaise' by Rude, for the Arc de Triomphe de l'Etoile, Paris **(Bulloz)**. **380.** The tree of liberty at Cassel, Germany; January 1793. **381.** The proclamation of the Roman Republic, on the Capitol. **382.** The insurrection of Pavia, the 7 prairial, year IV. **383.** Bonaparte. Medal by David d'Angers **(J. Roubier)**. **384.** Map of Napoleon's campaigns by Michel Fontaine. **385.** The emperors Napoleon and Alexandre II take leave of each other at Tilsitt, on the Niemen. **386.** 'Dos de Mayo', a painting by Goya. The mamelukes of Murat attacked by the population of Madrid, 2 May 1808. Prado Museum, Madrid **(Anderson)**. **387.** Fichte, a drawing by Henschel. **388.** Madame de Staël, detail from a painting by Gérard called 'Corinne au Cap Misène'. Lyons Museum, France **(Giraudon)**. **389.** The French army enters Moscow, 14 September 1812. **390.** The Chelsea pensioners read the dispatch of Waterloo. A painting by David Wilkie, 1822. Wellington Museum, London. **391.** Napoleon at St Helena. An English engraving. **392.** The Congress of Vienna. Meeting of the plenipotentiaries of the eight signatory powers of the Treaty of Paris. **393.** The Holy Alliance, an allegorical print. **394.** Chateaubriand at the age of 23. A portrait by Girodet **(Bulloz)**. **395.** Byron in Greek costume. A portrait by Philipp, National Gallery, London **(Bulloz)**. **396.** Leopardi, a portrait. **397.** Mickiewicz a portrait by Shyka. **398.** The last scene of 'Hernani', the play of Victor Hugo. Lithograph by Dévéria. **399.** Engraving from one of the original (1820) editions of 'Ivanhoe' by Walter Scott. **400.** Balzac, a portrait by Boulanger. Museum of Tours **(Bulloz)**. **401.** The entry of the crusaders into Constantinople, painting by Delacroix, 1840. Louvre **(Ektachrome Giraudon)**.

Pages 181/190

402. Schubert, a portrait in a private collection **(Giraudon)**. **403.** Chopin, a portrait by Delacroix. Louvre **(Bulloz)**. **404.** Berlioz. A satirical print. **405.** The waltz, lithograph by Langlumé. **406.** Liszt, lithograph by Dévéria (1832). **407.** Schumann, portrait by Kriehuber. **408.** Rossini, a portrait. **409.** Label of the liquor baptised 'Spirit of Bolivar' in honour of the South American general. **410.** Don Pedro is acclaimed emperor of an independent Brazil. **411.** The battle of Navarino, 20 October 1827. A painting by L. Garneray. Museum of Versailles **(Giraudon)**. **412.** Liberty leading the people, a painting by Delacroix. Louvre, Paris **(Giraudon)**. **413.** The entry of the king of the Belgians into Brussels. **414.** Label of the liquor baptised 'Liquor of the Brave Poles'. **415.** Satirical print concerning the 'events of July 183-...'. **416.** The insurrection of Frankfurt, April 1833. Imagerie Pellerin, Epinal, France. **417.** Volta presents his battery to Bonaparte. Drawing by Fragonard **(Bulloz)**. **418.** Trevithick's locomotive on show in London, 1809. **419.** The american steamer 'Savannah'. **420.** Textile works at Manchester, England. **421.** The Schneider metallurgic works at Creusot, France. **422.** The Borsig metallurgic works in Berlin, Germany. **423.** Interior of the London Stock Exchange, 1847 **(I.L.N.)**. **424.** Drawing from the English report on child labour. **425.** Engraving to celebrate **the guild of the farriers.** **426.** Mob at the entrance to the Trade Ministry of people with plans for railway construction. London 1845 **(I.L.N.)**. **427.** The Nuremberg-Furth railway. **428.** Traveller in a hurry, Austrian engraving.

Pages 191/200

429. A lady traveller, 1867 **(Picture Post Library)**. **430.** Charing Cross station, London, 1867 **(Picture Post Library)**. **431.** President Louis-Napoleon inaugurating the gare de Lyon, Paris. **432.** Railways in 1845. English colour prints. **433.** Mazzini. Openning pages of his works, with appeal for the 'Young Europe'. **434.** Storming of the Tuileries palace, 24 February 1848.

435. The throne of king Louis-Philippe burns in the place de la Bastille, Paris. **436.** The revolution at Milan. **437.** At the barricades — Berlin, the night of March 18th to 19th, 1848. Il.Z. **438.** At the barricades — Vienna, May 26th, 1848. Il.Z. **439.** The parliament at Frankfurt, May 18th, 1848. Il.Z. **440.** Kossuth's call to arms. Il.Z. **441.** An execution at Budapest. **442.** The german parliament dissolved, June 1849. **443.** The liberation of the negroes in the French Antilles. Museum of Clermont-Ferrand, France. **444.** Reception of Queen Victoria by the Emperor Napoleon III at Boulogne. 1855 **(I.L.N.)** **445.** William E. Gladstone. Photo collec. **(Sirot)**. **446.** The battle for Sebastopol, 18th to 19th April, 1855. A Russian print. **447. The** reception of the French troops in Genoa, 30th April, 1851. **448.** Victor Emmanuel, Cavour, Garibaldi **(R. Viollet)**. **449.** Henri Dunant. Engraved portrait. **450.** One of the first ambulances to carry the emblem of the Red Cross **(Gentina)**. **451.** At the Paris Bourse, 1854 **(I.L.N.)**. **452.** Smelting with the new Bessemer process. An American engraving.

Pages 201/210

453. The last of the **Téméraire,** painting by Turner, 1839 **(Ektachrome Editions P. Tisné)**. **454.** 'The emperor Napoleon and his august guests at the Exhibition of 1867'. From left to right: the sultan, the Taïcoun, the emperor of Austria, the king of Holland, the emperor of Russia, the king of Italy, the emperor of the French, the shah of Persia, the king of the Belgians, the king of the Hellenes, the prince of Wales, the queen of Spain, the king of Portugal, the king of Prussia. **455.** The boring of the Brenner Tunnel. 1867. Il.Z. **456.** The first engine passes through the Mont-Cenis tunnel. Illus. **457.** Reading the newspaper. Satirical French print. **458.** Printing press for the 'Petit Journal', **invented by** H. Marinoni, 1868. **459.** Deck of an emigrant ship sailing from Hamburg. Engraving by Knut Ekwall. Il.Z. **460.** The Champs-Elysées about 1860 — A stereoscopic photograph. **461.** Music in the Tuileries, detail of a painting by Edouard Manet. From left to right: Manet himself, behind A. de Balleroy, Zacharie Astruc seated, Eugène Manet, Offenbach, and behind, Baudelaire and Gautier. **462.** Illustration for Dickens' **'Oliver Twist',** **463.** A London omnibus, towards 1865 **(H.P.L.)**. **464.**

The Prater at Vienna, 1856. II.Z. **465.** Figures from a French fashion plate, 1856. **466.** The Leipziger Platz, Berlin, towards 1865 **(Ullstein bilderdienst).** **467.** The umbrellas, a painting by Renoir. National Gallery, London. **468.** View of Hamburg, 1870. **469.** View of Marseille, 1866. An engraving. **470.** View of Trieste, 1870. **471.** Bismarck. A portrait by Lombach **(Bay. Staat).** **472.** The German empire proclaimed at Versailles.

Pages 211/220

473. Women demonstrate outside the coal mines of Creusot, France, April 1870. Illus. **474.** Auguste Comte, a portrait. **475.** John Stuart Mill. Daguerreotype portrait. **476.** Herbert Spencer. A portrait by J. Bagnold Burgess (1872). **477.** Darwin. Photo collec. Sirot. **478.** Renan. A portrait by Bonnat (1892). **479.** Proudhon. A detail from Courbet's painting 'Proudhon et ses enfants'. Petit Palais, Paris **(Giraudon).** **480.** Ferdinand Lasalle. A popular drawing. **481.** Title page of Karl Marx's 'Das Kapital', Hamburg edition, 1877. **482.** Meeting of the first French workers' congress, Paris, 1874. **483.** Abraham Lincoln and his cabinet. An American painting. **484.** The execution of Maximilian. A painting by Manet **(Giraudon).** **485.** The inauguration of the Suez canal, 16th November, 1869. Photo collec. Sirot. **486.** Ferdinand de Lesseps. Caricature by E. Carjat. **487.** The allied troops enter Pekin, 22nd October, 1860. Illus. **488.** 'Dr. Livingstone, I Presume?' (1872). **489.** Queen Victoria proclaimed empress of India, Delhi, 1st January, 1877 **(I.L.N.).** **490.** Disraeli. Photo collec. Sirot. **491.** Brazza. Photo Nadar **(Archives photographiques, Paris).** **492.** The French attack Son Tay, June 1884. Popular Chinese print. **493.** Europeans at table. Print of Yoshikatsu. Collec. Jeannette Ostier, Paris **(Ekta Michaelides).** **494.** After the war of 1870, professors Edgar Quinet and Michelet resume their classes. Painting by A. Brouillet, Paris. **495.** The Flying Boat. An engraving from Jules Verne's 'Robur le Conquérant'. **496.** Justin Liebig, a portrait. **497.** Koch in his laboratory, 1890. **498.** Louis Pasteur. Photograph by Nadar **(Archives Photographiques Paris).** **499.** Krupp's giant cannon at the Paris Exhibition, 1867. II.Z.

Pages 221/230

500. Deprez' experiment at Munich, for the transmission of electricity over long distances. **501.** Alfred Nobel. A photograph **(Roger Viollet).** **502.** A textiles office at New Orleans. Painting by Degas. Musée de Paris **(Giraudon).** **503.** The 1889 Exhibition at the Champ-de-Mars, Paris **(Roger Viollet).** **504.** The Congress of Berlin, 1878 — Salisbury, Disraeli, Andrassy, Bismarck (standing), Waddington, Mohammed Ali (standing, right). **505.** Joseph Chamberlain. Photo collec. Sirot. **506.** Jules Ferry. Photo collec. Sirot. **507.** King Leopold of Belgium. Photo Nadar. **508.** The occupation of Ismailia by English troops, 1882 **(I.L.N.).** **509.** Kitchener. Photo collec. Sirot. **510.** The Cameroon chieftains received by the emperor of Germany. II.Z. **511.** The royal princesses preach the holy war in Madagascar, 1894 **(P.J.I.).** **512.** The Jameson raid. Photo collec. Sirot. **513.** The entry of William II into Jerusalem. Drawing by L. Sabatier, 1898. Illus. **514.** Marchand's mission. The S.S. **Faidherbe** carried across Africa in sections **(P.J.I.).** **515.** The Egyptian colours hoisted at Fashoda. **516.** Friendly greetings from the great wall. Humorous German postcard showing the international expeditionary force drawn up against the Chinese Empire **(Roger Viollet).** **517.** The Russian warship **Piobeda** passes through the Suez canal in 1903 to reinforce the squadron at Port Arthur **(P.J.I.).** **518.** The battle of Port Arthur. A Japanese engraving. **519.** The Moroccan delegation at the conference of Algeciras, 1906 **(P.J.I.).** **520.** Montenegrin women bringing supplies to the army **(P.J.I.).** **521.** A strike. Engraving by Steinlein. **522.** Disturbances in Trafalgar Square, London, 1886. Illus. **523.** The assassination of the emperor Alexander II at St Petersburg, 1881. **524.** Wagner. A photograph. **525.** Inauguration of the Wagner Theater at Bayreuth. **526.** Moussorgsky. A' portrait. **527.** The Foyer de la Danse at the Opéra in the rue Le Peletier. Painting by Degas. Louvre, Paris **(Giraudon).** **528.** Brahms. Photo collec. Sirot.

Pages 231/240

529. Verdi. A portrait. **530.** Grieg. A portrait, 1907. **531.** Verlaine (on the left) and Rimbaud. Detail from Fantin-Latour's painting 'Un coin de table'. Louvre, Paris **(Giraudon).** **532.** Tolstoy. Portrait by F. Repin. **533.** Dostoievsky. A portrait **(Giraudon).** **534.** Ibsen, after Nyblin's photograph, 1898. Illus. **535.** Nietzsche. A portrait. **536.** Rudyard Kipling. A pencil portrait in the National Portrait Gallery, London. **537.** Illustration from H.G. Wells' 'War in the air': the monorail crossing the Channel for the London-Paris railway. **538.** The painter's studio — 'Allégorie réelle' — a painting by G. Courbet. Louvre, Paris **(Giraudon).** **539.** The church at Auvers, a painting by Van Gogh, 1890. Musée du Jeu de Paume, Paris **(Ektachrome Editions Somogy).** **540.** The studio at the Batignolles, a painting by Fantin-Latour. From left to right: standing: Schoelderer, Renoir, Zola, Edmond Maitre, Basille, Claude Monet. Sitting: Manet, Zacharie Astruc. **541.** Sisley and his wife, a painting by Renoir. Wallraf Richartz Museum **(Rheinisches Bildarchiv).** **542.** Breton Landscape, a painting by Paul Gauguin **(Ektachrome Editions Somogy).** **543.** The first Daimler motor car, 1889. **544.** Walter Bersey in his vehicle 'motor car day' for the London-Brighton race, 1896 **(H.P.L.).** **545.** Santos Dumont airborne at Bagatelle, near Paris, 23rd October 1906. Illus. **546.** Roentgen's discovery, 1896. Illus. **547.** Pierre Curie teaching at the Sorbonne, 1906. **548.** Marconi in front of his apparatus. A photograph. **549.** Debussy. Photo Nadar **(Archives photographiques Paris).** **550.** Nijinsky. Photo collec. Sirot. **551.** Marcel Proust. Portrait by E. Blanche **(Bulloz).** **552.** Georges Méliès in 'Les cartes animées' **(Cinémathèque française).** **553.** Gerhart Hauptmann. Portrait by Max Liebermann. Kunsthalle, Hamburg.

Pages 241/250

554. George Bernard Shaw. A photograph **(Associated Press).** **555.** Sigmund Freud. A photograph **(Harlingue).** **556.** Man with a pipe. A painting by Picasso **(Giraudon).** **557.** Modigliani. A self-portrait. From a private collection at Sao Paolo, Brazil **(Giraudon).** **558.** The British royal family and the imperial family of Russia in London, 1906. Photograph **(Monde et Camera).** **559.** The heir to the Austrian throne assassinated at Sarajevo **(P.J.I.).** **560.** A German machine-gun post, 1914. Photo collec. Cossira. **561.** French trenches in the Champagne. Photo collec. Cossira. **562.** English trenches. Photo collec. Cossira. **563.** German infantry commencing an attack. **564.** An attack on Courcelles, 1918. Photo collec. Cossira. **565.** One of the earliest French tanks. Photo collec. Cossira. **566.** Ludendorff. A portrait. **567.** American infantry **(Monde et Camera).** **568.** Clemenceau, Foch and Weygand in May, 1918 **(Collec. J. Boudet).** **569.** Lenin haranguing the crowd. At the foot of the platform, Trotsky **(Roger Viollet).** **570.** Clemenceau, Wilson, Lloyd George (from left to right) after signing the treaty of Versailles. Photo collec. Cossira. **571.** Mussolini and his followers during the march on Rome **(Rizzoli Press Service).** **572.** Lloyd George and Briand. Photo collec. J. Boudet. **573.** Stresemann **(Monde et Camera).** **574.** The performance, in 1949, by the Piccolo Teatro of Milan, of Pirandello's 'Tonight we improvise'. **575.** Knut Hamsun. **576.** Thomas Mann at Munich. **577.** Henry Bergson. **578.** Ramuz. A lithograph portrait by R. Joël. **579.** Rainer Maria Rilke in 1906. **580.** Claudel's 'The Satin slipper' at the Comédie-Française **(Studio Lipnitzki).** **581.** Stravinsky. A portrait by E. Blanche. **582.** Hindemith. A portrait by R. Heirisch. **583.** Ravel playing a piano duet with Nijinsky. **584.** Bela Bartok.

Pages 251/260

585. Black lines. A painting by W. Kandinsky (1913) Guggenheim Collection, New York **(Giraudon).** **586** The Roumanian blouse. A painting by Matisse. Musée d'Art Moderne, Paris **(Giraudon).** **587.** 'Bella matribus detestata'. Engraving from Rouault's 'Miserere'. Collec Jacques Boudet. **588.** Charlie Chaplin **(Keystone).** **589** Falconetti in K. Dreyer's film 'Joan of Arc' (Jacques Boudet). **590.** Scene from Eisenstein's film 'The battleship Potemkin' **(Photo Cinémathèque française).** **591.** Hindenburg flanked by Hitler and Goering at Tannenberg August 1933 **(Keystone).** **592.** A crowd at the Berlin Lustgarten **(Keystone).** **593.** Hitler and Mussolini **(Rizzoli Press).** **594.** Prospectus of the 'Berliner Ensemble for Brecht's 'Mother courage'. **595.** Léon Blum at Luna Park, September 1936. Collec. Jacques Boudet. **596** Sharpshooters at the Alcazar during the Spanish civil war **(Monde et Camera).** **597.** André Malraux and Maxim Gorki. **598.** 'The fairy electricity'. Detail from a painting by Raoul Dufy **(Giraudon).** **599.** Saint-Exupéry in his aeroplane **(Monde et Camera).** **600.** Chamberlain, Daladier, Hitler, Mussolini, Ciano (from left to right) **(Deutsche Presse Agentur).** **601.** German and Russian forces meet in Poland, 4th October 1939 **(Keystone).** **602.** British troops evacuated from Dunkirk **(British War Office).** **603.** Refugees in France, June 1940 **(Agence diffusion presse).** **604.** London during the blitz **(Keystone).** **605.** Winston Churchill and the mayor of Dover watch an aerial combat 22 August 1940 **(Imperial War Museum).** **606.** A notice from the commandant of German occupation forces in France, concerning the shooting of hostages **(Monde et Camera).** **607.** Anne Frank. **608.** The Germans retreat in Russia **(Agence diffusion presse).** **609.** The bombardment of Berlin **(Keystone).**

Pages 261/270

610. American troops land in Normandy **(USIS).** **611.** Conference at Teheran: Stalin, Roosevelt, Churchill. In the background: Eisenhower, Alanbrooke, Cunningham, Leahy. **612.** Russian and American forces meet at Torgau on the Elbe **(USIS).** **613.** Eisenhower and Zhukov **(G. Séruzier).** **614.** The ruins of Berlin under the snow **(H. Cartier-Bresson).** **615.** Germans from the area ceded to Poland wait to be taken to the West **(Keystone).** **616.** Conference at Potsdam: Churchill, Truman, Stalin **(Keystone).** **617.** Coup d'Etat in Prague (from left to right): Gottwald, Benes, Zapotocky **(Keystone).** **618.** Demarcation line between British and Soviet zones of occupation in Germany **(Keystone).** **619.** The wall of the moon, by the painter Miro and the ceramist Artigas. Secretariat of UNESCO, Paris **(Ektachrome Roger Roche).** **620.** A V II base at Peenemünde **(Roger Viollet).** **621.** The Atomium, on view at the Brussels International Exhibition, 1958 **(Keystone).** **622.** Sir Alexander Fleming. **623.** Television transmitter north of Birmingham, England **(Interpress).** **624.** Scene from 'Bicycle thieves' by de Sica (Photo **Cinémathèque française).** **625.** Karl Jaspers. **626.** Albert Camus **(Keystone).** **627.** Olivetti factory at Barcelona, Spain. **628.** Monument commemorating the air lift, at Templehof airport, Berlin **(Gisele Freund).** **629.** Insurrection at Budapest. The statue of Stalin is thrown down **(Keystone).** **630.** Khrushchev visits Mao Tse Tung, 12th April, 1958 **(Assoc. Press).** **631.** United Nations battalion on guard at Suez.

Pages 271/280

632. Voting in Senegal **(Keystone).** **633.** Drilling for petroleum in the Sahara **(Keystone).** **634.** Winston Churchill. **635.** Spaak. **636.** De Gasperi. **637.** Robert Schuman. **638.** National flags outside the Council of Europe, Strasburg. **639.** Adenauer meets de Gaulle at Bad Kreuznach, Germany, 26th November 1958 **(Keystone).** **640.** Students from the University of Paris on a pilgrimage to Chartres (**Pierre Belzeaux, Rapho**). **641.** Students at the University of Upsala, Sweden (**Refat-Rapho**). **642.** At an air display in Great Britain (**Cornell Capa-Magnum**). **643.** The Olympic Games (**Brian Brake-Magnum**). **649.** The Venetian lagoon (**Rapho**). **650.** nini (**Keystone**). **646.** Einstein (**USIS**). **647.** Sir John Hunt. **648.** Fountain in Portugal (**H. Cartier-Bresson-Magnum**). **649.** The venetian lagoon (**Rapho**). **650.** Zermatt, Switzerland (**Atlas photo**). **651.** Windmill in the Greek islands (**Holmes**). **652.** Grenada, Spain (**Rapho**). **653.** Christmas decorations in Regent Street, London (**B.T.H.A.**). **654.** A Dutch town (**P. Molinard**). **655.** The Rhine valley, seen from Rheinstein Castle (**Holmes**). **656.** The Champs-Elysées at night (**Brassaï**). **657.** Stockholm at night (**Camera Press**). **658.** Performance in the Greek theatre, Taormina, Sicily (**Holmes**). **659.** The works at Lacq, France, seen at night (**Yan-Rapho**).

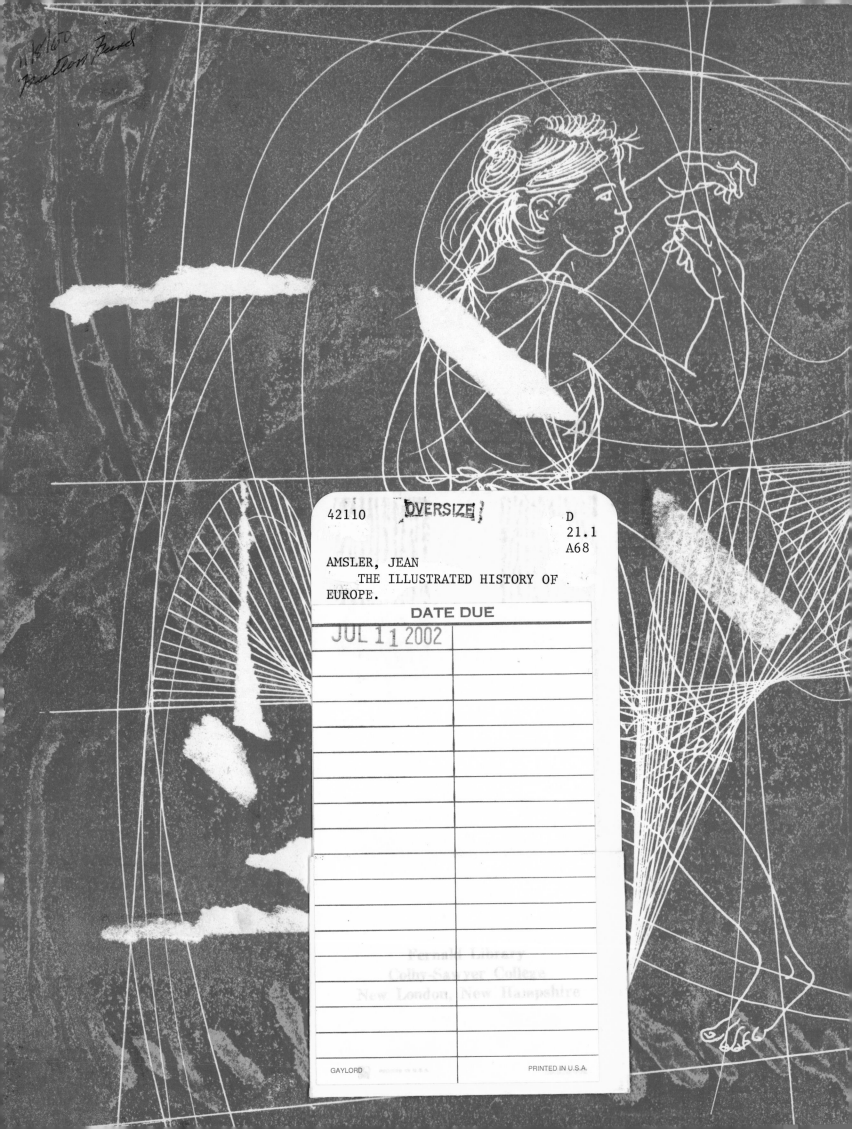